KAPLAN

PUBLISHING

D0352261

THIS EXAM KIT COMES WITH
FREE ONLINE ACCESS
TO EXTRA RESOURCES AIMED AT HELPING YOU PASS YOUR EXAMS

IN ADDITION TO THE OFFICIAL QUESTIONS AND ANSWERS IN THIS BOOK, GO ONLINE AND EN-gage WITH:

- An iPaper version of the Exam Kit
- Articles including Key Examinable Areas
- Material updates
- Latest Official ACCA exam questions
- Extra question assistance using the Signpost icon
- Timed Questions with an online tutor debrief using the Clock icon

And you can access all of these extra resources anytime, anywhere using your EN-gage account.

How to access your online resources

If you are a Kaplan Financial tuition, full-time or distance learning student

You will already have an EN-gage account and these extra resources will be available to you online. You do not need to register again, as this process was completed when you enrolled. If having problems accessing online materials, please ask your course administrator.

If you purchased through Kaplan Flexible Learning or via the Kaplan Publishing website

You will automatically receive an e-mail invitation to EN-gage online. Please register your details using this e-mail to gain access to your content. If you do not receive the e-mail or book content, please contact our Technical Support team at engage@twinsystems.com.

If you are already a registered EN-gage user

Go to www.EN-gage.co.uk and log in. Select the 'add a book' feature and enter the ISBN number of this book and the unique pass key at the bottom of this card. Then click 'finished' or 'add another book'. You may add as many books as you have purchased from this screen.

If you are a new EN-gage user

Register at www.EN-gage.co.uk and click on the link contained in the e-mail we sent you to activate your account. Then select the 'add a book' feature, enter the ISBN number of this book and the unique pass key at the bottom of this card. Then click 'finished' or 'add another book'.

Your Code and Information

This code can only be used once for the registration of one book online. This registration will expire when the final sittings for the examinations covered by this book have taken place. Please allow one hour from the time you submitted your book details for us to process your request.

Please scratch the film to access your Engage code

Please be aware that this code is case-sensitive and you will need to include the dashes within the passcode, but not when entering the ISBN. For further technical support, please visit www.EN-gage.co.uk

Paper F8 (INT & UK)

AUDIT AND ASSURANCE

EXAM KIT

KAPLAN

PUBLISHING

British Library Cataloguing-in-Publication Data

A catalogue record for this book is available from the British Library.

Published by:

Kaplan Publishing UK

Unit 2 The Business Centre

Molly Millar's Lane

Wokingham

Berkshire

RG41 2QZ

ISBN: 978 0 85732 315 6

© Kaplan Financial Limited, 2011.

Printed and bound by CPI Group (UK) Ltd, Croydon, CR0 4YY.

Acknowledgements

The past ACCA examination questions are the copyright of the Association of Chartered Certified Accountants. The original answers to the questions from June 1994 onwards were produced by the examiners themselves and have been adapted by Kaplan Publishing.

We are grateful to the Chartered Institute of Management Accountants and the Institute of Chartered Accountants in England and Wales for permission to reproduce past examination questions. The answers have been prepared by Kaplan Publishing.

CONTENTS

Section

Features in this edition

In addition to providing a wide ranging bank of real past exam questions, we have also included in this edition:

- An analysis of all of the recent new syllabus examination papers.

- Paper specific information and advice on exam technique.

- Our recommended approach to make your revision for this particular subject as effective as possible.

    This includes step by step guidance on how best to use our Kaplan material (Complete text, pocket notes and exam kit) at this stage in your studies.

- Enhanced tutorial answers packed with specific key answer tips, technical tutorial notes and exam technique tips from our experienced tutors.

- Complementary online resources including full tutor debriefs and question assistance to point you in the right direction when you get stuck.

December 2010, June and December 2011 – Real examination questions with enhanced tutorial answers

The real December 2010, June 2011, and December 2011 exam questions with enhanced "walk through answers" and full "tutor debriefs", updated in line with legislation relevant to your exam sitting, is available on Kaplan EN-gage at:

www.EN-gage.co.uk

You will find a wealth of other resources to help you with your studies on the following sites:

www.EN-gage.co.uk

www.accaglobal.com/students/

INDEX TO QUESTIONS AND ANSWERS

INTRODUCTION

The style of current Paper F8 exam questions is different to old syllabus Paper 2.6 questions and significant changes have had to be made to questions in light of the recent amendments to International Standards of Auditing, namely the Clarity Project.

Accordingly, many of the old ACCA questions within this kit have been adapted to reflect the new style of paper and the new guidance. If changed in any way from the original version, this is indicated in the end column of the index below with the mark *(A)*.

Note that the majority of the questions within the kit are past ACCA exam questions, the more recent questions are labelled as such in the index.

The pilot paper is included at the end of the kit.

KEY TO THE INDEX

PAPER ENHANCEMENTS

We have added the following enhancements to the answers in this exam kit:

Key answer tips

All answers include key answer tips to help your understanding of each question.

Tutorial note

All answers include more tutorial notes to explain some of the technical points in more detail.

Top tutor tips

For selected questions, we "walk through the answer" giving guidance on how to approach the questions with helpful 'tips from a top tutor', together with technical tutor notes.

These answers are indicated with the "footsteps" icon in the index.

ONLINE ENHANCEMENTS

 Timed question with Online tutor debrief

For selected questions, we recommend that they are to be completed under full exam conditions (i.e. properly timed in a closed book environment).

In addition to the examiner's technical answer, enhanced with key answer tips and tutorial notes in this exam kit, you can find an answer debrief online by a top tutor that:

- works through the question in full;

- discusses how to approach the question;

- discusses how to ensure that the easy marks are obtained as quickly as possible; and

- emphasises how to tackle exam questions and exam technique.

These questions are indicated with the "clock" icon in the index.

 Online question assistance

Have you ever looked at a question and not know where to start, or got stuck part way through?

For selected questions, we have produced "Online question assistance" offering different levels of guidance, such as:

- ensuring that you understand the question requirements fully, highlighting key terms and the meaning of the verbs used;

- how to read the question proactively, with knowledge of the requirements, to identify the topic areas covered;

- assessing the detailed content of the question body, pointing out key information and explaining why it is important;

- help to devise a plan of attack

With this assistance, you should be able to attempt your answer confident that you know what is expected of you.

These questions are indicated with the "signpost" icon in the index.

Online question enhancements and answer debriefs will be available from Spring 2010 on Kaplan EN-gage at:

www.EN-gage.co.uk

Systems and Audit Procedures

Risk and audit approach

Specialised audit areas

Completion and reporting

ISAs and other key areas

ANALYSIS OF PAST PAPERS

The table below summarises the key topics that have been tested in the new syllabus examinations to date.

	Pilot	Dec 07	June 08	Dec 08	June 09	Dec 09	June 10	Dec 10	June 11
Audit Framework									
Audit vs. assurance			✓				✓		
Statutory audits				✓					
Benefits of an audit									
The regulatory environment									
Corporate governance	✓					✓			
Ethics	✓	✓		✓	✓		✓		✓
Engagement letter	✓								✓
Internal Audit									
Scope/limitations		✓	✓	✓				✓	
Audit committee	✓				✓				
Differences external and internal					✓				
Outsourcing internal audit			✓						✓
Value for money								✓	
Planning and risk assessment									
Audit risk			✓	✓		✓	✓	✓	✓
Understanding the entity						✓		✓	
Materiality							✓		
Fraud & error	✓				✓				✓
Analytical procedures			✓					✓	
Audit strategy & plan					✓	✓			
Interim & final									
Audit documentation								✓	
The work of others/internal audit	✓			✓	✓				✓
Internal control									
Internal control questionnaires			✓						✓
Control Systems/tests of controls:									
Revenue system			✓		✓				✓
Purchases system	✓	✓				✓		✓	
Payroll system	✓			✓					
Capital system						✓			
Inventory system		✓							
Cash system		✓							

	Pilot	Dec 07	June 08	Dec 08	June 09	Dec 09	June 10	Dec 10	June 11
Audit Evidence									
The use of assertions	✓		✓	✓	✓	✓		✓	
Audit sampling					✓				
Sufficient appropriate evidence			✓	✓		✓			
CAAT's/audit software	✓	✓			✓				
Not for profit organisations				✓					
The audit of specific items:									
Sales					✓	✓			✓
Purchases	✓								✓
Payroll				✓					
Trade receivables			✓		✓				✓
Bank							✓		
Non-current assets									
Trade payables	✓							✓	
Other liabilities						✓	✓	✓	
Inventory		✓				✓	✓		
Completion & reporting									
Subsequent events	✓			✓					
Going concern		✓	✓				✓		
Management representations			✓					✓	
Audit reports/opinions	✓	✓			✓	✓	✓	✓	✓
Other reports to management				✓	✓	✓		✓	
Internal audit reports									

KAPLAN PUBLISHING

EXAM TECHNIQUE

- Use the allocated **15 minutes reading and planning time** at the beginning of the exam:
  - read the questions and examination requirements carefully, and
  - begin planning your answers.

  See the Paper Specific Information for advice on how to use this time for this paper.
- **Divide the time** you spend on questions in proportion to the marks on offer:
  - there are 1.8 minutes available per mark in the examination
  - within that, try to allow time at the end of each question to review your answer and address any obvious issues

  Whatever happens, always keep your eye on the clock and **do not over run on any part of any question!**
- Spend the last **five minutes** of the examination:
  - reading through your answers, and
  - **making any additions or corrections**.
- If you **get completely stuck** with a question:
  - leave space in your answer book, and
  - **return to it later.**
- Stick to the question and **tailor your answer** to what you are asked.
  - pay particular attention to the verbs in the question.
- If you do not understand what a question is asking, **state your assumptions**.

  Even if you do not answer in precisely the way the examiner hoped, you should be given some credit, if your assumptions are reasonable.
- You should do everything you can to make things easy for the marker.

  The marker will find it easier to identify the points you have made if your **answers are legible**.
- **Written questions**:

  Your answer should:
  - Have a clear structure
  - Be concise: get to the point!
  - Address a broad range of points: it is usually better to write a little about a lot of different points than a great deal about one or two points.
- **Reports, memos and other documents**:

  Some questions ask you to present your answer in the form of a report, a memo, a letter or other document.

  Make sure that you use the correct format – there could be easy marks to gain here.

PAPER SPECIFIC INFORMATION

THE EXAM

FORMAT OF THE F8 EXAM

		Number of marks
5 compulsory questions which will be **case study based**:		
Question 1:	Case study – cross syllabus	30
Question 2:	ISAs and other key areas	10
Question 3:	Cross syllabus	20
Question 4:	Cross syllabus	20
Question 5:	Completion and reporting	20
		————
		100
		————

Total time allowed: 3 hours plus 15 minutes reading and planning time.

Note that:

- Question 1 will focus on a reasonably large scenario. The requirements will be broken into numerous sub-requirements that tests a range of audit procedures:

- Most of the marks available for question 1 are for applying your knowledge of audit procedures to the scenario, rather than simple 'knowledge dumping.' For this reason most points of explanation or recommended procedure pick up 1 mark.

- Question 2 tests a number of basic auditing principles. Requirements are typically 'list and explain' based, where you pick up ½ for listing the point and ½ for explaining it. Knowledge of ISAs is usually required in this question.

- Typical areas of testing for question 3 and 4 include: audit planning, risk assessment, ethics, audit software, internal audit, audit committees/corporate governance and not for profit organisations. Questions are usually part knowledge recall and part application to a small scenario.

- Question 5 focuses on completion and reporting, so typical questions focus on post fieldwork reviews (including subsequent events and going concern), audit reports/opinions and reporting to those charged with governance.

PASS MARK

The pass mark for all ACCA Qualification examination papers is 50%.

READING AND PLANNING TIME

Remember that all three hour paper based examinations have an additional 15 minutes reading and planning time.

ACCA GUIDANCE

ACCA guidance on the use of this time is as follows:

This additional time is allowed at the beginning of the examination to allow candidates to read the questions and to begin planning their answers before they start to write in their answer books.

This time should be used to ensure that all the information and, in particular, the exam requirements are properly read and understood.

During this time, candidates may only annotate their question paper. They may not write anything in their answer booklets until told to do so by the invigilator.

KAPLAN GUIDANCE

As all questions are compulsory, there are no decisions to be made about choice of questions, other than in which order you would like to tackle them.

Therefore, in relation to F8, we recommend that you take the following approach with your reading and planning time:

- **Skim through the whole paper**, assessing the level of difficulty of each question.

- **Write down** on the question paper next to the mark allocation **the amount of time you should spend on each part.** Do this for each part of every question.

- **Decide the order** in which you think you will attempt each question:

    This is a personal choice and you have time on the revision phase to try out different approaches, for example, if you sit mock exams.

    A common approach is to tackle the question you think is the easiest and you are most comfortable with first.

    Others may prefer to tackle the longest questions first, or conversely leave them to the last.

    Psychologists believe that you usually perform at your best on the second and third question you attempt, once you have settled into the exam, so not tackling the longer question first may be advisable.

    It is usual, however, that students tackle their least favourite topic and/or the most difficult question last.

    Whatever your approach, you must make sure that you leave enough time to attempt all questions fully and be very strict with yourself in timing each question.

- **For each question** in turn, read the requirements and then the detail of the question carefully.

  Always read the requirement first as this enables you to **focus on the detail of the question with the specific task in mind**.

  For written questions:

  Take notice of the format required (e.g. letter, memo, notes) and identify the recipient of the answer . You need to do this to judge the level of sophistication required in your answer and whether the use of a formal reply or informal bullet points would be satisfactory.

  With F8, whilst there are occasions when you are requested to write a formal document, there are many times when you can use tables to present your answer. This is the case when you are asked to link answers together. Pay attention to the format of the answers in this text to help identify when such layouts are appropriate.

  Plan your beginning, middle and end and the key areas to be addressed and your use of titles and sub-titles to enhance your answer.

  For all questions:

  Spot the easy marks to be gained in a question.

  Make sure that you do these parts first when you tackle the question.

  Don't go overboard in terms of planning time on any one question – you need a good measure of the whole paper and a plan for all of the questions at the end of the 15 minutes.

  By covering all questions you can often help yourself as you may find that facts in one question may remind you of things you should put into your answer relating to a different question.

- With your plan of attack in mind, **start answering your chosen question** with your plan to hand, as soon as you are allowed to start.

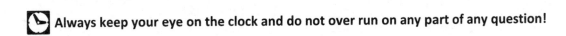 **Always keep your eye on the clock and do not over run on any part of any question!**

DETAILED SYLLABUS

The detailed syllabus and study guide written by the ACCA can be found at:

www.accaglobal.com/students/

KAPLAN'S RECOMMENDED REVISION APPROACH

QUESTION PRACTICE IS THE KEY TO SUCCESS

Success in professional examinations relies upon you acquiring a firm grasp of the required knowledge at the tuition phase. In order to be able to do the questions, knowledge is essential.

However, the difference between success and failure often hinges on your exam technique on the day and making the most of the revision phase of your studies.

The **Kaplan complete text** is the starting point, designed to provide the underpinning knowledge to tackle all questions. However, in the revision phase, pouring over text books is not the answer.

Kaplan Online fixed tests help you consolidate your knowledge and understanding and are a useful tool to check whether you can remember key topic areas.

Kaplan pocket notes are designed to help you quickly revise a topic area, however you then need to practice questions. There is a need to progress to full exam standard questions as soon as possible, and to tie your exam technique and technical knowledge together.

The importance of question practice cannot be over-emphasised.

The recommended approach below is designed by expert tutors in the field, in conjunction with their knowledge of the examiner and their recent real exams.

The approach taken for the fundamental papers is to revise by topic area. However, with the professional stage papers, a multi topic approach is required to answer the scenario based questions.

You need to practice as many questions as possible in the time you have left.

OUR AIM

Our aim is to get you to the stage where you can attempt exam standard questions confidently, to time, in a closed book environment, with no supplementary help (i.e. to simulate the real examination experience).

Practising your exam technique on real past examination questions, in timed conditions, is also vitally important for you to assess your progress and identify areas of weakness that may need more attention in the final run up to the examination.

In order to achieve this we recognise that initially you may feel the need to practice some questions with open book help and exceed the required time.

The approach below shows you which questions you should use to build up to coping with exam standard question practice, and references to the sources of information available should you need to revisit a topic area in more detail.

Remember that in the real examination, all you have to do is:

- attempt all questions required by the exam

- only spend the allotted time on each question, and

- get them at least 50% right!

Try and practice this approach on every question you attempt from now to the real exam.

EXAMINER COMMENTS

We have included the examiners comments to the specific new syllabus examination questions in this kit for you to see the main pitfalls that students fall into with regard to technical content.

However, too many times in the general section of the report, the examiner comments that students had failed due to:

- "misallocation of time"

- "running out of time" and

- showing signs of "spending too much time on an earlier questions and clearly rushing the answer to a subsequent question".

Good exam technique is vital.

THE KAPLAN PAPER F8 REVISION PLAN

Stage 1: Assess areas of strengths and weaknesses

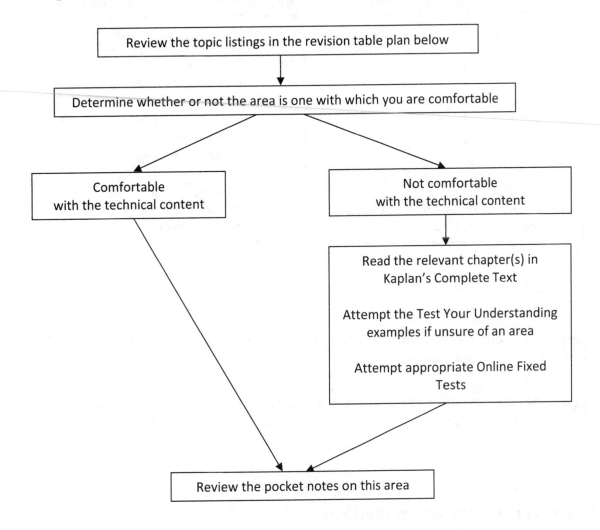

Stage 2: Practice questions

Follow the order of revision of topics as recommended in the revision table plan below and attempt the questions in the order suggested.

Try to avoid referring to text books and notes and the model answer until you have completed your attempt.

Try to answer the question in the allotted time.

Review your attempt with the model answer and assess how much of the answer you achieved in the allocated exam time.

Fill in the self-assessment box below and decide on your best course of action.

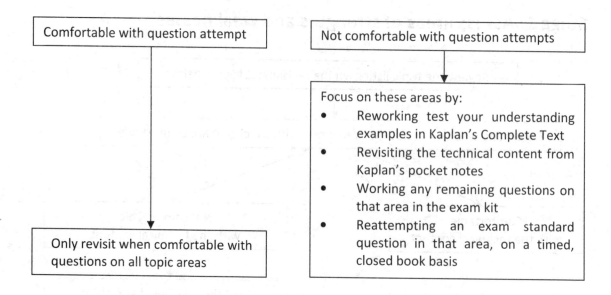

Note that :

 The "footsteps questions" give guidance on exam techniques and how you should have approached the question.

 The "clock questions" have an online debrief where a tutor talks you through the exam technique and approach to that question and works the question in full.

Stage 3: Final pre-exam revision

We recommend that you **attempt at least one three hour mock examination** containing a set of previously unseen exam standard questions.

It is important that you get a feel for the breadth of coverage of a real exam without advanced knowledge of the topic areas covered – just as you will expect to see on the real exam day.

Ideally this mock should be sat in timed, closed book, real exam conditions and could be:

- a mock examination offered by your tuition provider, and/or

- the pilot paper in the back of this exam kit, and/or

- the last real examination paper (available shortly afterwards on Kaplan EN-gage with "enhanced walk through answers" and a full "tutor debrief").

THE DETAILED REVISION PLAN

Topics (as per the "7 Capabilities" identified in the examiner's approach article)	Complete Text (and Pocket Note) Chapter	Questions to attempt	Tutor guidance	Date attempted	Self assessment
1. Nature, purpose & scope of assurance, the role of external audit and ethics	1, 2, & 4	17, 19, 23 & 26	Make sure that you can define the elements of the Code of Ethics and that you practice applying the concepts to specific scenarios. You must also be able to discuss the purpose of assurance and the levels of assurance offered by accountants.		
2. Nature of internal audit	12	10, 30, 32 & 38	Questions tend to focus on: differences between internal and external auditors; how internal audit helps meet corporate governance requirements and how internal and external auditors interact.		
3. Understanding clients: risk assessment and planning	5 & 6	16, 18, 24, & 31	Audit risk is a vital concept. You need to be able to: discuss what it is, including materiality; perform risk assessment for a client; and discuss its impact on audit strategy.		
4. Information systems & internal controls	8	1, 7, & 19	At a basic level you need to know how a simple financial control system (e.g. sales, purchases, payroll etc..) operates. You then need to be able to discuss how those systems should be tested, including CAATs. You may also be asked to identify weaknesses in control systems and recommend improvements.		

5. Audit procedures	7 & 9	3, 4, 5, 6, 7, 33 & 35	Question 1 tends to focus on a particular system and requires candidates to discuss a range of audit procedures relevant to those systems. It is vital that you identify **specifically** what procedures are required (e.g. tests of control, analytical procedures) and what assertions are being tested (e.g. completeness, existence, accuracy).
6. Evaluation of audit findings	10	43, 44 & 50	There are a wide range of issues that need to be considered at the completion phase of an audit, as well as performing normal reviews. Typical examples include: subsequent events and going concern reviews. You may also be asked to consider how you report on issues other than in an audit report (e.g. fraud and reporting to those charged with governance).
7. Audit reports	11	41, 45, & 47	One of the fundamental weaknesses identified by the examiner is a lack of understanding regarding the nature of audit report modifications. It is therefore important that you are able to assess a scenario and identify how it might impact upon your audit opinion. You also need to be able to discuss the content and purpose of the sections of an audit report.

Note that not all of the questions are referred to in the programme above. We have recommended an approach to build up from the basic to exam standard questions.

The remaining questions are available in the kit for extra practice for those who require more question on some areas.

Section 1

PRACTICE QUESTIONS

SYSTEMS & AUDIT PROCEDURES

1   **SHINY HAPPY WINDOWS CO** *Walk in the footsteps of a top tutor*

  (a) **(i)** Define a 'test of control' and a 'substantive procedure'; **(2 marks)**

        (ii) State ONE test of control and ONE substantive procedure in relation to sales invoicing. **(2 marks)**

  (b) Shiny Happy Windows Co (SHW) is a window cleaning company. Customers' windows are cleaned monthly, the window cleaner then posts a stamped addressed envelope for payment through the customer's front door.

      SHW has a large number of receivable balances and these customers pay by cheque or cash, which is received in the stamped addressed envelopes in the post. The following procedures are applied to the cash received cycle:

      (1) A junior clerk from the accounts department opens the post and if any cheques or cash have been sent, she records the receipts in the cash received log and then places all the monies into the locked small cash box.

      (2) The contents of the cash box are counted each day and every few days these sums are banked by which ever member of the finance team is available.

      (3) The cashier records the details of the cash received log into the cash receipts day book and also updates the sales ledger.

      (4) Usually on a monthly basis the cashier performs a bank reconciliation, which he then files, if he misses a month then he catches this up in the following month's reconciliation.

      Required:

      For the cash cycle of SHW:

      (i) Identify and explain THREE deficiencies in the system; **(3 marks)**

      (ii) Suggest controls to address each of these deficiencies; and **(3 marks)**

      (iii) List tests of controls the auditor of SHW would perform to assess if the controls are operating effectively. **(3 marks)**

  (c) Describe substantive procedures an auditor would perform in verifying a company's bank balance. **(7 marks)**

                      (Total: 20 marks)

(2) **REDBURN CO** *Walk in the footsteps of a top tutor*

(a) Explain the importance of audit planning and state TWO matters that would be included in an audit plan. **(6 marks)**

Redburn Co, a publisher and producer of books of poetry, has been a client of your firm of Chartered Certified Accountants for a number of years. The manager in overall charge of the audit has been discussing the audit plan with the audit team, of which you are a member, prior to commencement of the work. The audit manager has informed the team, among other things, that there has been a growing interest in poetry generally and that the company has acquired a reputation for publishing poets who are still relatively unknown.

During your audit you determine:

(i) Contracts with the poets state that they are given a royalty of 10% on sales. Free copies of the books are provided to the poets and to some organisations such as copyright libraries and to others, such as reviewers and university lecturers. No royalties are given on these free copies.

(ii) The computerised customer master file contains a code indicating whether a despatch is to earn a royalty for the author. This code is shown on the sales invoice and despatch note when they are prepared.

(iii) A computerised royalties file is held, all entries therein bearing the invoice number and date.

(iv) The company keeps detailed statistics of sales made, including trends of monthly sales by type of customer, and of colleges where its books are recommended as part of course material, based on reports from sales staff.

(v) Bookshops have the right to return books which are not selling well, but about 10% of these are slightly damaged when returned. The company keeps similar records of returns as it does for sales.

Required:

(b) Describe TWO procedures used to ensure that the sales statistics kept by the company may be relied upon. **(4 marks)**

(c) Describe THREE substantive tests you should perform to ensure that the royalties charge is accurate and complete, stating the objective of each test. **(6 marks)**

(d) A material figure in the statement of financial position of Redburn Co is the amount attributed to inventory of books.

Required:

State TWO inherent risks that may affect the inventory figure and suggest ONE control to mitigate each risk. **(4 marks)**

(e) The management of Redburn Co have told you that inventory is correctly valued at the lower of cost and netrealisable value. You have already satisfied yourself that cost is correctly determined.

Required:

(i) Define net realisable value; (2 marks)

(ii) State and explain the purpose of FOUR procedures that you should use to ensure that net realisable value of the inventory is at or above cost. (8 marks)

(Total: 30 marks)

3 **B-STAR** *Walk in the footsteps of a top tutor*

 Timed question with Online tutor debrief

Background information

B-Star is a theme park based on a popular series of children's books. Customers pay a fixed fee to enter the park, where they can participate in a variety of activities such as riding roller-coasters, playing on slides and purchasing themed souvenirs from gift shops.

The park is open all year and has been in operation for the last seven years. It is located in a country which has very little rainfall – the park is open-air so poor weather such as rain results in a significant fall in the number of customers for that day (normally by 50%). During the last seven years there have been on average 30 days each year with rain.

B-Star is now very successful; customer numbers are increasing at approximately 15% each year.

Ticket sales

Customers purchase tickets to enter the theme park from ticket offices located outside the park. Tickets are only valid on the day of purchase. Adults and children are charged the same price for admission to the park. Tickets are preprinted and stored in each ticket office.

Tickets are purchased using either cash or credit cards.

Each ticket has a number comprising of two elements – two digits relating to the ticket office followed by six digits to identify the ticket. The last six digits are in ascending sequential order.

Cash sales

(1) All ticket sales are recorded on a computer showing the amount of each sale and the number of tickets issued. This information is transferred electronically to the accounts office.

(2) Cash is collected regularly from each ticket office by two security guards. The cash is then counted by two accounts clerks and banked on a daily basis.

(3)   The total cash from each ticket office is agreed to the sales information that has been transferred from each office.

(4)   Total cash received is then recorded in the cash book, and then the general ledger.

Credit card sales

(1)   Payments by credit cards are authorised online as the customers purchase their tickets.

(2)   Computers in each ticket office record the sales information which is transferred electronically to the accounts office.

(3)   Credit card sales are recorded for each credit card company in a receivables ledger.

(4)   When payment is received from the credit card companies, the accounts clerks agree the total sales values to the amounts received from the credit card companies, less the commission payable to those companies. The receivables ledger is updated with the payments received.

You are now commencing the planning of the annual audit of B-Star. The date is 3 June 2009 and B-Star's year end is 30 June 2009.

Required:

(a)   List and explain the purpose of the main sections of an audit strategy and for each section, provide an example relevant to B-Star.   **(8 marks)**

(b)   (i)   For the cash sales system of B-Star, identify the risks that could affect the assertion of completeness of sales and cash receipts;   **(4 marks)**

       (ii)   Discuss the extent to which tests of controls and substantive procedures could be used to confirm the assertion of completeness of income in B-Star.
                                                                                          (6 marks)

(c)   (i)   List the substantive analytical procedures that may be used to give assurance on the total income from ticket sales for one day in B-Star;

       (ii)   List the substantive analytical procedures that may be used to give assurance on the total income from ticket sales in B-Star for the year.   **(8 marks)**

(d)   List the audit procedures you should perform on the credit card receivables balance.   **(4 marks)**

                                                                                   (Total: 30 marks)

 Calculate your allowed time, allocate the time to the separate parts...............

---

4   BLAKE *Walk in the footsteps of a top tutor*

Introduction

Blake Co assembles specialist motor vehicles such as lorries, buses and trucks. The company owns four assembly plants to which parts are delivered and assembled into the motor vehicles.

The motor vehicles are assembled using a mix of robot and manual production lines. The 'human' workers normally work a standard eight hour day, although this is supplemented by overtime on a regular basis as Blake has a full order book. There is one shift per day; mass production and around the clock working are not possible due to the specialist nature of the motor vehicles being assembled.

Wages system – shift workers

Shift-workers arrive for work at about 7.00 am and 'clock in' using an electronic identification card. The card is scanned by the time recording system and each production shift-worker's identification number is read from their card by the scanner. The worker is then logged in as being at work. Shift-workers are paid from the time of logging in. The logging in process is not monitored as it is assumed that shift-workers would not work without first logging in on the time recording system.

Shift-workers are split into groups of about 25 employees, with each group under the supervision of a shift foreman. Each day, each group of shift-workers is allocated a specific vehicle to manufacture. At least 400 vehicles have to be manufactured each day by each work group. If necessary, overtime is worked to complete the day's quota of vehicles. The shift foreman is not required to monitor the extent of any overtime working although the foreman does ensure workers are not taking unnecessary or prolonged breaks which would automatically increase the amount of overtime worked. Shift-workers log off at the end of each shift by re-scanning their identification card.

Payment of wages

Details of hours worked each week are sent electronically to the payroll department, where hours worked are allocated by the computerised wages system to each employee's wages records. Staff in the payroll department compare hours worked from the time recording system to the computerised wages system, and enter a code word to confirm the accuracy of transfer. The code word also acts as authorisation to calculate net wages. The code word is the name of a domestic cat belonging to the department head and is therefore generally known around the department.

Each week the computerised wages system calculates:

(i)   gross wages, using the standard rate and overtime rates per hour for each employee,

(ii)   statutory deductions from wages, and

(iii)   net pay.

The list of net pay for each employee is sent over Blake's internal network to the accounts department. In the accounts department, an accounts clerk ensures that employee bank details are on file. The clerk then authorises and makes payment to those employees using Blake's online banking systems. Every few weeks the financial accountant reviews the total amount of wages made to ensure that the management accounts are accurate.

Termination of employees

Occasionally, employees leave Blake. When this happens, the personnel department sends an e-mail to the payroll department detailing the employee's termination date and any unclaimed holiday pay. The receipt of the e-mail by the payroll department is not monitored by the personnel department.

Salaries system – shift managers

All shift managers are paid an annual salary; there are no overtime payments.

Salaries were increased in July by 3% and an annual bonus of 5% of salary was paid in November

Required:

(a) List FOUR control objectives of a wages system. **(2 marks)**

(b) As the external auditors of Blake Co, write a management letter to the directors in respect of the shift-workers wages recording and payment systems which:

    (i) Identifies and explains FOUR deficiencies in that system;

    (ii) Explains the possible effect of each deficiency;

    (iii) Provides a recommendation to alleviate each deficiency.

    Note up to two marks will be awarded within this requirement for presentation.

(14 marks)

(c) List THREE substantive analytical procedures you should perform on the shift managers' salary system. For each procedure, state your expectation of the result of that procedure. **(6 marks)**

(d) Audit evidence can be obtained using various audit procedures, such as inspection.

APART FROM THIS PROCEDURE, in respect of testing the accuracy of the time recording system at Blake Co, explain FOUR procedures used in collecting audit evidence and discuss whether the auditor will benefit from using each procedure.

(8 marks)

(Total: 30 marks)

5 BRENNON & CO

Introduction – audit firm

You are an audit senior in Brennon & Co, a firm providing audit and assurance services. At the request of an audit partner, you are preparing the audit programme for the income and receivables systems of Seeley Co.

Audit documentation is available from the previous year's audit, including internal control questionnaires and audit programmes for the despatch and sales system. The audit approach last year did not involve the use of computer assisted audit techniques (CAATs); the same approach will be taken this year. As far as you are aware, Seeley's system of internal control has not changed in the last year.

Client background – sales system

Seeley Co is a wholesaler of electrical goods such as kettles, televisions, MP3 players, etc. The company maintains one large warehouse in a major city. The customers of Seeley are always owners of small retail shops, where electrical goods are sold to members of the public. Seeley only sells to authorised customers; following appropriate credit checks, each customer is given a Seeley identification card to confirm their status. The card must be used to obtain goods from the warehouse.

Despatch and sales system

The despatch and sales system operates as follows:

(1)   Customers visit Seeley's warehouse and load the goods they require into their vans after showing their Seeley identification card to the despatch staff.

(2)   A pre-numbered goods despatch note (GDN) is produced and signed by the customer and a member of Seeley's despatch staff confirming goods taken.

(3)   One copy of the GDN is sent to the accounts department, the second copy is retained in the despatch department.

(4)   Accounts staff enter goods despatch information onto the computerised sales system. The GDN is signed.

(5)   The computer system produces the sales invoice, with reference to the inventory master file for product details and prices, maintains the sales day book and also the receivables ledger. The receivables control account is balanced by the computer.

(6)   Invoices are printed out and sent to each customer in the post with paper copies maintained in the accounts department. Invoices are compared to GDNs by accounts staff and signed.

(7)   Paper copies of the receivables ledger control account and list of aged receivables are also available.

(8)   Error reports are produced showing breaks in the GDN sequence.

Information on receivables

The chief accountant has informed you that receivables days have increased from 45 to 60 days over the last year. The aged receivables report produced by the computer is shown below:

Number of receivables	Range of debt	Total debt $	Current $	1 to 2 months old $	More than 2 months old $
15	Less than $0	(87,253)	(87,253)	-	-
197	$0 to $20,000	2,167,762	548,894	643,523	975,345
153	$20,001 to 50,000	5,508,077	2,044,253	2,735,073	728,751
23	$50,001 or more	1,495,498	750,235	672,750	72,513
388		9,084,084	3,256,129	4,051,346	1,776,609

In view of the deteriorating receivables situation, a direct confirmation of receivables will be performed this year.

Required:

(a)   Explain the steps necessary to check the accuracy of the previous year's internal control questionnaires.   **(4 marks)**

(b)   Using information from the scenario, list SIX tests of control that an auditor would normally carry out on the despatch and sales system at Seeley Co and explain the reason for each test.   **(12 marks)**

(c)   State and explain the meaning of FOUR assertions that relate to the direct confirmation of receivables.   (4 marks)

(d)   (i)   Describe the procedures up to despatch of letters to individual receivables in relation to a direct confirmation of receivables.   (5 marks)

        (ii)   Discuss which particular categories of receivables might be chosen for the sample.   (5 marks)

                                                                                          (Total: 30 marks)

 Online question assistance

---

6   METCALF CO

ISA 500 Audit Evidence requires that auditors 'obtain sufficient appropriate audit evidence to be able to draw reasonable conclusions on which to base the auditor's opinion'.

Required:

(a)   **List and explain the factors which will influence the auditor's judgement concerning the sufficiency of audit evidence obtained.**   **(4 marks)**

You are the audit senior in charge of the audit of Metcalf Co, a company that has been trading for over 50 years. Metcalf Co manufactures and sells tables and chairs directly to the public. The company's year end is 31 March.

Current liabilities are shown on Metcalf Co's balance sheet as follows:

	2007	2006
	$	$
Trade payables	884,824	816,817
Accruals	56,903	51,551
Provision for legal action	60,000	–
	1,001,727	868,368

The provision for legal action relates to a claim from a customer who suffered an injury while assembling a chair supplied by Metcalf Co. The directors of Metcalf Co dispute the claim, although they are recommending an out of court settlement to avoid damaging publicity against Metcalf Co.

Required:

(b)   **List the substantive audit procedures that you should undertake in the audit of current liabilities of Metcalf Co for the year ended 31 March 2007. For each procedure, explain the purpose of that procedure.**

        Marks are allocated as follows:

        (i)   **Trade payables;**   **(9 marks)**

        (ii)   **Accruals;**   **(3 marks)**

        (iii)   **The provision for legal action.**   **(4 marks)**

                                                                                          (Total: 20 marks)

---

7   DINZEE CO

DinZee Co assembles fridges, microwaves, washing machines and other similar domestic appliances from parts procured from a large number of suppliers. As part of the interim audit work two weeks prior to the company year-end, you are testing the procurement and purchases systems and attending the inventory count.

Procurement and purchases system

Parts inventory is monitored by the stores manager. When the quantity of a particular part falls below re-order level, an e-mail is sent to the procurement department detailing the part required and the quantity to order. A copy of the e-mail is filed on the store manager's computer.

Staff in the procurement department check the e-mail, allocate the order to an authorised supplier and send the order to that supplier using Electronic Data Interchange (EDI). A copy of the EDI order is filed in the order database by the computer system. The order is identified by a unique order number.

When goods are received at DinZee, the stores clerk confirms that the inventory agrees to the delivery note and checks the order database to ensure that the inventory were in fact ordered by DinZee. (Delivery is refused where goods do not have a delivery note.)

The order in the order database is updated to confirm receipt of goods, and the perpetual inventory system updated to show the receipt of inventory. The physical goods are added to the parts store and the paper delivery note is stamped with the order number and is filed in the goods inwards department.

The supplier sends a purchase invoice to DinZee using EDI; invoices are automatically routed to the accounts department. On receipt of the invoice, the accounts clerk checks the order database, matches the invoice details with the database and updates the database to confirm receipt of invoice. The invoice is added to the purchases database, where the purchase day book (PDB) and suppliers individual account in the payables ledger are automatically updated.

Required:

(a)   List SIX audit procedures that an auditor would normally carry out on the purchases system at DinZee Co, explaining the reason for each procedure.   **(12 marks)**

(b)   List FOUR audit procedures that an auditor will normally perform prior to attending the client's premises on the day of the inventory count.   **(2 marks)**

On the day of the inventory count, you attended depot nine at DinZee. You observed the following activities:

(1) Prenumbered count sheets were being issued to client's staff carrying out the count. The count sheets showed the inventory ledger balances for checking against physical inventory.

(2) All count staff were drawn from the inventory warehouse and were counting in teams of two.

(3) Three counting teams were allocated to each area of the stores to count, although the teams were allowed to decide which pair of staff counted which inventory within each area. Staff were warned that they had to remember which inventory had been counted.

(4) Information was recorded on the count sheets in pencil so amendments could be made easily as required.

(5) Any inventory not located on the pre-numbered inventory sheets was recorded on separate inventory sheets – which were numbered by staff as they were used.

(6) At the end of the count, all count sheets were collected and the numeric sequence of the sheets checked; the sheets were not signed.

Required:

(i) **List the deficiencies in the control system for counting inventory at depot nine.** **(3 marks)**

(ii) **For each deficiency, explain why it is a deficiency and state how that deficiency can be overcome.** **(9 marks)**

(d) (i) **State the aim of a test of control and the aim of a substantive procedure.**

(ii) **In respect of your attendance at DinZee Co's inventory count, state one test of control and one substantive procedure that you should perform. (4 marks)**

(Total: 30 marks)

8 **FIREFLY TENNIS CLUB** *Walk in the footsteps of a top tutor*

The FireFly Tennis Club owns 12 tennis courts. The club uses 'all weather' tarmac tennis courts, which have floodlights for night-time use. The club's year end is 30 September.

Members pay an annual fee to use the courts and participate in club championships. The club had 430 members as at 1 October 2005.

Income is derived from two main sources:

(1) Membership fees. Each member pays a fee of $200 per annum. Fees for the new financial year are payable within one month of the club year end. Approximately 10% of members do not renew their membership. New members joining during the year pay 50% of the total fees that would have been payable had they been members for a full year. During 2006, 50 new members joined the club. No members pay their fees before they are due.

(2) Court hire fees: Non-members pay $5 per hour to hire a court. Non-members have to sign a list in the club house showing courts hired. Money is placed in a cash box in the club house for collection by the club secretary.

All fees (membership and court hire) are paid in cash. They are collected by the club secretary and banked on a regular basis. The paying-in slip shows the analysis between fees and court hire income. The secretary provides the treasurer with a list of bankings showing member's names (for membership fees) and the amount banked. Details of all bankings are entered into the cash book by the treasurer.

Main items of expenditure are:

(1) Court maintenance including repainting lines on a regular basis.

(2) Power costs for floodlights.

(3) Tennis balls for club championships. Each match in the championship uses 12 tennis balls.

The treasurer pays for all expenditure using the club's debit card. Receipts are obtained for all expenses and these are maintained in date order in an expenses file. The treasurer also prepares the annual financial statements.

Under the rules of the club, the annual accounts must be audited by an independent auditor. The date is now 13 December 2006 and the treasurer has just prepared the financial statements for audit.

Required:

(a) Describe the audit work that should be performed to determine the completeness of income for the FireFly Tennis Club.   **(10 marks)**

(b) Describe the audit procedures that should be performed to check the completeness and accuracy of expenditure for the FireFly Tennis Club.   **(5 marks)**

(c) Discuss why internal control testing has limited value when auditing not-for-profit entities such as the FireFly Tennis Club.   **(5 marks)**

(Total: 20 marks)

9   ATLANTIS STANDARD GOODS (ASG) CO (A)

(a) State the control objectives for the ordering, despatch and invoicing of goods.
(5 marks)

Atlantis Standard Goods (ASG) Co has a year end of 30 June 2006. ASG is a retailer of kitchen appliances such as washing machines, fridges and microwaves. All sales are made via the company's Internet site with despatch and delivery of goods to the customer's house made using ASG's vehicles. Appliances are purchased from many different manufacturers.

The process of making a sale is as follows:

(1) Potential customers visit ASG's website and select the kitchen appliance that they require. The website ordering system accesses the inventory specification file to obtain details of products ASG sells.

(2) When the customer chooses an appliance, order information including price, item and quantity required are stored in the orders pending file.

(3)   Online authorisation of credit card details is obtained from the customer's credit card company automatically by ASG's computer systems.

(4)   Following authorisation, the sales amount is transferred to the computerised sales day book. At the end of each day the total from this ledger is transferred to the general ledger.

(5)   Reimbursement of the sales amount is obtained from each credit card company monthly, less the appropriate commission charged by the credit card company.

(6)   Following authorisation of the credit card, order details are transferred to a goods awaiting despatch file and allocated a unique order reference code. Order details are automatically transferred to the despatch department's computer system.

(7)   In the despatch department, goods are obtained from the physical inventory, placed on ASG vehicles and the computerised inventory system updated. Order information is downloaded on a hand held computer with a writable screen.

(8)   On delivery, the customer signs for the goods on the hand held computer. On return to ASG's warehouse, images of the customer signature are uploaded to the orders file which is then flagged as 'order complete'.

This year's audit planning documentation states that a substantive approach will be taken on the audit.

Required:

(b)   Tabulate the audit tests you should carry out on the sales and despatch system, explaining the reason for each test.   **(15 marks)**

(c)   Describe the audit work you will perform during and after ASG's year end inventory count.   **(10 marks)**

(Total: 30 marks)

10   DECE & CO

You are the audit manager in the firm of DeCe & Co, an audit firm with ten national offices.

One of your clients, Rocks Forever, purchases diamond jewellery from three manufacturers. The jewellery is then sold from Rocks Forever's four shops. This is the only client your firm has in the diamond industry.

You are planning to attend the physical inventory count for Rocks Forever. Inventory is the largest account on the statement of financial position with each of the four shops holding material amounts. Due to the high value of the inventory, all shops will be visited and test counts performed.

With the permission of the directors of Rocks Forever, you have employed UJ, a firm of specialist diamond valuers who will also be in attendance. UJ will verify that the jewellery is, in fact, made from diamonds and that the jewellery is saleable with respect to current trends in fashion. UJ will also suggest, on a sample basis, the value of specific items of jewellery.

Counting will be carried out by shop staff in teams of two using pre-numbered count sheets.

Required:

(a) List and explain the reason for the audit procedures used in obtaining evidence in relation to the inventory count of inventory held in the shops. **(10 marks)**

(b) Explain the factors you should consider when placing reliance on the work of UJ. **(5 marks)**

(c) Describe the audit procedures you should perform to ensure that jewellery inventory is valued correctly. **(5 marks)**

(Total: 20 marks)

11 TRACEY TRANSPORTERS

You are the external auditor of Tracey Transporters, a public limited company (TT). The company's year end is 31 March. You have been the auditor since the company was formed 24 years ago to take advantage of the increase in goods being transported by road. Many companies needed to transport their products but did not always have sufficient vehicles to move them. TT therefore purchased ten vehicles and hired these to haulage companies for amounts of time ranging from three days to six months.

The business has grown in size and profitability and now has over 550 vehicles on hire to many different companies. At any one time, between five and 20 vehicles are located at the company premises where they are being repaired; the rest could be anywhere on the extensive road network of the country it operates in. Full details of all vehicles are maintained in a non-current asset register.

Bookings for hire of vehicles are received either over the telephone or via e-mail in TT's offices. A booking clerk checks the customer's credit status on the receivables ledger and then the availability of vehicles using the Vehicle Management System (VMS) software on TT's computer network. E-mails are filed electronically by customer name in the e-mail program used by TT. If the customer's credit rating is acceptable and a vehicle is available, the booking is entered into the VMS and confirmed to the customer using the telephone or e-mail. Booking information is then transferred within the network from the VMS to the receivables ledger program, where a sales invoice is raised. Standard rental amounts are allocated to each booking depending on the amount of time the vehicle is being hired for. Hard copy invoices are sent in the post for telephone orders or via e-mail for e-mail orders.

The main class of asset on TT's statement of financial position is the vehicles. The net book value of the vehicles is $6 million out of total shareholders' funds of $15 million as at 31 March 20X5.

Required:

(a) List and explain the reason for the audit tests you should perform to check the completeness and accuracy of the sales figure in TT's financial statements. **(10 marks)**

(b) List and describe the audit work you should perform on the statement of financial position figure for vehicles in TT's financial statements for the year ended 31 March 20X5. **(10 marks)**

(Total: 20 marks)

12 BEARSWORLD (A)

You are the auditor of BearsWorld, a limited liability company which manufactures and sells small cuddly toys by mail order. The company is managed by Mr Kyto and two assistants. Mr Kyto authorises important transactions such as wages and large orders, one assistant maintains the payables ledger and orders inventory and pays suppliers, and the other assistant receives customer orders and despatches cuddly toys. Due to other business commitments Mr Kyto only visits the office once per week.

At any time, about 100 different types of cuddly toys are available for sale. All sales are made cash with order – there are no receivables. Customers pay using credit cards and occasionally by sending cash. Turnover is over $5.2 million.

You are planning the audit of BearsWorld and are considering using some of the procedures for gathering audit evidence recommended by ISA 500 as follows:

(i)   Analytical Procedures

(ii)   Inquiry

(iii)   Inspection

(iv)   Observation

(v)   Re-calculation

Required:

(a)   For EACH of the above procedures:

   (i)   Explain its use in gathering audit evidence.   (5 marks)

   (ii)   Describe one example for the audit of BearsWorld.   (5 marks)

(b)   Discuss the suitability of each procedure for BearsWorld, explaining the limitations of each.   (10 marks)

(c)   Tabulate FIVE key features of small companies such as BearsWorld and the impact these may have on your audit work.   (10 marks)

(Total: 30 marks)

RISK AND AUDIT APPROACH

13   LV FONES CO *Walk in the footsteps of a top tutor*

(a)   State the FIVE threats contained within ACCA's Code of Ethics and Conduct and for each threat list ONE example of a circumstance that may create the threat. (5 marks)

(b)   You are the audit manager of Jones & Co and you are planning the audit of LV Fones Co, which has been an audit client for four years and specialises in manufacturing luxury mobile phones.

During the planning stage of the audit you have obtained the following information. The employees of LV Fones Co are entitled to purchase mobile phones at a discount of 10%. The audit team has in previous years been offered the same level of staff discount.

During the year the financial controller of LV Fones was ill and hence unable to work. The company had no spare staff able to fulfil the role and hence a qualified audit senior of Jones & Co was seconded to the client for three months. The audit partner has recommended that the audit senior work on the audit as he has good knowledge of the client. The fee income derived from LV Fones was boosted by this engagement and along with the audit and tax fee, now accounts for 16% of the firm's total fees.

From a review of the correspondence files you note that the partner and the finance director have known each other socially for many years and in fact went on holiday together last summer with their families. As a result of this friendship the partner has not yet spoken to the client about the fee for last year's audit, 20% of which is still outstanding.

Required:

(i)   Explain the ethical threats which may affect the independence of Jones & Co's audit of LV Fones Co; and   **(5 marks)**

(ii)   For each threat explain how it might be avoided.   **(5 marks)**

(c)   Describe the steps an audit firm should perform prior to accepting a new audit engagement.   **(5 marks)**

(Total: 20 marks)

14   SMOOTHBRUSH PAINTS CO *Walk in the footsteps of a top tutor*

Introduction and client background

You are an audit senior in Staple and Co and you are commencing the planning of the audit of Smoothbrush Paints Co for the year ending 31 August 2010.

Smoothbrush Paints Co is a paint manufacturer and has been trading for over 50 years, it operates from one central site, which includes the production facility, warehouse and administration offices.

Smoothbrush sells all of its goods to large home improvement stores, with 60% being to one large chain store Homewares. The company has a one year contract to be the sole supplier of paint to Homewares. It secured the contract through significantly reducing prices and offering a four-month credit period, the company's normal credit period is one month.

Goods in/purchases

In recent years, Smoothbrush has reduced the level of goods directly manufactured and instead started to import paint from South Asia. Approximately 60% is imported and 40% manufactured. Within the production facility is a large amount of old plant and equipment that is now redundant and has minimal scrap value. Purchase orders for overseas paint are made six months in advance and goods can be in transit for up to two months. Smoothbrush accounts for the inventory when it receives the goods.

To avoid the disruption of a year end inventory count, Smoothbrush has this year introduced a continuous/perpetual inventory counting system. The warehouse has been divided into 12 areas and these are each to be counted once over the year. The counting team includes a member of the internal audit department and a warehouse staff member. The following procedures have been adopted;

(1) The team prints the inventory quantities and descriptions from the system and these records are then compared to the inventory physically present.

(2) Any discrepancies in relation to quantities are noted on the inventory sheets, including any items not listed on the sheets but present in the warehouse area.

(3) Any damaged or old items are noted and they are removed from the inventory sheets.

(4) The sheets are then passed to the finance department for adjustments to be made to the records when the count has finished.

(5) During the counts there will continue to be inventory movements with goods arriving and leaving the warehouse.

At the year end it is proposed that the inventory will be based on the underlying records. Traditionally Smoothbrush has maintained an inventory provision based on 1% of the inventory value, but management feels that as inventory is being reviewed more regularly it no longer needs this provision.

Finance Director

In May 2010 Smoothbrush had a dispute with its finance director (FD) and he immediately left the company. The company has temporarily asked the financial controller to take over the role while they recruit a permanent replacement. The old FD has notified Smoothbrush that he intends to sue for unfair dismissal. The company is not proposing to make any provision or disclosures for this, as they are confident the claim has no merit.

Required:

(a) Identify and explain the audit risks identified at the planning stage of the audit of Smoothbrush Paints Co. (10 marks)

(b) Discuss the importance of assessing risks at the planning stage of an audit. (4 marks)

(c) List and explain suitable controls that should operate over the continuous/perpetual inventory counting system, to ensure the completeness and accuracy of the existing inventory records at Smoothbrush Paints Co. (10 marks)

(d) Describe THREE substantive procedures the auditor of Smoothbrush Paints Co should perform at the year end in confirming each of the following:

(i) The valuation of inventory;   (3 marks)

(ii) The completeness of provisions or contingent liabilities.   (3 marks)

(Total: 30 marks)

15 LETHAM CO   *Walk in the footsteps of a top tutor*

ISA 315 (Redrafted) *Identifying and Assessing the Risks of Material Misstatement Through Understanding the Entity and Its Environment* requires auditors to obtain an understanding of the entity and its environment, including its internal control.

Required:

(a) Explain why obtaining an understanding of the entity and its environment is important for the auditor.   (4 marks)

Letham Co is a large engineering company with ten manufacturing units throughout the country in which it is located. The manufacturing process is capital intensive and the company holds a wide variety of plant and equipment.

The finance director is responsible for the preparation of a detailed non-current assets budget annually, which is based on a five-year budget approved by the whole board of directors after consultation with the audit committee. This annual budget, which is also approved by the full board, is held on computer file and is the authority for the issue of a purchase order.

When the item of plant and equipment is delivered to the company, a pre-numbered goods received note (GRN) is prepared, a copy of which is sent to the accounting department, and used to update the non-current assets budget to reflect the movement. The equipment is carefully inspected by production personnel and tested for proper operation. An operational certificate is prepared by the production department and this is used by the accounting department, together with the GRN, to check against the purchase invoice when it is received.

At the same time as the purchase invoice enters the purchasing system, a computerised non-current assets register is updated. Access to the non-current assets register is restricted to personnel in the accounting department. On a rolling basis throughout the year the non-current assets register is compared to plant and equipment on site by accounting department personnel, using identification numbers in the register and permanently marked onto each item in the factory.

The internal audit department also tests on a sample basis the operation of the system from budget preparation to entry in the non-current assets register. Internal audit staff also compare a sample of entries in the non-current assets register with equipment on the shop floor.

Required:

(b) Identify SIX STRENGTHS in Letham's control environment in respect of non-current assets and explain why they may reduce control risk.   (12 marks)

(c) As part of your work as external auditor you are reviewing the non-current assets audit programme of the internal auditors and notice that the basis of their testing is a representative sample of purchase invoices. They use this to test entries in the non-current assets register and the updating movements on the annual budget.

Required:

(i) Explain why this is not a good test for completeness;

(ii) State a more appropriate test to prove completeness of the non-current assets records, including the non-current assets register. **(4 marks)**

(Total: 20 marks)

16 TIRROL *Walk in the footsteps of a top tutor*

 Timed question with Online tutor debrief

Following a competitive tender, your audit firm Cal & Co has just gained a new audit client Tirrol Co. You are the manager in charge of planning the audit work. Tirrol Co's year end is 30 June 2009 with a scheduled date to complete the audit of 15 August 2009. The date now is 3 June 2009.

Tirrol Co provides repair services to motor vehicles from 25 different locations. All inventory, sales and purchasing systems are computerised, with each location maintaining its own computer system. The software in each location is the same because the programs were written specifically for Tirrol Co by a reputable software house. Data from each location is amalgamated on a monthly basis at Tirrol Co's head office to produce management and financial accounts.

You are currently planning your audit approach for Tirrol Co. One option being considered is to re-write Cal & Co's audit software to interrogate the computerised inventory systems in each location of Tirrol Co (except for head office) as part of inventory valuation testing. However, you have also been informed that any computer testing will have to be on a live basis and you are aware that July is a major holiday period for your audit firm.

Required:

(a) **(i)** Explain the benefits of using audit software in the audit of Tirrol Co;

(4 marks)

(ii) Explain the problems that may be encountered in the audit of Tirrol Co and for each problem, explain how that problem could be overcome. **(10 marks)**

(b) Following a discussion with the management at Tirrol Co you now understand that the internal audit department are prepared to assist with the statutory audit. Specifically, the chief internal auditor is prepared to provide you with documentation on the computerised inventory systems at Tirrol Co. The documentation provides details of the software and shows diagrammatically how transactions are processed through the inventory system. This documentation can be used to significantly decrease the time needed to understand the computer systems and enable audit software to be written for this year's audit.

Required:

Explain how you will evaluate the computer systems documentation produced by the internal audit department in order to place reliance on it during your audit.   **(6 marks)**

(Total: 20 marks)

 Calculate your allowed time, allocate the time to the separate parts...............

17   **STARK** *Walk in the footsteps of a top tutor*

You are a manager in the audit firm of Ali & Co; and this is your first time you have worked on one of the firm's established clients, Stark Co. The main activity of Stark Co is providing investment advice to individuals regarding saving for retirement, purchase of shares and securities and investing in tax efficient savings schemes. Stark is regulated by the relevant financial services authority.

You have been asked to start the audit planning for Stark Co, by Mr Son, a partner in Ali & Co. Mr Son has been the engagement partner for Stark Co, for the previous nine years and so has excellent knowledge of the client. Mr Son has informed you that he would like his daughter Zoe to be part of the audit team this year; Zoe is currently studying for her first set of fundamentals papers for her ACCA qualification. Mr Son also informs you that Mr Far, the audit senior, received investment advice from Stark Co during the year and intends to do the same next year.

In an initial meeting with the finance director of Stark Co, you learn that the audit team will not be entertained on Stark Co's yacht this year as this could appear to be an attempt to influence the opinion of the audit. Instead, he has arranged a balloon flight costing less than one-tenth of the expense of using the yacht and hopes this will be acceptable. The director also states that the fee for taxation services this year should be based on a percentage of tax saved and trusts that your firm will accept a fixed fee for representing Stark Co in a dispute regarding the amount of sales tax payable to the taxation authorities.

Required:

(a)   (i)   Explain the ethical threats which may affect the auditor of Stark Co.

(6 marks)

(ii)   For each ethical threat, discuss how the effect of the threat can be mitigated.

(6 marks)

(b)   Discuss the benefits of Stark Co establishing an internal audit department.

(8 marks)

(Total: 20 marks)

18   ZAK CO

(a)   With reference to ISA 520 *Analytical Procedures* explain

(i)   what is meant by the term 'analytical procedures';   **(2 marks)**

(ii)   the different types of analytical procedures available to the auditor; and   **(3 marks)**

(iii)   the situations in the audit when analytical procedures can be used.   **(3 marks)**

Zak Co sells garden sheds and furniture from 15 retail outlets. Sales are made to individuals, with income being in the form of cash and debit cards. All items purchased are delivered to the customer using Zak's own delivery vans; most sheds are too big for individuals to transport in their own motor vehicles. The directors of Zak indicate that the company has had a difficult year, but are pleased to present some acceptable results to the members.

The income statements for the last two financial years are shown below

	31 March 2008	31 March 2007
	$000	$000
Revenue	7,482	6,364
Cost of sales	(3,520)	(4,253)
Gross profit	3,962	2,111
Operating expenses		
Administration	(1,235)	(1,320)
Selling and distribution	(981)	(689)
Interest payable	(101)	(105)
Investment income	145	–
Profit/(loss) before tax	1,790	(3)
Financial statement extract		
Cash and bank	253	(950)

Required:

(b)   As part of your risk assessment procedures for Zak Co, identify and provide a possible explanation for unusual changes in the income statement.   **(9 marks)**

(c)   Confirmation of the end of year bank balances is an important audit procedure.

Required:

Explain the procedures necessary to obtain a bank confirmation letter from Zak Co's bank.   **(3 marks)**

(Total: 20 marks)

 Online question assistance

19 MATALAS CO

Matalas Co sells cars, car parts and petrol from 25 different locations in one country. Each branch has up to 20 staff working there, although most of the accounting systems are designed and implemented from the company's head office. All accounting systems, apart from petty cash, are computerised, with the internal audit department frequently advising and implementing controls within those systems.

Matalas has an internal audit department of six staff, all of whom have been employed at Matalas for a minimum of five years and some for as long as 15 years. In the past, the chief internal auditor appoints staff within the internal audit department, although the chief executive officer (CEO) is responsible for appointing the chief internal auditor. The chief internal auditor reports directly to the finance director. The finance director also assists the chief internal auditor in deciding on the scope of work of the internal audit department.

You are an audit manager in the internal audit department of Matalas. You are currently auditing the petty cash systems at the different branches. Your initial systems notes on petty cash contain the following information:

(1)   The average petty cash balance at each branch is $5,000.

(2)   Average monthly expenditure is $1,538, with amounts ranging from $1 to $500.

(3)   Petty cash is kept in a lockable box on a bookcase in the accounts office.

(4)   Vouchers for expenditure are signed by the person incurring that expenditure to confirm they have received re-imbursement from petty cash.

(5)   Vouchers are recorded in the petty cash book by the accounts clerk; each voucher records the date, reason for the expenditure, amount of expenditure and person incurring that expenditure.

(6)   Petty cash is counted every month by the accounts clerk, who is in charge of the cash. The petty cash balance is then reimbursed using the 'imprest' system and the journal entry produced to record expenditure in the general ledger.

(7)   The cheque to reimburse petty cash is signed by the accountant at the branch at the same time as the journal entry to the general ledger is reviewed.

Required:

(a)   **Explain the issues which limit the independence of the internal audit department in Matalas Co. Recommend a way of overcoming each issue.**   **(8 marks)**

(b)   **Explain the internal control deficiencies in the petty cash system at Matalas Co. For each deficiency, recommend a control to overcome that deficiency.**   **(12 marks)**

(Total: 20 marks)

20 SPECS4YOU

ISA 230 *Audit Documentation* establishes standards and provides guidance regarding documentation in the context of the audit of financial statements.

Required:

(a)   **List the purposes of audit working papers.**   **(3 marks)**

(b)   You have recently been promoted to audit manager in the audit firm of Trums & Co. As part of your new responsibilities, you have been placed in charge of the audit of

Specs4You Co, a long established audit client of Trums & Co. Specs4You Co sells spectacles; the company owns 42 stores where customers can have their eyes tested and choose from a range of frames.

Required:

List the documentation that should be of assistance to you in familiarising yourself with Specs4You Co. Describe the information you should expect to obtain from each document. **(8 marks)**

(c) The time is now towards the end of the audit, and you are reviewing working papers produced by the audit team. An example of a working paper you have just reviewed is shown below.

Client Name **Specs4You Co**	Year **end 30 April**	Page **xxxxxxx**
Working paper **Payables transaction testing**		
	Prepared by	Date
	Reviewed by **CW**	Date **12 June 2007**

Audit assertion: To make sure that the purchases day book is correct.

Method: Select a sample of 15 purchase orders recorded in the purchase order system. Trace details to the goods received note (GRN), purchase invoice (PI) and the purchase day book (PDB) ensuring that the quantities and prices recorded on the purchase order match those on the GRN, PI and PDB.

Test details: In accordance with audit risk, a sample of purchase orders were selected from a numerically sequenced purchase order system and details traced as stated in the method. Details of items tested can be found on another working paper.

Results: Details of purchase orders were normally correctly recorded through the system. Five purchase orders did not have any associated GRN, PI and were not recorded in the PDB. Further investigation showed that these orders had been cancelled due to a change in spectacle specification. However, this does not appear to be a system deficiency as the internal controls do not allow for changes in specification.

Conclusion: Purchase orders are completely recorded in the purchase day book.

Required:

Explain why the working paper shown above does not meet the standards normally expected of a working paper. *Note:* **You are not required to reproduce the working paper.** **(9 marks)**

(Total: 20 marks)

21 MAL & CO

(a) **ISA 315 Understanding the Entity and its Environment and Assessing the Risks of Material Misstatement states:**

'the auditor should perform . . . risk assessment procedures to obtain an understanding of the entity and its environment, including its internal control.'

Required:

(i) **Explain the purpose of risk assessment procedures.** **(3 marks)**

(ii)   Outline the sources of audit evidence the auditor can use as part
assessment procedures.   (3 m

(b)   Mal & Co, an audit firm, has seven partners. The firm has a number of audit clie
in different industrial sectors, with a wide range of fee income.

An audit partner of Mal & Co has just delegated to you the planning work for the
audit of Serenity Co. This company provides a range of mobile communication
facilities and this will be the second year your firm has provided audit services.

You have just met with the financial controller of Serenity prior to agreeing the
engagement letter for this year.

The controller has informed you that Serenity has continued to grow quickly, with
financial accounting systems changing rapidly and appropriate control systems being
difficult to maintain. Additional services in terms of review and implementation of
control systems have been requested. An internal audit department has recently
been established and the controller wants you to ensure that external audit work is
limited by using this department.

You have also learnt that Serenity is to market a new type of mobile telephone,
which is able to intercept messages from law enforcement agencies. The legal status
of this telephone is unclear at present and development is not being publicised.

The granting of the licence to market the mobile telephone is dependent on the
financial stability of Serenity. The financial controller has indicated that Mal & Co
may be asked to provide a report to the mobile telephone licensing authority
regarding Serenity's cash flow forecast for the year ending December 2007 to
support the licence application.

Required:

As part of your risk assessment procedures for the audit of Serenity Co for the year
ending 31 December 2006, identify and describe the issues to be considered when
providing services to this client.   **(10 marks)**

(c)   When reporting on a cash flow forecast, explain the term 'negative
assurance' and why this is used.   **(4 marks)**

(Total: 20 marks)

22   WEAR WRAITH CO

Wear Wraith (WW) Co's main activity is the extraction and supply of building materials
including sand, gravel, cement and similar aggregates. The company's year-end is 31 May
and your firm has audited WW for a number of years. The main asset on the balance sheet
relates to non-current assets. A junior member of staff has attempted to prepare the non-
current asset note for the financial statements. The note has not been reviewed by the
senior accountant and so may contain errors.

	Land and buildings	Plant and machinery	Motor vehicles	Railway trucks	Total
COST	$	$	$	$	$
01-Jun-05	100,000	875,000	1,500,000	–	2,475,000
Additions	10,000	125,000	525,000	995,000	1,655,000
Disposals	–	(100,000)	(325,000)	–	(425,000)
31-May-06	110,000	900,000	1,700,000	995,000	3,705,000
Depreciation					
01-Jun-05	60,000	550,000	750,000	–	1,360,000
Charge	2,200	180,000	425,000	199,000	806,200
Disposals	–	(120,000)	(325,000)	–	(445,000)
31-May-06	62,200	610,000	850,000	199,000	1,721,200
Net Book Value					
31-May-06	47,800	290,000	850,000	796,000	1,983,800
31-May-05	40,000	325,000	750,000	–	1,115,000

- Land and buildings relate to company offices and land for those offices.

- Plant and machinery includes extraction equipment such as diggers and dumper trucks used to extract sand and gravel etc.

- Motor vehicles include large trucks to transport the sand, gravel etc.

- Railway trucks relate to containers used to transport sand and gravel over long distances on the railway network.

Depreciation rates stated in the financial statements are all based on cost and calculated using the straight line basis. The rates are:

Land and buildings   2%

Plant and machinery   20%

Motor vehicles   33%

Railway trucks   20%

Disposals in the motor vehicles category relates to vehicles which were five years old.

Required:

(a)   List the audit work you should perform on railway trucks.   **(10 marks)**

(b)   You have just completed your analytical procedures of the non-current assets note.

   (i)   Excluding railway trucks, identify and explain any issues with the non-current asset note to raise with management.

   (ii)   Explain how each issue could be resolved.   **(10 marks)**

   Note: you do not need to re-cast the schedule.

(Total: 20 marks)

23   MCKAY & CO

(a)   Explain the situations where an auditor may disclose confi[...]
about a client.

(b)   You are an audit manager in McKay & Co, a firm of Chartered Ce[...]
You are preparing the engagement letter for the audit of Ancie[...]
company, for the year ending 30 June 2006.

Ancients has grown rapidly over the past few years, and is now one of your firm's
most important clients.

Ancients has been an audit client for eight years and McKay & Co has provided audit,
taxation and management consultancy advice during this time. The client has been
satisfied with the services provided, although the taxation fee for the period to
31 December 2005 remains unpaid.

Audit personnel available for this year's audit are most of the staff from last year,
including Mr Grace, an audit partner and Mr Jones, an audit senior. Mr Grace has
been the audit partner since Ancients became an audit client. You are aware that
Allyson Grace, the daughter of Mr Grace, has recently been appointed the financial
director at Ancients.

To celebrate her new appointment, Allyson has suggested taking all of the audit staff
out to an expensive restaurant prior to the start of the audit work for this year.

Required:

**Identify and explain the risks to independence arising in carrying out your audit of
Ancients for the year ending 30 June 2006, and suggest ways of mitigating each of
the risks you identify.**   **(12 marks)**

                                                                (Total: 20 marks)

24   TEMPEST (A)

(a)   International Standard on Auditing 300 *Planning an Audit of Financial Statements*,
states that an auditor must plan the audit.

Explain why it is important to plan an audit.   **(5 marks)**

(b)   You are the audit manager in charge of the audit of Tempest, a limited liability
company. The company's year end is 31 December, and Tempest has been a client
for seven years. The company purchases and resells fittings for ships including
anchors, compasses, rudders, sails etc. Clients vary in size from small businesses
making yachts to large companies maintaining large luxury cruise ships. No
manufacturing takes place in Tempest.

Information on the company's financial performance is available as follows:

	2005 Forecast $000	2004 Actual $000
Revenue	45,928	40,825
Cost of sales	(37,998)	(31,874)
Gross profit	7,930	8,951
Administration costs	(4,994)	(4,758)
Distribution costs	(2,500)	(2,500)
Net profit	436	1,693
Non-current assets (at net book value)	3,600	4,500
Current assets		
Inventory	200	1,278
Receivables	6,000	4,052
Cash and bank	500	1,590
Total assets	10,300	11,420
Capital and reserves		
Share capital	1,000	1,000
Accumulated profits	5,300	5,764
Total shareholders' funds	6,300	6,764
Non-current liabilities	1,000	2,058
Current liabilities	3,000	2,598
	10,300	11,420

Other information

The industry that Tempest trades in has seen moderate growth of 7% over the last year.

- Non-current assets mainly relate to company premises for storing inventory. Ten delivery vehicles are owned with a net book value of $300,000.

- One of the directors purchased a yacht during the year.

- Inventory is stored in ten different locations across the country, with your firm again having offices close to seven of those locations.

- A computerised inventory control system was introduced in August 2005. Inventory balances are now obtainable directly from the computer system. The client does not intend to count inventory at the year end but rely instead on the computerised inventory control system.

Required:

Using the information provided above, prepare the audit strategy for Tempest for the year ending 31 December 2005. **(15 marks)**

(Total: 20 marks)

25 ROCK

You are an audit senior responsible for understanding the entity and its environmen, assessing the risk of material misstatements for the audit of Rock for the year ending 31 December 20X4. Rock is a company listed on a stock exchange. Rock is engaged in the wholesale import, manufacture and distribution of basic cosmetics and toiletries for sale to a wide range of stores, under a variety of different brand names. You have worked on the audit of this client for several years as an audit junior.

Required:

(a)   **Describe the information you will seek, and procedures you will perform in order to understand the entity and its environment and assess risk for the audit of Rock for the year ending 31 December 20X4.** **(10 marks)**

(b)   You are now nearing the completion of the audit of Rock for the year ending 31 December 20X4. Draft financial statements have been produced. You have been given the responsibility of performing a review of the audit files before they are passed to the audit manager and the audit partner for their review. You have been asked to concentrate on the proper completion of the audit working papers. Some of the audit working papers have been produced electronically but all of them have been printed out for you.

Describe the types of audit working papers you should expect to see in the audit files and the features of those working papers that show that they have been properly completed. **(10 marks)**

(Total: 20 marks)

26 EXTERNAL AUDIT

The purpose of an external audit and its role are not well understood. You have been asked to write some material for inclusion in your firm's training materials dealing with these issues in the audit of large companies.

Required:

(a)   **Draft an explanation dealing with the purpose of an external audit and its role in the audit of large companies, for inclusion in your firm's training materials.** **(10 marks)**

(b)   The external audit process for the audit of large entities generally involves two or more recognisable stages. One stage involves understanding the business and risk assessment, determining the response to assessed risk, testing of controls and a limited amount of substantive procedures. This stage is sometimes known as the interim audit. Another stage involves further tests of controls and substantive procedures and audit finalisation procedures. This stage is sometimes known as the final audit.

Describe and explain the main audit procedures and processes that take place during the interim and final audit of a large entity. **(10 marks)**

(Total: 20 marks)

27 CLIFF

Day-to-day internal controls are important for all businesses to maximise the efficient use of resources and profitability.

Your firm has recently been appointed as auditor to Cliff, a private company that runs a chain of small supermarkets selling fresh and frozen food, and canned and dry food. Cliff has very few controls over inventory because the company trusts local managers to make good decisions regarding the purchase, sale and control of inventory, all of which is done locally. Pricing is generally performed on a cost-plus basis.

Each supermarket has a stand-alone computer system on which monthly accounts are prepared. These accounts are mailed to head office every quarter. There is no integrated inventory control, sale or purchasing system and no regular system for inventory counting. Management accounts are produced twice a year.

Trade at the supermarkets has increased in recent years and the number of supermarkets has increased. However, the quality of staff that has been recruited has fallen. Senior management at Cliff are now prepared to invest in more up-to-date systems.

Required:

(a) **Describe the problems that you might expect to find at Cliff resulting from poor internal controls.** (8 marks)

(b) **Make FOUR recommendations to the senior management of Cliff for the improvement of internal controls, and explain the advantages and disadvantages of each recommendation.** (12 marks)

(Total: 20 marks)

28 TOUREX AND PUDCO

Your firm is the external auditor to two companies. One is a hotel, Tourex, the other is a food wholesaler, Pudco, that supplies the hotel. Both companies have the same year-end. Just before that year-end, a large number of guests became ill at a wedding reception at the hotel, possibly as a result of food poisoning.

The guests have taken legal action against the hotel and the hotel has taken action against the food wholesaler. Neither the hotel nor the food wholesaler have admitted liability. The hotel is negotiating out-of-court settlements with the ill guests, the food wholesaler is negotiating an out-of-court settlement with the hotel. At the statement of financial position date, the public health authorities have not completed their investigations.

Lawyers for both the hotel and the food wholesaler say informally that negotiations are 'going well' but refuse to confirm this in writing. The amounts involved are material to the financial statements of both companies.

Required:

(a) **Describe how ACCA's *Rules of Professional Conduct* apply to this situation and explain how the external auditors should manage this conflict of interest.** (6 marks)

(b) **Outline the main requirements of IAS 37 *Provisions, Contingent Liabilities and Contingent Assets* and apply them to this case.** (7 marks)

(c)   Assuming that your firm continues with the audit of both companies, for each company, describe the difficulties you foresee in obtaining sufficient audit evidence for potential provisions, contingent liabilities and contingent assets, and describe how this could affect your audit reports on their financial statements.   **(7 marks)**

(Total: 20 marks)

SPECIALISED AUDIT AREAS

29   BRAMPTON CO *Walk in the footsteps of a top tutor*

(a)   **Explain the difference between the interim audit and the final audit.**   **(4 marks)**

You are the senior in charge of the audit of Brampton Co for the year ending 31 January 2010 and are currently planning the year-end audit. Brampton specialises in the production of high quality bread of various kinds.

During the interim audit you noted that, in the present economic down-turn, the company has suffered as its costs are increasing and its prices have been higher than its competitors because of lower production runs. One indicator of the problems facing the company is that it has consistently used a bank overdraft facility to finance its activities.

At the time of the interim audit you had discussed with company management what actions were being taken to improve the liquidity of the company and you were informed that the company plans to expand its facilities for producing white bread as this line had maintained its market share. The company has asked its bank for a loan to finance the expansion and also to maintain its working capital generally.

To support its request for a loan, the company has prepared a cash flow forecast for the two years from the end of the reporting period and the internal audit department has reported on the forecast to the board of directors. However, the bank has said it would like a report from the external auditors to confirm the accuracy of the forecast. Following this request the company has asked you to examine the cash flow forecast and then to report to the bank.

Required:

(b)   **Explain whether you would be able to rely on the work of the internal auditors.**
      (6 marks)

(c)   **Describe THREE procedures you would adopt in your examination of the cash flow forecast.**   **(6 marks)**

(d)   **Explain the kind of assurance you could give in the context of the request by the bank.**   **(4 marks)**

(Total: 20 marks)

30 CONOY *Walk in the footsteps of a top tutor*

 Timed question with Online tutor debrief

(a) Contrast the role of internal and external auditors. **(8 marks)**

(b) Conoy Co designs and manufactures luxury motor vehicles. The company employs 2,500 staff and consistently makes a net profit of between 10% and 15% of sales. Conoy Co is not listed; its shares are held by 15 individuals, most of them from the same family. The maximum shareholding is 15% of the share capital.

The executive directors are drawn mainly from the shareholders. There are no non-executive directors because the company legislation in Conoy Co's jurisdiction does not require any. The executive directors are very successful in running Conoy Co, partly from their training in production and management techniques, and partly from their 'hands-on' approach providing motivation to employees.

The board are considering a significant expansion of the company. However, the company's bankers are concerned with the standard of financial reporting as the financial director (FD) has recently left Conoy Co. The board are delaying provision of additional financial information until a new FD is appointed.

Conoy Co does have an internal audit department, although the chief internal auditor frequently comments that the board of Conoy Co do not understand his reports or provide sufficient support for his department or the internal control systems within Conoy Co. The board of Conoy Co concur with this view. Anders & Co, the external auditors have also expressed concern in this area and the fact that the internal audit department focuses work on control systems, not financial reporting. Anders & Co are appointed by and report to the board of Conoy Co.

The board of Conoy Co are considering a proposal from the chief internal auditor to establish an audit committee. The committee would consist of one executive director, the chief internal auditor as well as three new appointees. One appointee would have a non-executive seat on the board of directors.

Required:

Discuss the benefits to Conoy Co of forming an audit committee. **(12 marks)**

(Total: 20 marks)

 Calculate your allowed time, allocate the time to the separate parts...............

31   EUKARE   *Walk in the footsteps of a top tutor*

(a)   **Explain the term 'audit risk' and the three elements of risk that contribute to total audit risk.**   **(4 marks)**

The EuKaRe charity was established in 1960. The charity's aim is to provide support to children from disadvantaged backgrounds who wish to take part in sports such as tennis, badminton and football.

EuKaRe has a detailed constitution which explains how the charity's income can be spent. The constitution also notes that administration expenditure cannot exceed 10% of income in any year.

The charity's income is derived wholly from voluntary donations. Sources of donations include:

(i)   Cash collected by volunteers asking the public for donations in shopping areas,

(ii)   Cheques sent to the charity's head office,

(iii)   Donations from generous individuals. Some of these donations have specific clauses attached to them indicating that the initial amount donated (capital) cannot be spent and that the income (interest) from the donation must be spent on specific activities, for example, provision of sports equipment.

The rules regarding the taxation of charities in the country EuKaRe is based are complicated, with only certain expenditure being allowable for taxation purposes and donations of capital being treated as income in some situations.

Required:

(b)   **Identify areas of inherent risk in the EuKaRe charity and explain the effect of each of these risks on the audit approach.**   **(12 marks)**

(c)   **Explain why the control environment may be weak at the charity EuKaRe.** **(4 marks)**

                                                                    (Total: 20 marks)

32   MONTEHODGE CO

(a)   **Discuss the advantages and disadvantages of outsourcing an internal audit department.**   **(8 marks)**

(b)   MonteHodge Co has a sales income of $253 million and employs 1,200 people in 15 different locations. MonteHodge Co provides various financial services from pension and investment advice to individuals, to maintaining cash books and cash forecasting in small to medium-sized companies. The company is owned by six shareholders, who belong to the same family; it is not listed on any stock-exchange and the shareholders have no intention of applying for a listing. However, an annual audit is required by statute and additional regulation of the financial services sector is expected in the near future.

Most employees are provided with on-line, real-time computer systems, which present financial and stock market information to enable the employees to provide up-to-date advice to their clients. Accounting systems record income, which is based on fees generated from investment advice. Expenditure is mainly fixed, being salaries, office rent, lighting and heating, etc. Internal control systems are limited; the directors tending to trust staff and being more concerned with making profits than implementing detailed controls.

Four of the shareholders are board members, with one member being the chairman and chief executive officer. The financial accountant is not qualified, although has many years experience in preparing financial statements.

Required:

Discuss the reasons for and against having an internal audit department in MonteHodge Co. (12 marks)

(Total: 20 marks)

33 DELPHIC

Delphic Co is a wholesaler of furniture (such as chairs, tables and cupboards). Delphic buys the furniture from six major manufacturers and sells them to over 600 different customers ranging from large retail chain stores to smaller owner-controlled businesses. The receivables balance therefore includes customers owing up to $125,000 to smaller balances of about $5,000, all with many different due dates for payments and credit limits. All information is stored on Delphic's computer systems although previous audits have tended to adopt an 'audit around the computer' approach.

You are the audit senior in charge of the audit of the receivables balance. For the first time at this client, you have decided to use audit software to assist with the audit of the receivables balance. Computer staff at Delphic are happy to help the auditor, although they cannot confirm completeness of systems documentation, and warn that the systems have very old operating systems in place, limiting file compatibility with more modern programs.

The change in audit approach has been taken mainly to fully understand Delphic's computer systems prior to new internet modules being added next year. To limit the possibility of damage to Delphic's computer files, copy files will be provided by Delphic's computer staff for the auditor to use with their own audit software.

Required:

(a) **Explain the audit procedures that should be carried out using audit software on the receivables balance at Delphic Co. For each procedure, explain the reason for that procedure.** (9 marks)

(b) **Explain the potential problems of using audit software at Delphic Co. For each problem, explain how it can be resolved.** (8 marks)

(c) **Explain the concept of 'auditing around the computer' and discuss why this increases audit risk for the auditor.** (3 marks)

(Total: 20 marks)

34 KLE CO

(a) **Explain the purpose of the three 'Es' in relation to a value for money audit.** (4 marks)

(b) You are an audit manager in the internal audit department of KLE Co. The internal audit department is auditing the company's procurement system in the company. Extracts from your system notes, which are correct and contain no errors, are provided below.

Details on ordering department:

- Six members of staff – one buyer and five purchasing clerks.

- Receives about 75 orders each day, many orders for duplicate items come from different departments in the organisation.

- Initial evaluation of internal controls is high.

Procurement systems

Ordering department

All orders are raised on pre-numbered purchase requisitions and sent to the ordering department.

In the ordering department, each requisition is signed by the chief buyer. A purchasing clerk transfers the order information onto an order form and identifies the appropriate supplier for the goods.

Part one of the two part order form is sent to the supplier and part two to the accounts department. The requisition is thrown away.

Goods inwards department

All goods received are checked for damage. Damaged items are returned to the supplier and a damaged goods note completed.

For undamaged items a two-part pre-numbered Goods Received Note (GRN) is raised.

- Part one is sent to the ordering department with the damaged goods notes.

- Part two is filed in order of the reference number for the goods being ordered (obtained from the supplier's goods despatched documentation), in the goods inwards department.

Ordering department

GRNs are separated from damaged goods notes, which are filed. The GRN is forwarded to the accounts department.

Accounts department

GRNs matched with the order awaiting the receipt of the invoice.

Required:

Using the system notes provided

(i) **Identify and explain the internal control deficiencies and provide a recommendation to overcome each deficiency.** (10 marks)

(ii) **Identify and explain the additional deficiencies that should be raised by a value for money audit and provide a suitable recommendation to overcome each deficiency.** (6 marks)

(Total: 20 marks)

35   WALSH

Walsh Co sells motor vehicle fuel, accessories and spares to retail customers. The company owns 25 shops.

The company has recently implemented a new computerised wages system. Employees work a standard eight hour day. Hours are recorded using a magnetic card system; when each employee arrives for work, they hold their card close to the card reader; the reader recognises the magnetic information on the card identifying the employee as being 'at work'. When the employee leaves work at the end of the day the process is reversed showing that the employee has left work.

Hours worked are calculated each week by the computer system using the magnetic card information. Overtime is calculated as any excess over the standard hours worked. Any overtime over 10% of standard hours is sent on a computer generated report by e-mail to the financial accountant. If necessary, the accountant overrides overtime payments if the hours worked are incorrect. Statutory deductions and net pay are also computer calculated with payments being made directly into the employee's bank account. The only other manual check is the financial accountant authorising the net pay from Walsh's bank account, having reviewed the list of wages to be paid.

Required:

(a)   Using examples from Walsh Co, explain the benefits of using Computer-Assisted Audit Techniques to help the auditor to obtain sufficient appropriate audit evidence to be able to draw reasonable conclusions on which to base the audit opinion.   **(8 marks)**

(b)   List SIX examples of audit tests on Walsh Co's wages system using audit software.   **(6 marks)**

(c)   Explain how using test data should help in the audit of Walsh Co's wages system, noting any problems with this audit technique.   **(6 marks)**

(Total: 20 marks)

36   JAYNE

(a)   ISA 505, *External Confirmations*, states that 'the auditor should determine whether the use of external confirmations is necessary to obtain sufficient appropriate audit evidence at the assertion level'.

Required:

(i)   List FOUR examples of external confirmations.   **(2 marks)**

(ii)   For EACH of the examples in (i) above explain:

ONE audit assertion that the external confirmation supports, and

ONE audit assertion that the external confirmation does NOT support.   **(8 marks)**

(b)   Jayne Co has a significant number of cash transactions and recent non-current asset purchases have been financed by a bank loan. This loan is repayable in equal annual instalments for the next five years.

Required:

(i)   Explain the procedures to obtain a bank report for audit purposes from Jayne Co's bank and the substantive procedures that should be carried out on that report.   **(5 marks)**

(ii)   List the further substantive procedures that should be carried out on the bank balances in Jayne Co's financial statements.   **(5 marks)**

(Total: 20 marks)

37   TELA & CO   *Walk in the footsteps of a top tutor*

You are the audit manager of Tela & Co, a medium sized firm of accountants. Your firm has just been asked for assistance from Jumper & Co, a firm of accountants in an adjacent country. This country has just implemented the internationally recognised codes on corporate governance and Jumper & Co has a number of clients where the codes are not being followed. One example of this, from SGCC, a listed company, is shown below. As your country already has appropriate corporate governance codes in place, Jumper & Co have asked for your advice regarding the changes necessary in SGCC to achieve appropriate compliance with corporate governance codes.

Extract from financial statements regarding corporate governance

Mr Sheppard is the Chief Executive Officer and board chairman of SGCC. He appoints and maintains a board of five executive and two non-executive directors. While the board sets performance targets for the senior managers in the company, no formal targets or review of board policies is carried out. Board salaries are therefore set and paid by Mr Sheppard based on his assessment of all the board members, including himself, and not their actual performance.

Internal controls in the company are monitored by the senior accountant, although detailed review is assumed to be carried out by the external auditors; SGCC does not have an internal audit department.

Annual financial statements are produced, providing detailed information on past performance.

Required:

Write a memo to Jumper & Co which:

(a)   Explains why SGCC does not meet international codes of corporate governance

(b)   Explains why not meeting the international codes may cause a problem for SGCC, and

(c)   Recommends any changes necessary to implement those codes in the company.
                                                                                                       (20 marks)

38   ZPM

ISA 610 *Using the Work of Internal Auditors* states that 'when the external auditor intends to use specific work of internal auditing, the external auditor should evaluate and perform audit procedures on that work to confirm its adequacy for the external auditor's purposes.'

Required:

(a)   **In relation to ISA 610, explain the factors the external auditor will consider when evaluating the work of the internal auditor.**   **(5 marks)**

(b)   ZPM is a listed limited liability company with a year end of 30 June. ZPM's main activity is selling home improvement or 'Do-It-Yourself' (DIY) products to the public. Products sold range from nails, paint and tools to doors and showers; some stores also sell garden tools and furniture. Products are purchased from approximately 200 different suppliers. ZPM has 103 stores in eight different countries.

ZPM has a well-staffed internal audit department, who report on a regular basis to the audit committee. Areas where the internal and external auditors may carry out work include:

(1)   Attending the year end inventory count in 30 stores annually. All stores are visited on a rotational basis.

(2)   Checking the internal controls over the procurement systems (e.g. ensuring a liability is only recorded when the inventory has been received).

(3)   Reviewing the operations of the marketing department.

Required:

For each of the above three areas, discuss

(i)   **the objectives of the internal auditor;**   **(5 marks)**

(ii)   **the objectives of the external auditor; and**   **(5 marks)**

(iii) **whether the external auditor will rely on the internal auditor, and if reliance is required, the extent of that reliance.**   **(5 marks)**

(Total: 20 marks)

39   OCTBALL

You are the senior manager in the internal audit department of Octball, a limited liability company. You report to the chief internal auditor and have a staff of six junior auditors to supervise, although the budget allows for up to ten junior staff.

In a recent meeting with the chief internal auditor, the difficulty of staff recruitment and retention was discussed. Over the past year, five junior internal audit staff have left the company, but only two have been recruited. Recruitment problems identified include location of Octball's head office in a small town over 150 kilometres from the nearest major city and extensive foreign travel, often to cold climates.

Together with the chief internal auditor you believe that outsourcing the internal audit department may be a way of alleviating the staffing problems. You would monitor the new outsourced department in a part-time role taking on additional responsibilities in other departments, and the chief internal auditor would accept the post of Finance Director (FD) on the board, replacing the retiring FD.

Two firms have been identified as being able to provide the internal audit service:

- The NFA Partnership, a local firm specialising in provision of accountancy and internal audit services. NFA does not audit financial statements or report to members, and

- T&M, Octball's external auditors, who have offices in 75 countries and employ in excess of 65,000 staff.

Required:

(a) **Discuss the advantages and disadvantages of appointing NFA as internal auditors for Octball.** **(8 marks)**

(b) **Discuss the issues T&M need to consider before they could accept appointment as internal auditors for Octball.** **(7 marks)**

(c) **Assume that an outsourcing company has been chosen to provide internal audit services.**

Describe the control activities that Octball should apply to ensure that the internal audit service is being maintained to a high standard. **(5 marks)**

(Total: 20 marks)

COMPLETION AND REPORTING

40 MEDIMADE CO *Walk in the footsteps of a top tutor*

(a) **Define the going concern assumption.** **(2 marks)**

Medimade Co is an established pharmaceutical company that has for many years generated 90% of its revenue through the sale of two specific cold and flu remedies. Medimade has lately seen a real growth in the level of competition that it faces in its market and demand for its products has significantly declined. To make matters worse, in the past the company has not invested sufficiently in new product development and so has been trying to remedy this by recruiting suitably trained scientific staff, but this has proved more difficult than anticipated.

In addition to recruiting staff the company also needed to invest $2m in plant and machinery. The company wanted to borrow this sum but was unable to agree suitable terms with the bank; therefore it used its overdraft facility, which carried a higher interest rate. Consequently, some of Medimade's suppliers have been paid much later than usual and hence some of them have withdrawn credit terms meaning the company must pay cash on delivery. As a result of the above the company's overdraft balance has grown substantially.

The directors have produced a cash flow forecast and this shows a significantly worsening position over the coming 12 months.

The directors have informed you that the bank overdraft facility is due for renewal next month, but they are confident that it will be renewed. They also strongly believe that the new products which are being developed will be ready to market soon and hence trading levels will improve and therefore that the company is a going concern. Therefore they do not intend to make any disclosures in the accounts regarding going concern.

Required:

(b) Identify any potential indicators that the company is not a going concern and describe why these could impact upon the ability of the company to continue trading on a going concern basis. **(8 marks)**

(c) Explain the audit procedures that the auditor of Medimade should perform in assessing whether or not the company is a going concern. **(6 marks)**

(d) The auditors have been informed that Medimade's bankers will not make a decision on the overdraft facility until after the audit report is completed. The directors have now agreed to include going concern disclosures.

Required:

Describe the impact on the audit report of Medimade if the auditor believes the company is a going concern but a material uncertainty exists. **(4 marks)**

(Total: 20 marks)

41 HAVE A BITE CO *Walk in the footsteps of a top tutor*

(a) Identify and explain FOUR assertions relevant to accounts payable at the year-end date. **(6 marks)**

You are the audit senior responsible for the audit of Have A Bite Co, a company that runs a chain of fast food restaurants. You are aware that a major risk of their sector is that poor food quality might result in damage claims by customers.

You had satisfied yourself at the interim audit that the company's control risk as regards purchases of food and its preparation in the kitchen was low. However, during your final audit it comes to your attention that one month before the year-end, a customer has sued the company for personal injury caused by food poisoning, claiming an amount of $200,000 in compensation. This amount is material to the stated profit of the company, but management believes that it has good defences against the claim.

Required:

(b) (i) State TWO controls that the company should have in place to reduce the risk associated with purchases of food and its preparation in the kitchen; and

(ii) State TWO audit procedures you should carry out during controls testing to satisfy yourself that control risk in this area is low. **(4 marks)**

(c) In respect of the potential claim state THREE items of evidence you should obtain and explain how they might enable you to form a conclusion on the likelihood of the claim being successful. **(6 marks)**

Following your audit you have concluded that there is a possibility, but not a probability, that the claim will be successful. However, management have decided not to make a provision or disclosure in the financial statements in respect of this matter.

Required:

(d) Describe how the matter should be reported in the financial statements and explain the effect on your audit report. **(4 marks)**

(Total: 20 marks)

42 TYE *Walk in the footsteps of a top tutor*

 Timed question with Online tutor debrief

One of your audit clients is Tye Co a company providing petrol, aviation fuel and similar oil based products to the government of the country it is based in. Although the company is not listed on any stock exchange, it does follow best practice regarding corporate governance regulations. The audit work for this year is complete, apart from the matter referred to below.

As part of Tye Co's service contract with the government, it is required to hold an emergency inventory reserve of 6,000 barrels of aviation fuel. The inventory is to be used if the supply of aviation fuel is interrupted due to unforeseen events such as natural disaster or terrorist activity.

This fuel has in the past been valued at its cost price of $15 a barrel. The current value of aviation fuel is $120 a barrel. Although the audit work is complete, as noted above, the directors of Tye Co have now decided to show the 'real' value of this closing inventory in the financial statements by valuing closing inventory of fuel at market value, which does not comply with relevant accounting standards. The draft financial statements of Tye Co currently show a profit of approximately $500,000 with net assets of $170 million.

Required:

(a) **List the audit procedures and actions that you should now take in respect of the above matter.** **(6 marks)**

(b) For the purposes of this section assume from part (a) that the directors have agreed to value inventory at $15/barrel.

Having investigated the matter in part (a) above, the directors present you with an amended set of financial statements showing the emergency reserve stated not at 6,000 barrels, but reported as 60,000 barrels. The final financial statements now show a profit following the inclusion of another 54,000 barrels of oil in inventory. When queried about the change from 6,000 to 60,000 barrels of inventory, the finance director stated that this change was made to meet expected amendments to emergency reserve requirements to be published in about six months time. The inventory will be purchased this year, and no liability will be shown in the financial statements for this future purchase. The finance director also pointed out that part of Tye Co's contract with the government requires Tye Co to disclose an annual profit and that a review of bank loans is due in three months. Finally the finance director stated that if your audit firm qualifies the financial statements in respect of the increase in inventory, they will not be recommended for re-appointment at the annual general meeting. The finance director refuses to amend the financial statements to remove this 'fictitious' inventory.

Required:

(i) **State the external auditor's responsibilities regarding the detection of fraud;** **(4 marks)**

(ii) **Discuss to which groups the auditors of Tye Co could report the 'fictitious' aviation fuel inventory;** **(6 marks)**

(iii)   Discuss the safeguards that the auditors of Tye Co can use in an attempt to overcome the intimidation threat from the directors of Tye Co.   (4 marks)

(Total: 20 marks)

> Calculate your allowed time, allocate the time to the separate parts...............

43   ZEEDIEM (A) Walk in the footsteps of a top tutor

The date is 3 December 2008. The audit of ZeeDiem Co is nearly complete and the financial statements and the audit report are due to be signed next week. However, the following additional information on two material events has just been presented to the auditor. The company's year end was 30 September 2008.

Event 1 – Occurred on 10 October 2008

The springs in a new type of mattress have been found to be defective making the mattress unsafe for use. There have been no sales of this mattress; it was due to be marketed in the next few weeks. The company's insurers estimate that inventory to the value of $750,000 has been affected. The insurers also estimate that the mattresses are now only worth $225,000. No claim can be made against the supplier of springs as this company is in liquidation with no prospect of any amounts being paid to third parties. The insurers will not pay ZeeDiem for the fall in value of the inventory as the company was underinsured. All of this inventory was in the finished goods store at the end of the year and no movements of inventory have been recorded post year-end.

Event 2 – Occurred 5 November 2008

Production at the ShamEve factory was halted for one day when a truck carrying dye used in colouring the fabric on mattresses reversed into a metal pylon, puncturing the vehicle allowing dye to spread across the factory premises and into a local river. The Environmental Agency is currently considering whether the release of dye was in breach of environmental legislation. The company's insurers have not yet commented on the event.

Required:

(a)   For each of the two events above:

(i)   Explain whether the events are adjusting or non-adjusting according to IAS 10 *Events After the Reporting Period*.   (4 marks)

(ii)   Explain the auditors' responsibility and the audit procedures and actions that should be carried out according to ISA 560 *Subsequent Events*.   (12 marks)

(b)   Assume that the date is now 20 December 2008, the financial statements and the audit report have just been signed, and the annual general meeting is to take place on 10 January 2009. The Environmental Agency has issued a report stating that ZeeDiem Co is in breach of environmental legislation and a fine of $900,000 will now be levied on the company. The amount is material to the financial statements.

Explain the additional audit work the auditor should carry out in respect of this fine.   (4 marks)

(Total: 20 marks)

44   SMITHSON CO (A)

Smithson Co provides scientific services to a wide range of clients. Typical assignments range from testing food for illegal additives to providing forensic analysis on items used to commit crimes to assist law enforcement officers.

The annual audit is nearly complete. As audit senior you have reported to the engagement partner that Smithson is having some financial difficulties. Income has fallen due to the adverse effect of two high-profile court cases, where Smithson's services to assist the prosecution were found to be in error. Not only did this provide adverse publicity for Smithson, but a number of clients withdrew their contracts. A senior employee then left Smithson, stating lack of investment in new analysis machines was increasing the risk of incorrect information being provided by the company.

A cash flow forecast prepared internally shows Smithson requiring significant additional cash within the next 12 months to maintain even the current level of services. Smithson's auditors have been asked to provide a negative assurance report on this forecast.

Required:

(a)   Define 'going concern' and discuss the auditor's responsibilities in respect of going concern.   (4 marks)

(b)   State the audit procedures that may be carried out to try to determine whether or not Smithson Co is a going concern.   (8 marks)

(c)   Explain the audit procedures the auditor may take where the auditor has decided that Smithson Co is unlikely to be a going concern.   (4 marks)

(d)   In the context of the cash flow forecast, define the term 'negative assurance' and explain how this differs from the assurance provided by an audit report on statutory financial statements.   (4 marks)

(Total: 20 marks)

45   JONARC & CO (A)

(a)   You are the audit manager in JonArc & Co. One of your new clients this year is Galartha Co, a company having net assets of $15 million. The audit work has been completed, but there is one outstanding matter you are currently investigating; the directors have decided not to provide depreciation on buildings in the financial statements, although International Accounting Standards suggest that depreciation should be provided.

Required:

State the additional audit procedures and actions you should now take in respect of the above matter.   (6 marks)

(b)   Unfortunately, you have been unable to resolve the matter regarding depreciation of buildings; the directors insist on not providing depreciation. You have therefore drafted the following extracts for your proposed audit report.

(1)   'We conducted our audit in accordance with International Standards on Auditing. Those Standards require that we comply with ethical requirements and plan and perform the audit to obtain reasonable assurance about whether

the financial statements are free of material misstatement (remaining words are the same as a normal unmodified report).

(2) *Basis for Qualified Opinion*

As discussed in Note 15 to the financial statements, no depreciation has been provided in the financial statements which practice, in our opinion, is not in accordance with International Accounting Standards.

(3) The provision for the year ended 31 September 2007, should be $420,000 based on the straight-line method of depreciation using an annual rate of 5% for the buildings.

(4) Accordingly, the non-current assets should be reduced by accumulated depreciation of $1,200,000 and the profit for the year and accumulated reserve should be decreased by $420,000 and $1,200,000, respectively.

(5) *Qualified Opinion*

In our opinion, except for the effect on the financial statements of the matter referred to in the preceding paragraph, the financial statements give a true and fair view ... (remaining words are the same as for an unmodified opinion paragraph).'

The extracts have been numbered to help you refer to them in your answer.

Required:

Explain the meaning and purpose of each of the above extracts in your draft audit report. **(10 marks)**

(c) **State the effect on your audit report of the following alternative situations:**

(i) **Depreciation had not been provided on any non-current asset for a number of years, the effect of which if corrected would be to turn an accumulated profit into a significant accumulated loss.**

(ii) **JonArc & Co were appointed auditors after the end of the financial year of Galartha Co. Consequently, the auditors could not attend the year end inventory count. Inventory is material to the financial statements.**

Note: **You are not required to draft any audit reports.** **(4 marks)**

(Total: 20 marks)

 Online question assistance

46 GREEN CO (A)

Green Co grows crops on a large farm according to strict organic principles that prohibits the use of artificial pesticides and fertilizers. The farm has an 'organic certification', which guarantees its products are to be organic. The certification has increased its sales of flour, potatoes and other products, as customers seek to eat more healthily.

Green Co is run by two managers who are the only shareholders. Annual revenue is $50 million with a net profit of 5%. Both managers have run other businesses in the last 10 years. One business was closed due to suspected tax fraud (although no case was ever brought to court).

Green Co's current auditors provide audit services. Additional assurance on business controls and the preparation of financial statements are provided by a different accountancy firm.

Last year, a neighbouring farm, Black Co started growing genetically modified (GM) crops, the pollen from which blows over Green Co's fields on a regular basis. This is a threat to Green Co's organic status because organic crops must not be contaminated with GM material. Green Co is considering court action against Black Co for loss of income and to stop Black Co growing GM crops.

You are an audit partner in Lime & Co, a 15 partner firm of auditors and business advisors. You have been friends with the managers of Green Co for the last 15 years, advising them on an informal basis. The managers of Green Co have indicated that the audit will be put out to tender next month and have asked your audit firm to tender for the audit and the provision of other professional services.

Required:

(a) Using the information provided, identify and explain the ethical threats that could affect Lime & Co. **(8 marks)**

(b) In respect of the going concern concept:

(i) Define 'going concern' and state two situations in which it should NOT be applied in the preparation of financial statements; **(3 marks)**

(ii) Explain the directors' responsibilities and the auditors' responsibilities regarding financial statements prepared on the going concern principle. **(4 marks)**

(c) List the audit procedures that should be carried out to determine whether or not the going concern basis is appropriate for Green Co. **(5 marks)**

(Total: 20 marks)

47 MSV

(a) ISA 700 *Forming an Opinion and Reporting on Financial Statements* indicates the basic elements that will ordinarily be included in the audit report.

Required:

List SIX basic elements of an auditor's report. Briefly explain why each element is included in the report. **(6 marks)**

(b) You are the audit manager in charge of the audit of MSV Co for the year ended 28 February 2007. MSV Co is based in a seaside town and hires motor boats and yachts to individuals for amounts of time between one day and one week. The majority of receipts are in cash, with a few customers paying by debit card. Consequently, there are no receivables on the statement of financial position. The main non-current assets are the motor boats and yachts. The company is run by four directors who are also the major shareholders. Total income for the year was about $10m.

The following issues have been identified during the audit:

Issue 1

Audit tests on sales indicate a deficiency in the internal control system, with a potential understatement of income in the region of $500,000. The deficiency

occurred because sales invoices are not sequentially numbered, allowing one of the directors to remove cash sales prior to recording in the sales day book. This was identified during analytical procedures of sales, when the audit senior noted that on the days when this director was working, sales were always lower than on the days when the director was not working. **(8 marks)**

Issue 2

During testing of non-current assets, one yacht was found to be located at the property of one of the directors. This yacht has not been hired out during the year and enquiries indicate that the director makes personal use of it. The yacht is included in the non-current assets balance in the financial statements. **(6 marks)**

Required:

For each of the issues above:

(i)   **List the audit procedures you should conduct to reach a conclusion on these issues;**

(ii)   **Assuming that you have performed all the audit procedures that you can, but the issues are still unresolved, explain the potential effect (if any) on the audit report.**

Note: The mark allocation is shown against each of the two issues.

(Total: 20 marks)

48   TAM (A)

(a)   (i)   **In the context of ISA 530** *Audit Sampling*, **explain and provide examples of the terms 'sampling risk' and 'non-sampling' risk.** **(4 marks)**

        (ii)   **Briefly explain how sampling and non-sampling risk can be controlled by the audit firm.** **(2 marks)**

(b)   Tam Co, is owned and managed by two brothers with equal shareholdings. The company specialises in the sale of expensive motor vehicles. Annual revenue is in the region of $70,000,000 and the company requires an audit under local legislation. About 500 cars are sold each year, with an average value of $140,000, although the range of values is from $130,000 to $160,000. Invoices are completed manually with one director signing all invoices to confirm the sales value is correct. All accounting and financial statement preparation is carried out by the directors. A recent expansion of the company's showroom was financed by a bank loan, repayable over the next five years.

The audit manager is starting to plan the audit of Tam Co. The audit senior and audit junior assigned to the audit are helping the manager as a training exercise.

Comments are being made about how to select a sample of sales invoices for testing. Audit procedures are needed to ensure that the managing director has signed them and then to trace details into the sales day book and sales ledger.

'We should check all invoices' suggests the audit manager.

'How about selecting a sample using statistical sampling techniques' adds the audit senior.

'Why waste time obtaining a sample?' asks the audit junior. He adds 'taking a random sample of invoices by reviewing the invoice file and manually choosing a few important invoices will be much quicker.'

Required:

Briefly explain each of the sample selection methods suggested by the audit manager, audit senior and audit junior, and discuss whether or not they are appropriate for obtaining a representative sample of sales invoices. **(9 marks)**

(c) **Define 'materiality' and explain why the auditors of Tam must form an opinion on whether the financial statements are free from material misstatement.** **(5 marks)**

(Total: 20 marks)

49   LALD

You are the auditor of LALD, a limited liability company. The main activity of the company is the construction of buildings ranging in size from individual houses to large offices and blocks of flats.

Under the laws of the country LALD operates in, LALD must add sales tax to all buildings sold and they pay this tax to the government at the end of each month.

The largest non-current asset on LALD's statement of financial position is the plant and machinery used in the construction of buildings. Due to the variety of different assets used, four different sub-classes of plant and machinery are recognised, each with its own rate of depreciation.

You are now reaching the end of the audit work for the year ended 30 September 2005. There are two specific matters where additional audit work is required:

(i)   The sales tax for the month of August was not paid to the government. This appears to have been an accidental error and the amount involved is not material to the financial statements.

(ii)   The complicated method of calculating depreciation for plant and machinery appears to have resulted in depreciation being calculated incorrectly, with the result that depreciation may have been under-provided in the financial statements.

Required:

(a)   **Explain the additional audit procedures you should take regarding the accidental underpayment of sales tax.** **(7 marks)**

(b)   **Explain the additional audit procedures you should take regarding the possible underprovision of depreciation.** **(7 marks)**

(c)   You have determined that the under-provision is material to the financial statements and therefore need to modify the audit report. The directors have informed you that they do not intend to take any action regarding the underprovision of depreciation. They also disagree with your action and have threatened to remove your company as the auditors of LALD unless you agree not to modify your report.

Required:

Explain the procedures that the directors must follow in order to remove your company as the auditors of LALD. **(6 marks)**

(Total: 20 marks)

50 CRIGHTON-WARD (A) *Walk in the footsteps of a top tutor*

(a)   Explain the purpose of a management representation letter.   **(5 marks)**

(b)   You are the manager in charge of the audit of Crighton-Ward, a public limited liability company which manufactures specialist cars and other motor vehicles for use in films. Audited turnover is $140 million with profit before tax of $7.5 million.

All audit work up to, but not including, the obtaining of management representations has been completed. A review of the audit file has disclosed the following outstanding points:

Lion's Roar

The company is facing a potential legal claim from the Lion's Roar company in respect of a defective vehicle that was supplied for one of their films. Lion's Roar maintains that the vehicle was not built strongly enough while the directors of Crighton-Ward argue that the specification was not sufficiently detailed. Dropping a vehicle 50 metres into a river and expecting it to continue to remain in working condition would be unusual, but this is what Lion's Roar expected. Solicitors are unable to determine liability at the present time. A claim for $4 million being the cost of a replacement vehicle and lost production time has been received by Crighton-Ward from Lions' Roar. The directors' opinion is that the claim is not justified.

Depreciation

Depreciation of specialist production equipment has been included in the financial statements at the amount of 10% pa based on reducing balance. The treatment is consistent with prior accounting periods (which received an unmodified auditor's report) and other companies in the same industry and sales of old equipment show negligible profit or loss on sale. The audit senior, who is new to the audit, feels that depreciation is being undercharged in the financial statements.

Required:

For each of the above matters:

(i)   discuss whether or not a paragraph is required in the representation letter; and

(ii)   if appropriate, draft the paragraph for inclusion in the representation letter.
                                                                          (10 marks)

(c)   A suggested format for the letter of representation has been sent by the auditors to the directors of Crighton-Ward. The directors have stated that they will not sign the letter of representation this year on the grounds that they believe the additional evidence that it provides is not required by the auditor.

Required:

Discuss the actions the auditor may take as a result of the decision made by the directors not to sign the letter of representation.   **(5 marks)**

                                                                          (Total: 20 marks)

ISAs AND OTHER KEY AREAS

51   ASSURANCE/ISA 320 *Walk in the footsteps of a top tutor*

(a)   Auditors are frequently required to provide assurance for a range of non-audit engagements.

Required:

List and explain the elements of an assurance engagement.   **(5 marks)**

(b)   ISA 320 *Materiality in Planning and Performing an Audit* provides guidance on the concept of materiality in planning and performing an audit.

Required:

Define materiality and determine how the level of materiality is assessed. (5 marks)

(Total: 10 marks)

52   ISA 500/260 *Walk in the footsteps of a top tutor*

(a)   ISA 500 *Audit Evidence* requires audit evidence to be reliable.

Required:

List FOUR factors that influence the reliability of audit evidence.   **(4 marks)**

(b)   ISA 260 (Revised and Redrafted) *Communication with Those Charged with Governance* deals with the auditor's responsibility to communicate with those charged with governance in relation to an audit of financial statements.

Required:

(i)   Describe TWO specific responsibilities of those charged with governance;
                                                                                    (2 marks)

(ii)   Explain FOUR examples of matters that might be communicated to them by the auditor.   **(4 marks)**

(Total: 10 marks)

53   ISA 530/315/AUDIT REPORTS (A) *Walk in the footsteps of a top tutor*

 Timed question with Online tutor debrief

(a)   **List and explain FOUR methods of selecting a sample of items to test from a population in accordance with ISA 530 *Audit Sampling*.**   **(4 marks)**

(b) List and explain FOUR assertions from ISA 315 *Identifying and Assessing the Risk of Material Misstatement Through Understanding the Entity and its Environment* that relate to the recording of classes of transactions. (4 marks)

(c) In terms of audit reports, explain the term 'modified'. (2 marks)

(Total: 10 marks)

 Calculate your allowed time, allocate the time to the separate parts...............

54   ISA 620/AUDITOR RIGHTS/ASSERTIONS *Walk in the footsteps of a top tutor*

(a) ISA 620 *Using the Work of an Auditor's Expert* explains how an auditor may use an expert to obtain audit evidence.

Required:

Explain THREE factors that the external auditor should consider when assessing the competence and objectivity of the expert. (3 marks)

(b) Auditors have various duties to perform in their role as auditors, for example, to assess the truth and fairness of the financial statements.

Required:

Explain THREE rights that enable auditors to carry out their duties. (3 marks)

(c) List FOUR assertions relevant to the audit of tangible non-current assets and state one audit procedure which provides appropriate evidence for each assertion. (4 marks)

(Total: 10 marks)

55   INTERNAL AUDIT

(a) Explain the factors to be taken into account when assessing the need for internal audit. (6 marks)

(b) List and explain the contents of a typical internal audit review report. (4 marks)

(Total: 10 marks)

56   AUDITOR'S RESPONSIBILITIES

(a) Explain the auditor's responsibility for the prevention and detection of fraud and error. (5 marks)

(b) Explain the auditor's responsibility to consider laws and regulations (5 marks)

(Total: 10 marks)

Section 2

ANSWERS TO PRACTICE QUESTIONS

SYSTEMS AND AUDIT PROCEDURES

1   SHINY HAPPY WINDOWS CO *Walk in the footsteps of a top tutor*

Key answer tips

This question was off the first paper written by the new F8 examiner. As per her "Examiner's Approach" article she has not followed the previous examiner's lead of always having the systems/procedures style question as the 30 mark question 1. This featured on the June 2010 paper as a 20 mark question 3.

Part (a) requires little more than pre-learnt knowledge.

Part (b) is a typical systems review question. You are asked to prepare a management letter of deficiencies to those charged with governance. This is a very common style of question and should be rehearsed before sitting the actual exam. Note that the question requires you to link parts (ii) and (iii) to the deficiencies you identified in part (i). For this reason a table format is appropriate for your answer. Your answer to part (b) requires application of knowledge to the specific information given in the question. You cannot "knowledge dump" in your answer.

Part (c) asks for tests you could perform on any company's bank balance. You can therefore suggest general tests learnt from your study texts. You do not have to apply your answer to the scenario.

The highlighted words are key phases that markers are looking for.

(a)   (i)   Tests of control test the operating effectiveness of controls in preventing, detecting or correcting material misstatements.

Substantive procedures are aimed at detecting material misstatements at the assertion level. They include tests of detail of transactions, balances, disclosures and substantive analytical procedures.

(ii)   Example tests of control over sales invoicing

- Inspect numerical sequence of sales invoices, if any breaks in the sequence noted, enquire of management as to missing invoices.

- Review a sample of sales invoices for evidence of authorisation by a responsible official of any discounts allowed.
- Inspect customer statements for evidence of regular preparation.

Example substantive procedures over sales invoicing

- Select a sample of pre and post year end goods despatch notes and follow through to pre or post year end sales invoices, to ensure the sales cut-off has been correctly applied.
- Perform an analytical review of monthly sales, compare any trends to prior years and discuss significant fluctuations with management.
- Review post year end credit notes to identify if any pre year end sales should be removed.

(b)

Deficiency	Control	Test of Control
A junior clerk opens the post unsupervised. This could result in cash being misappropriated.	A second member of the accounts team or staff independent of the accounts team should assist with the mail, one should open the post and the second should record cash received in the cash log.	Observe the mail opening process, to assess if the control is operating effectively.
Cash and cheques are secured in a small locked box and only banked every few days. A small locked box is not adequate for security of considerable cash receipts, as it can easily be stolen.	Cash and cheques should be ideally banked daily, if not then it should be stored in a fire proof safe, and access to this safe should be restricted to supervised individuals.	Enquire of management where the cash receipts not banked are stored. Inspect the location to ensure cash is suitably secure.
Cash and cheques are only banked every few days and any member of the finance team performs this.	Cash and cheques should be banked every day.	Inspect the paying-in-books to see if cash and cheques have been banked daily or less frequently. Review bank statements against the cash received log to confirm all amounts were banked promptly.
Cash should ideally not be held over-night as it is not secure. Also if any member of the team banks cash, then this could result in very junior clerks having access to significant amounts of money.	The cashier should prepare the paying-in-book from the cash received log. Then a separate responsible individual should have responsibility for banking this cash.	Enquire of staff as to who performs the banking process and confirm this person is suitably responsible.
The cashier updates both	The cashier should update	Observe the process for

Deficiency	Control	Test of Control
the cash book and the sales ledger. This is weak segregation of duties, as the cashier could incorrectly enter a receipt and this would impact both the cash book and the sales ledger. In addition weak segregation of duties could increase the risk of a 'teeming and lading' fraud.	the cash book from the cash received log. A member of the sales ledger team should update the sales ledger.	recording cash received into the relevant ledgers and note if the segregation of duties is occurring.
Bank reconciliations are not performed every month and they do not appear to be reviewed by a senior member of the finance department. Errors in the cash cycle may not be promptly identified if reconciliations are performed infrequently.	Bank reconciliations should be performed monthly. A responsible individual should then review them.	Review the file of reconciliations for evidence of regular performance and review by senior finance team members.

(c) **Substantive procedures over bank balance:**

- Obtain the company's bank reconciliation and check the additions to ensure arithmetical accuracy.
- Obtain a bank confirmation letter from the company's bankers.
- Verify the balance per the bank statement to an original year end bank statement and also to the bank confirmation letter.
- Verify the reconciliation's balance per the cash book to the year end cash book.
- Trace all of the outstanding lodgements to the pre year end cash book, post year end bank statement and also to paying-in-book pre year end.
- Examine any old unpresented cheques to assess if they need to be written back into the purchase ledger as they are no longer valid to be presented.
- Trace all unpresented cheques through to a pre year end cash book and post year end statement. For any unusual amounts or significant delays obtain explanations from management.
- Agree all balances listed on the bank confirmation letter to the company's bank reconciliations or the trial balance to ensure completeness of bank balances.
- Review the cash book and bank statements for any unusual items or large transfers around the year end, as this could be evidence of window dressing.
- Examine the bank confirmation letter for details of any security provided by the company or any legal right of set-off as this may require disclosure.

ACCA marking scheme		
		Marks
(a) Up to 1 mark each for definition of test of control and substantive procedures and up to 1 mark each for example test given		
– Definition of test of control (toc)		
– Definition of substantive test		
		2
– Example toc		
– Example substantive test		
		2
(b) Up to 1 mark for each deficiency identified and explained, up to 1 mark for each suitable control and up to 1 mark per test of control.		
– Junior clerk opens post		
– Small locked box		
– Cash not banked daily		
– Cashier updates cash book and sales ledger		
– Bank reconciliation not performed monthly		
	Maximum for deficiencies	3
	Maximum for controls	3
	Maximum for test of controls	3
(c) Up to 1 mark per substantive procedure		
– Check additions bank reconciliation		
– Obtain bank confirmation letter		
– Bank balance to statement/bank confirmation		
– Cash book balance to cash book		
– Outstanding lodgements		
– Unpresented cheques review		
– Old cheques write back		
– Agree all balances on bank confirmation		
– Unusual items/window dressing		
– Security/legal right set-off		
		7
Total		20

2 REDBURN CO *Walk in the footsteps of a top tutor*

Key answer tips

Part (a) requires little more than pre-learnt knowledge from your study texts. However, if you struggle without your notes employ a little common sense and simple ask the question; "why is it important to plan anything, e.g. a holiday?"

Parts (b) and (c) require you to recommend audit procedures. You must take care to answer the specific requirement, which focuses on certain assertions. If you procedures do not test the **reliability** of sales statistics and the **completeness/accuracy** of the royalty charge they will be irrelevant and not score. Do not just read the word "sales" and write all the procedures you can remember relevant to this.

For part (d) you need to remember that inherent risk is one that increases the risk of misstatement occurring in the first instance (e.g. a complex accounting requirement, constantly changing legal environment).

Part (e) then requires you to think about the net realisable value of inventory and how you test it. This is largely pre-learnt knowledge from your study texts.

The highlighted words are key phases that markers are looking for.

(a) Audit planning is addressed by ISA 300 (Redrafted) Planning an Audit of Financial Statements. The standard notes that an audit plan will be developed after the overall audit strategy has been established and then states that adequate planning benefits the audit of financial statements in several ways, including the following:

- Helping the auditor to devote appropriate attention to important areas of the audit.

- Helping the auditor identify and resolve potential problems on a timely basis.

- Helping the auditor properly organise and manage the audit engagement so that it is performed in an effective and efficient manner.

- Assisting in the selection of engagement team members with appropriate levels of capabilities and competence to respond to anticipated risks and the proper assignment of work to them.

- Facilitating the direction and supervision of engagement team members and the review of their work.

- Assisting, where applicable, in coordination of work done by experts.

The following are examples of matters that would be included in the audit plan:

(i) A description of the nature, timing and extent of planned risk assessment procedures sufficient to assess the risks of material misstatement.

(ii) This would include assessment of inherent risk and control risk at both the entity and assertion level. An important element of the plan would be the understanding and assessment of the control environment of the organisation.

(iii) A description of the nature, timing and extent of planned further procedures at the assertion level for each material class of transactions, account balance, and disclosure.

(iv) This would include an explanation of the decision

- whether to test the operating effectiveness of controls (an important decision is whether reliance is to be placed on controls).

- on the nature, timing and extent of planned substantive procedures (this would depend on the decision as to the level of control risk).

(v) Audit procedures required to be carried out for the engagement in order to comply with ISAs, for example, the use of external confirmations to obtain sufficient appropriate evidence at the assertion level.

Tutorial note

These model Marks would also be available for additional points such as:

- Materiality
- Timetable of detailed audit work
- Allocation of work to team members.)

(b) Appropriate procedures would include:

- Reconcile the sales statistics to the recorded sales in the accounting records.

- Compare trends this year to those of prior years to ensure they are reasonable.

- In this connection consider any changes in client circumstances and exercise professional scepticism as these statistics are produced internally.

- Discuss with management the analyses they have made and the actions they have taken as a result of the statistical information available to them. They would probably use them, for example, in deciding whether reprints of books are necessary.

- On a test basis check that the customer codes on the customer master file are properly entered to ensure that the type of customer is properly identified.

- Review reports from sales staff to ensure that information on college take-up of books is accurate.

Tutorial note

As a general rule statistics that are kept on a day-to-day basis for the company's own purposes, will be much more reliable than those prepared especially for the auditor. However, the auditor should carry out procedures to ensure that they are accurate enough for audit purposes.

(c) Appropriate substantive tests to satisfy the auditor that the royalties charge is accurate and complete include:

	Test	Objective
(i)	Compare the royalties charge with stated sales income and obtain explanations from management if the figures do not appear reasonable.	To satisfy the auditor that the royalties charge in the income statement is reasonable in relation to stated sales income.
(ii)	Compare budgeted royalties figure with actual figures. If variations are significant, obtain explanations from management.	To satisfy the auditor that the actual figures had been anticipated by management, thus providing evidence as to their reliability.
(iii)	Review the sales statistics (proven in (b) above) to ascertain those despatches that attract royalties.	This would be evidence that the royalties charge was soundly based.

	Test	Objective
(iv)	Take a sample of recorded sales entries and check: whether royalties are due in respect of the customer if they are, that the entry in the computerised royalties file has been calculated at 10% according to the contracts agreed with the published poets.	These are detailed tests to prove that royalties were due on despatches and that the calculation of the royalty was accurate
(v)	Take a sample of royalty payments and agree to supporting despatch and sales documentation, checking in particular that all despatches are to individuals and organisations attracting royalties.	This is a test to prove that recorded royalty payments have resulted from despatches and sales attracting royalties.
(vi)	Select sales for 15 days before the year end and 15 days afterwards and compare with the dates of despatch notes.	This is to check that cut-off is accurate. The royalties charge should only include royalties on sales up to the cut-off date.
(vii)	Calculate the expected level of royalty payments based on monthly trend information for type of customer. Obtain sales figures and multiply by 10%. Compare expectation to actual royalties and obtain explanations from management for any significant variations.	This test should provide the auditor with evidence as to the completeness and accuracy of royalties paid.

This list is not exhaustive and other procedures may be appropriate.

(d) There are many inherent risks that may affect the inventory of books and some of these are set out below, together with controls that would mitigate each risk.

Inherent risks	Mitigating controls
Risk of deterioration.	Books should be stored in a location with air conditioning to keep them in saleable state.
Some books may not be saleable because of lack of demand.	Maintenance of movement records to identify slow-moving items.
Books may be defective and therefore not saleable.	Inspection of books returned from customers to identify those that are not in good condition. Identification of defective items at interim or period-end inventory counts.
Books may be attractive and easily transportable, making attempted theft likely.	Books to be kept in a secure location with restriction of entry to authorised personnel.

Inherent risks	Mitigating controls
Poor counting of inventory at the period end.	The use of independent and experienced inventory counters. The use of teams to cover specific areas of the locations where inventory is held. The use of pre-numbered inventory count sheets. And other inventory count procedures.
Poor cut-off as there may be movements of goods during the inventory count.	Movement of books out stopped during the count or only allowed by permission of authorised official in charge of the count. Book returns received during count held in separate area. Identification of last movements in and out.
Goods on sale or return are held by customers but should be included within inventory until the return period is passed.	Detailed records should be maintained of goods on sale or return and this should be reviewed at the year end to ensure that any goods within the return period have been included in inventory.

(e) (i) Net realisable value is defined in IAS 2 Inventories as: 'the estimated selling price in the ordinary course of business less the estimated costs of completion and the estimated costs necessary to make the sale.'

(ii) Appropriate procedures to determine that net realisable value of book inventory is above cost would include:

(1) Assessment of estimated proceeds from the sale of items of inventory. Sales price in the period following the year-end is one important element of net realisable value. Procedures to determine sales prices include:

- Obtain actual sales prices by reference to invoices issued after the year-end and determine that the sales were genuine by vouching sales invoices to orders, despatch notes and subsequent receipt of cash.

- If actual sales prices are not available, the auditor should obtain estimated sales prices from management. It would be necessary to assess how reasonable these estimated prices were. The auditor might be aided in this respect by reviewing the reports from sales staff backed up by discussions with management.

- Particular attention should be paid to sales prices of books identified as slow-moving.

- For damaged books disposal price may be nil or very low and the auditor should examine records of disposal of such books in the past.

(2) Determine estimated costs to completion. These costs represent another important element of net realisable value. Relevant procedures include:

- Some books may still be in production and will initially be included in inventory at cost to date; for example, they may have been printed but not bound. The auditor should examine production budgets and actual costs (for binding, for example) to determine actual costs to completion. (Tutorial note: It is not uncommon for publishers to print books but leave them unbound until sales in the immediate future are expected.)

- Books returned may incur extra costs before they can be made ready for resale and the auditor should examine cost records to obtain a reasonable estimate of such costs.

(3) Determine costs to be incurred in marketing, selling and distributing directly related to the items in question.

- In general terms the auditor may determine the percentage relationship between sales and selling and distribution expenses.

- However, the distribution costs of heavy books are likely to be higher than for (say) light paperback books and the auditor should assess whether the cost weighting is reasonable.

(4) All of the above matters should be discussed with management bearing in mind that, although they represent an internal source of evidence, they are the most informed people regarding the saleability of books on hand and regarding determination of the various elements of net realisable value.

(5) Discuss with management the need for an inventory provision for slow moving and/or obsolete books.

	ACCA marking scheme	Marks
(a)	**Audit planning** Up to 1 mark for any of the following, but maximum 4. Important areas of the audit Potential problems Effective and efficient audit Selection of engagement team members and assignment of work Direction, supervision and review Coordination of work	4.0
	Two matters Up to 1 mark for relevant matters, but maximum 2. Risk assessment generally Assessment of control environment Decision to test controls Scope of substantive testing Procedures to comply with ISAs Materiality Timetable of detailed audit work Allocation of work to team members	2.0
	Maximum marks	6.0
(b)	**Sales statistics** 1 mark each for each relevant procedure and up to 1 for each explanation of how the procedure operates, but maximum 4. Reconcile to recorded sales Compare trends Discuss with management Customer codes Reports from sales staff	
	Maximum marks	4.0

(c)		**Substantive tests on royalties**	
		Up to 1½ marks for description of test and ½ mark for stating objective, but maximum 6.	
		Compare royalties with sales income	
		Compare budgeted and actual royalties	
		Review sales statistics	
		Check whether royalties due and correctly calculated	
		Agree royalty payments to supporting documentation	
		Check cut-off	
		Compare expected and actual royalties	
		Maximum marks	6.0
(d)		**Inventory risks**	
		Up to 1 mark for each identified risk and up to 1 mark for mitigating control, but maximum 4.	
		Deterioration	
		Unsaleable – lack of demand	
		Unsaleable – defective	
		Theft likely	
		Poor inventory counting	
		Poor cut-off	
		Sale or return	
		Maximum marks	4.0
(e)	(i)	**Define net realisable value**	
		1 mark for each element of definition.	
		Selling price Less estimated costs to completion, marketing, selling and distribution costs	
		Maximum marks	2.0
	(ii)	**Four procedures**	
		Up to 1 mark for stating procedure and up to 1 further mark for explanation, but maximum 8.	
		On sales price	
		On costs to completion	
		On selling and distribution cost	
		Discussion with management	
		Inventory provision	
		Maximum marks	8.0
		Total	30.0

3   B-STAR *Walk in the footsteps of a top tutor*

Key answer tips

This question exemplifies the importance of reading the question **properly** (i.e. by taking time to understand the requirements and the marks available) and of allocating time effectively. Remember, once your reading time has finished you have 1.8 minutes per mark. There are six separate requirements, so ensuring you leave enough time to tackle each is vital.

Part (a) is basic knowledge. However, an simpler way of referring to strategy is "how does the auditor get from A to B?" 'A' represents the point where the auditor begins the process of planning the audit and point B represents the signing the audit report.

Part (b)(ii) asks you to discuss the extent to which certain tests can be used during the audit of B-Star. It does not ask for a list of example procedures.

Part (c) requires you to list substantive **analytical procedures**. Remember: these are comparisons of data to identify underlying trends. Recommendations of inspections and enquiries will not score.

Making sure you are clear of these issues before you attempt the question will significantly improve your mark.

The highlighted words are key phases that markers are looking for.

(a) Audit strategy document

Section of document	Purpose	Example from B-Star
Understanding the entity's environment	Provides details of the industry area that the company is in along with specific information about the activities and strategies of the individual client.	Size of the theme park sector and expected growth over the next few years.
Understand the accounting and internal control systems	Details of accounting policies of the client and previous assessments of internal control systems indicating the expected extent of reliance on those systems.	Accounting policy for sales – sales are stated net of sales taxes. Reliance on control systems in B-Star may be limited due to lack of documentation of controls.
Risk and materiality	The assessment of risk for the client and risk of fraud and error and the identification of significant audit areas. The materiality level for audit planning purposes.	Materiality for sales to be 5% of turnover. B-Star receives cash sales – audit work required to determine the completeness of sales.
Consequent nature, timing and extent of audit procedures specific areas. Detail on the extent of use	Details of the focus on audit work on specific areas. Detail on the extent and use of audit software and possible reliance on internal audit.	Audit software could be used to provide analytical procedures on the sales of B-Star.
Co-ordination, supervision and review of audit work	Details the extent of involvement of experts, client locations and staffing requirements for the audit.	B-Star has only one location – audit staff will be required to work there for X weeks.

(b) (i) Risk affecting completeness

- The computer system does not record sales accurately and/or information is lost or transferred incorrectly from the ticket office computer to the accounts department computer.
- Cash sales are not recorded in the cash book; cash is stolen by the accounts clerks.

- Tickets are issued but no payment is received – that is the sale is not recorded.
- Cash is removed by the ticket office personnel, by the security guards or by the account clerks.
- The account clerks miscount the amount of cash received from a ticket office.

(ii) **Use of tests of controls and substantive procedures**

Tests of controls

Tests of control are designed to ensure that documented controls are operating effectively. If controls over the completeness of income were expected to operate correctly, then the auditor would test those controls.

In B-Star, while controls could be in operation, e.g. the account clerks agreeing physical cash to computer summaries, there is no indication that the control is documented; that is the computer summary is not signed to show the comparison has taken place. The auditor could use the test of inquiry – asking the clerks whether the control has been used, and observation – actually watching the clerks carry out the controls. As noted above though, lack of documentation of the control does mean relying on tests of control for the assertion completeness of income has limited value.

Substantive procedures

Substantive procedures include analytical procedures and other procedures.

Analytical procedures include the analysis of significant ratios and trends and subsequent investigation of any trends or relationships that appear to be abnormal. These procedures can be used effectively in B-Star as an approximation of income that can be obtained from sources other than the cash receipt records.

Other procedures, or tests of detail, are normally used to verify statement of financial position assertions and include obtaining audit evidence relevant to specific assertions. However, they could be used in B-Star to trace individual transactions through the sales/cash systems to ensure all ticket sales have been recorded (completeness assertion). The use of other procedures will be time consuming.

(c) (i) **Substantive analytical procedures – completeness of income for one day**

- Obtain proof in total. Tickets sold times price should equal day's income.
- Compare daily sales to budgeted daily sales (for example weekends and bank holidays would expect more income).
- Compare sales with previous days and account for changes such as variations for weather.
- Compare sales to souvenirs sales (more people in park means more souvenir sales).
- Compare ticket offices day-by-day and staff rotation to see if sales lower some day/some staff (attempt to identify fraud also).
- Compare the expected sales from ticket numbers to the total sales amount from cash and credit sales for each ticket office.

(ii)   **Substantive analytical procedures – completeness of income for the year**

- Obtain the sales income from the previous year. Multiply this by 115% to provide a rough estimate of the income for this year.

- Obtain information on the number of days with rain during the last year. Where this is more or less than 30, adjust the income estimate by 1/730 down for each day of rain above 30 or 1/730 up for each day of rain less than 30. (**Note:** B-Star only attracts 50% of the normal number of customers on a rainy day; hence one day of rain decreases total customers by 1/730 in the year.)

- Compare actual income to budgeted income for the year. Ask the directors to explain any significant deviations.

- Obtain industry information on the popularity of theme parks, and change in customer numbers. Compare these trends to the results obtained by B-Star. Where B-Star performed significantly better or worse than average, obtain explanations from the directors.

(d)   Audit of year end credit card receivable

- Agree the balances on each credit card company's ledger account to the list of receivables.

- Cast the list of receivables and agree the total to the total on the receivables ledger control account.

- For the last day of the financial year and the first day of the new financial year, agree total sales income from ticket office records to the cash book and receivables ledger ensuring they are recorded in the correct period.

For a sample of material balances and a random sample of immaterial items,

- Obtain direct confirmation from the credit card company of the amount due to B-Star using a receivables confirmation letter.

- Where direct confirmation is not possible, obtain evidence of cash receipt after the end of the financial year. Agree the amount on the bank statements post year end of B-Star to the amount due in the receivables ledger (less any commission due).

- Review after date sales day book for debit notes indicating that sales may have been overstated in the prior year.

- Obtain the financial statements of B-Star and ensure that the receivables amount is disclosed as a current asset net of commission due to the credit card companies.

Marking scheme		Marks
(a)	**Audit strategy document** 0.5 for each section of audit strategy document, 0.5 for explaining the purpose of that section, 1 for the relevant example from B-Star scenario. ***Ideas*** Understand the entity's environment Understand the accounting and control systems Risk and materiality Timing and extent of audit procedures Co-ordination, supervision and review of work	
	Maximum	**8**

(b)	**(i) Risks re completeness of sales and cash receipts** 1 for each risk *Ideas* The computer system does not record sales accurately Cash not recorded Tickets are issued but no payment is received – that is the sale is not recorded Cash is removed by the ticket office personnel, etc The account clerks miscount the amount of cash received from a ticket office **Maximum**	**4**
	(ii) Use of tests of controls and substantive procedures Up to 1 for each valid response and up to 2 for showing whether the procedure is valid for B-Star case. Deficiencies Tests of controls Substantive procedures **Maximum**	**6**
(c)	**Analytical procedures** 1 mark each for each valid procedure **(i) Ticket sales for one day** Proof in total Compare sales day-by-day Compare sales to souvenirs sales Compare ticket offices day-by-day and staff rotation Compare cash receipts to ticket sales **Maximum**	**4**
	(ii) Ticket sales for year Prior year income * 15% Adjust for rainy days Compare actual and budget Industry trends **Maximum**	**4**
(d)	**Year end receivables** Individual balances to list of receivables – Cast list Cut-off Direct confirmation Alternative procedures to direct confirmation After date sales – debit notes Presentation in financial statements **Maximum**	**4**
	Total	**30**

Examiner's comments

Part (a)

A significant number of candidates did not appear to be aware of what an audit strategy is. Many candidates did not even attempt the question. Of those candidates attempting the question, answers tended to fall into two main categories:

- Firstly, setting out sections of the strategy, and providing clear examples. Answers in this category included candidates who were not clear of the actual headings of the strategy, but even so attempted to think 'big picture' about the audit and make comments accordingly. For example, candidates were aware that setting out audit procedures were important for planning and attempted to explain the approach to sales testing even if the reason for this was not specifically mentioned. These answers were usually satisfactory.

- Secondly, focusing on the detail of the audit. Answers in this category listed income, expenditure, asset and liability headings and then attempted to show the detailed testing required for each section. While comments made were normally correct, the lack of focus on the overall audit approach limited the marks that could be awarded. This type of answer was unsatisfactory.

Most candidates provided a list of controls, although a minority did provide significant explanation of the controls; detail that was not needed for this answer.

Other common errors included:

- Not linking points made to the scenario. For example, mentioning the need to determine risk and materiality but then not mentioning key risk areas such as cash sales.

- Lack of breadth of points made. For example, mentioning scope and direction of the audit but not risk, materiality, assessment of control systems, etc.

Part (b)

Part (i) was generally answered well with many candidates being quite realistic and/or inventive regarding how either cash could be stolen or visitors to the park obtain entry without paying. As well as points mentioned in the marking scheme, more innovative comments including ticket staff giving away free tickets to family members and two security guards being insufficient to guard the cash.

A minority of answers tended to focus on control deficiencies without actually stating how this affecting completeness of income. For example, answers could mention not reconciling tickets sold to cash received without specifically stating that an error would indicate tickets had been 'sold' for no income, which affected the completeness assertion.

Part (ii) was almost always answered inadequately. Almost all candidates appeared to see the words 'tests *of controls and substantive* procedures' and therefore provided a long list of possible tests of control and substantive procedures on the sale system. Unfortunately, the question requirement was '*discuss the extent to which* tests *of control and substantive procedures could be used to confirm the assertion of completeness of income...*', a completely different question. In other words, the question was asking for some commentary on the effectiveness of audit testing in a cash based environment focusing on areas such as the need for clear segregation of duties and authorisation of cash/ticket reconciliations in the company to be confirmed in tests of control.

Part (c)

The main weakness in many answers was the lack of discrimination between substantive procedures and substantive *analytical* procedures. Almost all answers included one or more pure substantive procedures with a minority focusing on this type of procedure to the exclusion of analytical procedures. In other words, many comments related to the substantive testing of the cash receipts system including counting cash in the tickets offices through to confirming the amounts recorded in the cash books to the bank statements. While these procedures were not incorrect in themselves, they were not analytical procedures required by the question.

Regarding analytical procedures, most candidates managed to compare daily/yearly income with other days/years as well as budgets, forecasts and other similar theme parks. Only a minority used other information in the scenario such as comparing ticket receipts to gift shops sales.

Part (d)

Most candidates appeared to understand the question and provided an appropriate range of procedures. In other words, even though the concept of a credit card receivable may have been unfamiliar, candidates were able to apply their knowledge to the audit of receivables in general terms and therefore mentioned relevant procedures such as direct confirmation using after-date receipts to confirm year-end balances.

The main weakness in many answers was the confusion between the audit of sales and the audit of receivables. A significant minority of candidates explained how the total sales figure could be audited, for example, testing receipts through the sales day book to recording in the sales ledger. While answers were factually correct, they did not relate to receivables testing and could not therefore be awarded credit.

Other common errors included:

- Listing the methods of collecting audit evidence such as inspection and enquiry.
- Listing audit assertions for receivables without linking these to valid audit procedures.

---

4   BLAKE *Walk in the footsteps of a top tutor*

Key answer tips

The question requires an understanding of the purpose of control systems, namely payroll in this scenario. The student is also required to identify deficiencies relevant to the scenario and suggest improvements. This should not present any real challenge to a well prepared student as it is typical of the F8 exam. *Note:* There are 2 presentation marks for adopting a management letter style.

The remainder of the question focuses on audit evidence/procedures. Once again students should be prepared for this. However, be careful to respond to the specific requirement, i.e.: (c) requires *analytical procedures* and (d) requires tests conducted to assess the *accuracy* of the time recording system.

The highlighted words are key phases that markers are looking for.

(a)   **Control Objectives – wages system**
- Employees are only paid for work that they have done
- Gross pay has been calculated correctly
- Gross pay has been authorised
- Net pay has been calculated correctly
  Gross and net pay have been recorded accurately in the general ledger
- Only genuine employees are paid
- Correct amounts are paid to taxation authorities.

(b)   **The Directors**
        Blake Co
        110 High Street
        Littlehampton
        HH1 7YY

        3 December 2008

        Dear Sirs

        Management letter

        As usual at the end of our audit, we write to bring to your attention deficiencies in your company's internal control systems and provide recommendations to alleviate those deficiencies.

(i) Deficiency:	(ii) Possible effect:	(iii) Recommendation:
The logging in process for employees is not monitored.	Employees could bring cards for absent employees to the assembly plant and scan that card for the employee; absent employees would effectively be paid for work not done.	The shift manager should reconcile the number of workers physically present on the production line with the computerised record of the number of employees logged in for work each shift.
Overtime is not authorised by a responsible official.	Employees may get paid for work not done e.g. they may clock-off late in order to receive 'overtime' payments.	All overtime should be authorised, either by the shift manager authorising an estimated amount of overtime prior to the shift commencing or by the manager confirming the recorded hours in the payroll department computer system after the shift has been completed.
The code word authorising the accuracy of time worked to the wages system is the name of the cat of the department head.	The code work is not secure and could be easily guessed by an employee outside the department (names of pets are commonly used passwords).	The code work should be based on a random sequence of letters and numbers and changed on a regular basis.
The total amount of net wages transferred to employees is not agreed to the total of the list of wages produced by the payroll department.	'Dummy' employees – payments that do not relate to any real employee – could be added to the payroll payments list in the accounts department.	Prior to net wages being sent to the bank for payment, the financial accountant should cast and agree the total of the payments list to the total of wages from the payroll department.

(i) Deficiency:	(ii) Possible effect:	(iii) Recommendation:
Details of employees leaving the company are sent on an e-mail from the personnel department to payroll.	There is no check to ensure that all e-mails sent are actually received in the payroll department.	There needs to be a control to ensure all e-mails are received in personnel — pre-numbering of e-mails or tagging the e-mail to ensure a receipt is sent back to the personnel department will help meet this objective.
In the accounts department, the accounts clerk authorises payment of net wages to employees.	It is inappropriate that a junior member of staff should sign the payroll; the clerk may not be able to identify errors in the payroll or could even have included 'dummy employees' and is now authorising payments to those 'people'.	The payroll should be authorised by a senior manager or finance director.

If you require further information on the above, please do not hesitate to contact us.

Yours faithfully

Global Audit Co.

(c)

Substantive analytical procedure	Expectation
Compare total salaries cost this year to total salaries cost last year.	As the number of shift managers has remained unchanged, the total salary expenditure should have increased by inflation only.
Ascertain how many shift managers are employed by Blake and the average salary from the personnel department. Calculate managers' average salary.	Total salary should be approximately number of managers multiplied by average salary.
Obtain a listing of total salary payments made each month.	The total payments should be roughly the same apart from July onwards when salaries increased and November when the annual bonus was paid.

(d)

Audit procedure	Applicability in testing accuracy of time recording system
Confirmation Confirmation is the process of obtaining a representation of information or of an existing condition directly from a third party.	Confirmation that the time recording system has worked could be obtained from the shift foreman, although this evidence would not be reliable as the time-recording system is not monitored. Similarly, confirmation could also be obtained from staff in the payroll department that hours worked appear to be correct. Again, this would not confirm the accuracy of the recording – only the reasonableness of the amounts
Observation This procedure involves watching a procedure being performed by others – in this case watching shift-workers using the time recording system.	Testing will be limited to ensuring all shift-workers actually clock in and out when they arrive to and depart from work. The procedure has limited use as it only confirms it worked when shift-workers were observed. It also cannot confirm that hours have been recorded accurately.
Inquiry Inquiry involves obtaining information from client staff or external sources.	Inquiry only confirms that shirt-workers confirm they clock-in or out. It does not directly confirm the action actually happened or the accuracy of the recording of hours worked.
Recalculation Recalculation means re-checking the arithmetical accuracy of the client's records; in this case the hours worked by the time-recording system.	Recalculation can confirm the hours worked are correctly calculated as the difference between the clocking in and out times in the time recording system. When used with reperformance evidence this will confirm the overall accuracy of the time recording system.
Reperformance Means collecting audit evidence that controls have actually worked.	If the auditor notes the time of clocking in and out, then these times can be agreed to the time recording system confirming the accuracy of recording. Reperformance is therefore a good source of audit evidence.
Analytical procedures Analytical procedures involve comparing financial or non-financial data for plausible relationships.	This procedure will be useful for the auditor as the total time recorded for each employee should be standard hours plus any estimate of the overtime worked.

Marking scheme		Marks
(a)	½ mark for each valid objective	**2**
(b)	Management letter – 1 mark for each deficiency, 1 for each possible effect and 1 for each recommendation = 3 marks × 4 sets of points = 12 marks Logging in process not monitored Overtime not authorised Poor password control (cat's name) Transfer total wages not checked Employees leaving details sent on e-mail Other valid points 4 points × 3 marks each = 12 Letter format Introduction and conclusion to letter Maximum marks	**14**
(c)	1 mark for each valid procedure and 1 for expectation of result of procedure = 2 marks for each procedure Total salary cost Average salary List of payments each month Other valid points Maximum marks	**6**
(d)	½ mark for stating each procedure, ½ for explaining each procedure and 1 mark for discussing the use of that procedure = 2 marks for each procedure Confirmation Observation Inquiry Recalculation Reperformance Analytical procedures Note inspection procedure not valid as stated in question. Maximum marks	**8**
	Total	**30**

Examiner's comments

Part (a)

The requirement verb "list" indicated that no explanation of the control objective was needed; however a minority of candidates did provide a detailed explanation which was not required.

Other common errors included:

- Listing controls over computer systems, not the wages system (e.g. access controls or backup of computer data).

- Provided detailed explanation of each control, which as noted above was not required.

- Stating possible controls from the scenario when generic control objectives of a wages system were required. For example, stating that foremen should observe the clocking in process but the control objective was to ensure accuracy of hours worked.

Part (b)

The requirement stated that 4 deficiencies were required and that 2 marks were available for presentation. A minority of candidates provided more than 4 deficiencies in which case only the best 4 were marked.

Most candidates provided a brief introductory comment in a letter or report format, followed by a table with three columns normally headed Deficiency, Effect and Recommendation. This clear presentation made the answers easy to follow. Two other answer formats were also adopted:

- Firstly, using a heading for the deficiency (eg lack of authorisation of overtime) and then providing the deficiency, effect and recommendation as three paragraphs under this heading. This format was again clear and easy to follow.
- Secondly, listing all the deficiencies in one section, then all the effects in another and finally the recommendations in a third section. Answers taking this latter approach were of a lower standard simply because the logic of points could not be followed.

There was also some confusion regarding the requirement to "write a letter". A significant number of candidates used a report or memo format which was clearly inappropriate. Provision of basic information such as addresses, heading and an introductory paragraph, as outlined in the suggested answers, was expected.

Other common errors included:

- Explaining deficiencies that were not part of the scenario. These points normally started "there is no mention of.." indicating that the candidate was attempting to write deficiencies into the scenario which were not evident from the information given. While this may be correct, the question requirement was clearly focused on the recording and payment systems as given in the scenario; there was no need to "make up" additional deficiencies.
- Not always fully explaining the points being made. For example, the code word being generally know so any employee could authorise wages does not, in itself, constitute a problem. It is the unauthorised amendment of wages information increasing hours worked, adding "dummy employees," etc that is the problem. In situations such as these candidates were not always awarded a full mark as points had not been fully explained.

Part (c)

Candidates were expected to provide valid substantive analytical procedures such as a month by month analysis of salaries and then state expectations in terms of some months salaries being higher because of bonus payments or salary increases.

Common errors included:

- Stating procedures in very general terms such as reviewing salaries to show that a bonus was paid.
- Inclusion of comments relating to checking overtime amounts; managers were not paid overtime.
- Inclusion of comments relating to the accuracy of the time recording system; not relevant as managers receive a standard amount each month so again they do not receive overtime payments.

The standard of answers for this question was inadequate. Many candidates did not distinguish between substantive procedures and substantive analytical procedures, or simply provided vague points, as noted above.

Part (d)

Candidates were required to explain various procedures for collecting audit evidence and then to discuss whether the auditor will benefit from that evidence.

Most candidates appeared to understand the question and provided an appropriate range of procedures. A minority of candidates mentioned and explained audit procedures such as observation to obtain the first mark for that procedure, but then discussed the benefit by including an actual procedure e.g. observing the clocking in process to ensure this was being followed. This interpretation of the question requirement was acceptable and marked accordingly.

Other common errors included:

- Explaining the audit procedure inspection although this was specifically excluded by the question requirement.

- Using a list of assertions instead of audit procedures

- Including comments about wages systems in general when the question requirement was to focus on the time recording system.

The standard of answers was variable. Inadequate answers tended only to list procedures and then provide little or no detail on the procedure itself. Many candidates obtained between 6 and 8 marks for clearly stating procedures and explaining them per the question requirement. There tended to be relatively few answers between these extremes.

5   BRENNON & CO

Key answer tips

A question testing your knowledge of the practical application of verification techniques to the audit of trade receivables. This question is focusing on the manual records therefore CATT's are not required here.

Part (a) is asking for audit procedures to confirm the accuracy of an **existing** system via the ICQ.

Part (b) 6 tests are required, the marking scheme was 1 mark for the test and 1 for the explanation.

A student needs to clearly identifying the tests of control and reasons for each test. Therefore a solid understanding of what a test of control is required as students often confuse substantive for test of control. Ket words, review, observe and comply.

Part (c) To state assertions that are relevant for a **balance sheet item**.

As far as part (d) is asking you to set out the steps in performing a positive receivables circularisation exercise, up to despatch. These steps should be well known to you – but make sure you identify ALL relevant steps, starting at a logical point (obtaining an aged listing). It is also sensible to ensure that the more important points are fully reflected in your answer – such matters as obtaining agreement of management to the sample selected, and making sure that the auditor checks and retains control of the circularisation letters until posting.

(a)   **Prior year internal control questionnaires**

- Obtain the audit file from last year's audit. Ensure that the documentation on the sales system is complete. Review the audit file for indications of deficiencies in the sales system and note these for investigation this year.

- Obtain system documentation from the client. Review this to identify any changes made in the last 12 months.

- Interview client staff to ascertain whether systems have changed this year and to ensure that the internal control questionnaires produced last year are correct.

- Perform walk-through checks. Trace a few transactions through the sales system to ensure that the internal control questionnaires on the audit file are accurate and can be relied upon to produce the audit programmes for this year.

- During walk-through checks, ensure that the controls documented in the system notes are actually working, for example, verifying that documents are signed as indicated in the notes.

(b) **Tests of control**

Test of control	Reason for test
Review a sample of goods despatch notes (GDN) for signatures of the goods despatch staff and customer.	Ensures that the goods despatched are correctly recorded on the GDNs.
Review a sample of GDNs for signature of the accounts staff.	Ensures that the GDN details have been entered onto the computer system.
Observe despatch system ensuring Seeley staff have seen the customers' identification card prior to goods being loaded into customers' vans.	Ensures that goods are only despatched to authorised customers.
Review the error report on numeric sequence of GDNs produced in the accounts department and enquire action taken regarding omissions.	Ensures that the sequence of GDNs is complete.
Observe despatch process to ensure that the customers' credit limit is reviewed prior to goods being despatched.	Ensures that goods are not despatched to poor/bad credit risks. **Note:** Reviewing credit limits is not specifically stated in the scenario; however, most despatch/ sales systems will have this control and most candidates mentioned this in their answers. Hence marks were awarded for this point.
Review a selection of invoices ensuring they have been signed by accounts staff.	Ensures the accurate transfer of goods despatched information from the GDN to the invoice.

(c) **Assertions – receivables**

Assertion	Application to direct confirmation of receivables
Existence	The receivable actually exists which is confirmed by the receivable replying to the receivables confirmation.
Rights and obligations	The receivable belongs to Seeley Co. The receivable confirms that the amount is owed to Seeley again by replying to the confirmation.
Valuation and allocation	Receivables are included in the financial statements at the correct amount – the receivable will dispute any amounts that do not relate to that account.
Cut-off	Transactions and events have been recorded in the correct accounting period. The circularisation will identify reconciling items such as sales invoices/cash in transit.

(d) (i) **Receivables circularisation – procedures**

  – Obtain a list of receivables balances, cast this and agree it to the receivables control account total at the end of the year. Ageing of receivables may also be verified at this time.

  – Determine an appropriate sampling method (cumulative monetary amount, value-weighted selection, random, etc.) using materiality for the receivable balance to determine the sampling interval or number of receivables to include in the sample.

  – Select the balances to be tested, with specific reference to the categories of receivable noted below.

  – Extract details of each receivable selected from the ledger and prepare circularisation letters.

  – Ask the chief accountant at Seeley Co (or other responsible official) to sign the letters.

  – The auditor posts or faxes the letters to the individual receivables.

(ii) **Specific receivables for selection:**

  (1) Large or material items. These will be selected partly to ensure that no material error has occurred and partly to increase the overall value of items tested.

  (2) Negative balances. There are 15 negative balances on Seeley's list of receivables. Some of these will be tested to ensure the credit balance is correct and to ensure that payments have not been posted to the wrong ledger account.

  (3) Receivables in the range $0 to $20,000. This group is unusual because it has a relatively higher proportion of older debts. Additional testing may be necessary to ensure that the receivables exist and to confirm that Seeley is not overstating sales income by including many smaller receivables balances in the ledger.

  (4) Receivables with balances more than two months old. Receivables with old balances may indicate a provision is required for non-payment. The lack of analysis in Seeley Co's receivable information indicates a high risk of non-payment as the age of many debts is unknown.

  (5) Random sample of remaining balances to provide an overall view of the accuracy of the receivables balance.

Examiner's comments

Part (a)

To be clear, the question requirement was checking the accuracy of, not the specific content or production of the control questionnaires. Most candidates recognised this distinction and provided some appropriate content. A minority of candidates proceeded to explain how the whole despatch and sales system could be audited. This approach was inappropriate for two reasons:

- Firstly, with only 4 marks available for the question, explaining how to audit an entire system would take much more than 4 marks.
- Secondly, explaining how to audit a system was not relevant to the question requirement of checking the accuracy of some documentation.

Other common errors included:

- In a minority of situations, assuming that the client would produce and review the questionnaires. As with any audit documentation, it is the auditor who will obtain evidence on that item, not simply relying on the ability of the client.

Part (b)

Some candidates provided normally brief and succinct answers, clearly identifying the tests of control and reasons for each test. However, many candidates did not seem to appreciate the difference between a test of control and a substantive procedure.

A significant number of the points made were actually substantive procedures, which did limit the number of marks awarded for this section. This lack of knowledge was the main reason for the average mark in this section being far below a pass standard. Unfortunately, many candidates appear to list every single substantive procedure they could think of, making so very long and largely irrelevant answers.

Other common errors included:

- Stating deficiencies in the control systems, without mentioning any test of control.
- Including comments on the debtors/receivables systems. The question requirement was for tests on the sales and despatch systems, not debtors.
- Providing detailed examples of substantive procedures. Marks would be obtained for listing an appropriate control such as the GDN being signed in the accounts department to confirm details had been entered onto the computer system.

Part (c)

The overall standard for this question was relatively satisfactory; it was the application of the assertion that appeared to be problematic. Most candidates identified four assertions, but were unclear how this related to debtors/receivables.

Other common errors in this section included:

- Explaining the assertion "measurement". This is no longer a relevant assertion since the revision of ISA 500 and so no marks could be awarded for points made regarding this assertion.
- Listing four assertions – literally giving four words. These type of answers did not either state what the assertion was or explain the relevance to debtors/receivables.

Part (d)(i)

There was no limit to the number of procedures that could be mentioned in the answer, although most candidates included five, showing an appreciation of the requirement and mark allocation. Most answers were clear and to the point. A minority of answers either mentioned other parts of the debtors circularisation or testing of the sales system, as mentioned below, which was not relevant for this specific question.

Other common errors included:

- Mentioning other audit procedures on debtors such as reviewing after date cash to confirm that debtors had paid the year-end balance. While the procedures were normally valid, they did not relate to the preparation of the debtor's circularisation and therefore did not gain any marks.
- Explaining audit work on the replies received from debtors. Again this was outwith the question requirement and so not relevant.
- Explaining how the debtors balances were accumulated in the ledger; that is how invoices, payments received and credit notes were posted into the ledger.

Part (d)(ii)

The scenario did include an analysis of debtor balances which could be used as examples of the different categories of debtors – and many candidates focused their answer on this information. A minority of candidates stated other categories such as "material" or "potentially bad debts," correctly explained these and obtained similar marks.

There was no limit to the number of categories that could be mentioned in the answer, although most candidates included up to five, showing an appreciation of the requirement and mark allocation.

A significant minority of candidates spent the whole of the answer explaining one or two categories at the most, limiting the number of marks which could be awarded.

Other common errors included:

- Focusing the entire answer on explaining how to extract a sample of debtors using some form of statistical sampling technique. While the marking scheme did allow some credit for this approach, the answer was effectively only explaining one categorisation method, which therefore limited the marks that could be awarded.

- Repeating the points made. In other words, a minority of answers provided little or no structure. Adequate answers tended to work down the categorisation presented in the scenario. Other answers tended to mention categories of debtors in a random order, sometimes duplicating categories of debtors, and then fail to mention why that category was to be chosen anyway.

	Marking scheme	
(a)	**Accuracy of internal control questionnaires**	*Marks*
	1 for each well-explained step	
	– Prior year audit file	
	– System deficiencies identified not actioned by client	
	– Review system documentation	
	– Interview client staff	
	– Walk-through check	
	– Identify controls in above	**4**
(b)	**Tests of control despatch and sales system**	
	1 for procedure and 1 for reason for procedure.	
	Limit to ½ where the reason is not explained.	
	Maximum 2 marks per point.	
	Procedure	
	– GDN signature – despatch staff	
	– GDN signature – accounts staff	
	– Observe despatch system	
	– Error report GDN numeric sequence	
	– Credit limit control	
	– Invoices – signed	
	– Credit checking	
	– GDN signed by customer	
	– Observe the despatch system	**12**

(c)	Assertions – direct confirmation of receivables 1 for each explanation. *Assertions* – Existence – Rights and obligations – Valuation and allocation – Completeness	4

(d)	**Receivables circularisation procedures**
	1 mark per procedure
	(i) Procedure
	– List of receivables
	– Sampling method
	– Select balances for testing
	– Extract details from ledger
	– Prepare letters – client sign
	– Post letters
	– Choose date if not year end
	– Confirm with mgt can circularise receivables
	(ii) Specific receivables for selection – 1 mark each explained point (must include reason for selection for full mark)
	    – Negative balances
	    – Material balances
	    – \$0 to \$20,000 balances
	    – Old balances
	    – Random sample remaining balances
		5
		
		5

	Total	**30**

6   METCALF CO

Key answer tips

Part (a): Sufficiency of evidence is about quantity of evidence. Remember to consider the relationship between sufficiency and appropriateness of evidence, as well as the need to obtain more evidence to reduce audit risk (and therefore factors that increase audit risk also increase the need for more evidence). For four marks, an explanation of four different factors is needed.

Part (b): Linking audit procedures to assertions will produce a high score for this part of the question, and note the marks available for each sub-component.

(a)   Factors affecting sufficiency:

Assessment of inherent risk

As inherent risk increases, then more audit evidence will be required to reduce detection risk.

Materiality of the item

A decrease in materiality means that more audit evidence will be required to ensure that no material error has occurred.

Nature of the accounting and control systems

Where the accounting and control systems are poor then more audit evidence is necessary as less reliance can be placed on those systems.

Control risk

Determine the extent to which the directors have implemented a sound system of internal control; poor internal controls increase control risk, decreasing reliance that can be placed on those controls.

Experience from previous audits

Good experience from previous audits will decrease the amount of evidence required as the auditor can place reliance on previous review of clients' systems.

Result of audit procedures

Where the results of different audit procedures agree with each other then overall less evidence is needed – overall the evidence is more persuasive; however, where results are in conflict then more evidence is required.

Quality of information available

Some sources of audit evidence are more reliable than others – meaning less evidence is needed when relying on those sources for example, documentary evidence is more reliable than oral evidence.

(b) (i) **Audit procedures trade payables**

Procedure	Reason for procedure
Cast the list of trade payables and agree the total to the payables ledger and then to the general ledger.	To confirm that the list is complete, is accurately stated in the general ledger and contains no unusual or reconciling items which must be investigated.
Test, on a sample basis that payables on the list agree to the individual ledger balance and from the ledger to the list.	To confirm that the list agrees to the payables ledger.
Compare trade payables individually and in total to prior year balances and explain any unusual changes.	To explain changes in the balances. For example, the increase in payables could indicate cash flow problems and Metcalf & Co is delaying payment to suppliers in response to this. Comparison may also indicate lack of completeness of the list where payables balances have been omitted.
Select a sample of individual payables accounts for testing, focusing on material balances, zero balances and a sample of other items.	Material balances should always be tested to ensure correctness and test a large amount of payables by value. Some zero balances are tested to ensure that invoices have not been omitted from one supplier.
Select population from purchase invoices received after the year-end. Trace to evidence of goods receipt and where goods received prior year-end, ensure invoice amount included in purchase accrual.	Confirm completeness of recording of purchase invoices.
Obtain year-end supplier statements (either from Metcalf & Co or direct from the individual supplier via a circularisation letter). Agree the balance	Agree the payables balance to independent third party evidence to confirm accuracy, completeness and existence of the ledger balance.

Procedure	Reason for procedure
on the statement to the individual account in Metcalf & Co's payables ledger. Where necessary, reconcile the balances taking into account cash and invoices in transit.	
Take a sample of purchase invoices recorded in the purchase day book (PDB) just prior to the year end and trace to goods received note (GRN), ensuring that the goods were received prior to the end of the year.	To ensure that liabilities recorded in the PDB are represented by goods received during that year, and recorded in the correct period (cut-off testing).
Take a sample of GRNs prior to the end of the year and trace to purchase invoice or the 'goods received not invoiced' accrual in the financial statements.	To ensure completeness of recording of amounts payable.
Take a sample of GRNs just after the end of the year and trace to purchase invoice. Ensure that the invoice is recorded in the PDB after the year-end.	To ensure that the purchases figure is not overstated in this year's financial statements.
List all debit balances and obtain an explanation from the client.	To confirm why the balance arose and consider re-classifying the amounts as receivables. Debit balances may indicate control deficiencies with additional implications for audit testing.

(i)   Audit procedures accruals

Procedure	Reason for procedure
Cast the list of accruals and agree individual amounts to the general ledger accounts.	Confirm that the list is complete, the balances are accurately stated in the general ledger and contains no unusual or reconciling items which must be investigated.
Compare individual accruals with amount in the prior year accounts.	To account for unusual differences and identify omissions from the list this year.
Agree accruals to payments made after the end of the year for example, amounts payable for tax deducted from wages payments to remittance to the tax authority.	To help ensure the accuracy of the amounts paid and confirm that the accruals are genuine.
Review payments after the year-end to determine whether any accruals are required. Where the need for an accrual is identified, ensure this is included in the accruals list.	To confirm completeness of the accruals listing.

Procedure	Reason for procedure
Check calculations of individual accruals to supporting documentation for example, tax deductions from wages to the amount shown on the payroll as deducted from wages for the last month of the year.	To check that the accrual has been calculated correctly and therefore testing for over or understatement of each accrual.

(iii)   **Audit procedures provision for legal action**

Procedure	Reason for procedure
Discuss the provision with the directors.	To attempt to confirm whether the company is liable for the payment and confirm that an out-of-court settlement is appropriate.
Obtain a letter from Metcalf & Co's lawyers.	To provide evidence on whether Metcalf may be liable for payment and check the amount provided is approximately correct.
Review any correspondence with the customer.	To help determine Metcalf & Co's liability and determine whether the customer may accept the out-of-court settlement.
Obtain a letter of representation from the directors.	To confirm that the directors are considering settlement out of court.
If possible, trace the payment made after the end of the year to receipt from the customer stating that the payment is accepted in 'full and final settlement' i.e. no other payments are expected to be made.	To confirm the accuracy of the amount stated in accruals.

7   DINZEE CO

Key answer tips

Part (a): Candidates were required to use information concerning the purchases system provided in the scenario, students need to avoid the word 'check' as this is too vague.

Part (b): They key word to take from the requirements is 'prior' in order to score highly on this section.

Part (c): This is a time pressured exam plenty to write here, so the first thing do is identify how many deficiencies are required.

Part (d): Solid knowledge of test of control and substantive testing is required here to gain full marks.

(a)   **Audit procedures procurement and purchases system**

Procedure	Reason for procedure
Obtain a sample of e-mails from the store manager's computer. Trace details to the order database.	Ensure that all orders are recorded and that the order details are correct.
Obtain a sample of orders in the order database, record details of the order and trace to the paper delivery note filed in the goods inwards department.	To confirm that all goods ordered were received.
For the sample of orders above, agree to the inventory database.	To confirm that goods received were completely and accurately recorded in the inventory database.
Obtain a sample of paper delivery notes and agree to the order database and inventory database.	To confirm that inventory received has been recorded in DinZee's accounting system and that liabilities are therefore not understated
For a sample of orders in the orders database, agree details to the payables ledger database, confirming details against the purchase invoice.	To confirm complete and accurate recording of the inventory liability in the payables database. **Note:** To ensure goods received have been recorded as a payables liability the sample selected from the order database should be only those orders that have been received. The invoice number in the order database is then noted and traced to the payables ledger in the purchase database.
Within the purchase database, obtain a sample of invoices recorded in the purchase day book, agree details of price and supplier to the purchase invoice record in the database.	To confirm that purchase invoice details have been correctly recorded in the payables database.
For a sample of purchase invoices in the purchase day book, agree details to the delivery notes for items on that invoice.	To confirm that the purchase liability has been recorded only for goods actually received.
For the sample of purchase invoices above, agree details to the individual payables account in the payables database.	To confirm that the liability has been recorded in the correct payables account.
For a sample of supplier invoices, cast and cross cast invoice price and quantities confirming price to the original order.	To confirm the arithmetical accuracy of invoices and ensure the company was charged the correct price for goods received.
Select increases in the purchase daybook and vouch to the order database.	To ensure that invoiced goods have been ordered, confirming the occurrence assertion.
Using computer-assisted audit techniques, cast the purchase day book and agree total of liability incurred to the general ledger.	To confirm the completeness and accuracy of the liability recorded in the general ledger.

(b)   **Audit procedures prior to inventory count attendance**

Procedure

- Review prior year working papers.
- Contact client to obtain stocktaking instructions.
- Book audit staff to attend the inventory counts.
- Obtain copy of inventory count instructions from client.
- Ascertain whether any inventory is held by third parties.

- Obtain last year's inventory count memo.
- Prepare audit programme for the count.

(c) **Deficiencies in counting inventory**

Deficiency	Reason for deficiency	How to overcome deficiency:
Inventory sheets stated the quantity of items expected to be found in the store	Count teams will focus on finding that number of items making undercounting of inventory more likely – teams stop counting when 'correct' number of items found.	Count sheets should not state the quantity of items so as not to pre-judge how many units will be found.
Count staff were all drawn from the stores	Count staff are also responsible for the inventory. There could be a temptation to hide errors or missing inventory that they have removed from the store illegally.	Count teams should include staff who are not responsible for inventory to provide independence in the count.
Count teams allowed to decide which areas to count	There is a danger that teams will either omit inventory from the count or even count inventory twice due to lack of precise instructions on where to count.	Each team should be given a precise area of the store to count.
Count sheets were not signed by the staff carrying out the count	Lack of signature makes it difficult to raise queries regarding items counted because the actual staff carrying out the count are not known.	All count sheets should be signed to confirm who actually carried out the count of individual items.
Inventory not marked to indicate it has been counted	As above, there is a danger that inventory will be either omitted or included twice in the count.	Inventory should be marked in some way to show that it has been counted to avoid this error.
Recording information on the count sheets in pencil	Recording in pencil means that the count sheets could be amended after the count has taken place, not just during the count. The inventory balances will then be incorrectly recorded.	Count sheets should be completed in ink.
Count sheets for inventory not on the pre-numbered count sheets were only numbered when used	It is possible that the additional inventory sheets could be lost as there is no overall control of the sheets actually being used. Sheets may not be numbered by the teams, again giving rise to the possibility of loss.	All inventory sheets, including those for 'extra' inventory, should be pre-numbered.

(d) (i) The aim of a test of control is to check that an audit client's internal control systems are operating effectively.

The aim of a substantive procedure is to ensure that there are no material errors at the assertion level in the client's financial statements.

(ii)   Regarding the inventory count:

Test of control

Observe the count teams ensuring that they are counting in accordance with the client's inventory count instructions.

Substantive procedure

Record the condition of items of inventory to ensure that the valuation of those items is correct on the final inventory summaries.

Examiner's comments

Part (a)

Pass standard candidates provided between four and six good procedures, with some explanation of each procedure. However, only a minority of candidates demonstrated a good understanding of audit procedures and the reasons for those procedures.

Many candidates struggled with the scenario, particularly regarding the use of the purchases system and partly in respect to the computerisation of that system. Candidates who recognised that basic audit procedures such as tracing information through a system or ensuring that details were recorded in specific ledgers or books did obtain a pass standard.

Common errors and reasons why those errors did not obtain marks included:

- Testing the controls over the computer system, such as; passwords and backup systems. These were tests of the general controls over the computer rather than tests on the purchases system.

- Procedures relating to the payment of suppliers including recording of transactions in the cash book and supplier ledger accounts. These procedures related to the payments systems not the purchases systems.

- Procedures relating to cut-off. This assertion relates to year-end testing of stock and purchases. The scenario was dated prior to the year-end making these comments irrelevant.

- Just stating an assertion word as a reason for performing a procedure.

- Writing out what the purchase system should do without actually stating any audit procedures. No marks could be awarded because no audit procedure was actually stated.

- Other answers failed to provide sufficient detail to obtain either the procedure mark or the explanation mark.

Many candidates also continued to "check" documents rather than actually show clear what procedures were. For example, typical comments in this respect were:

- Check the invoice

- Check the goods received note

- Check return of goods.

Unfortunately, it was not clear exactly what was being checked or why; more detail was needed to earn the procedure mark.

Regarding the explanation mark, many candidates correctly attempted to link audit procedures to the audit assertions. However, the quoting of assertions was not always clear or accurate. For example:

- Suggesting that agreeing purchase order details to the inventory ledgers confirmed the completeness of invoices – when the correct assertion was occurrence.

- Tracing details from the delivery note to the purchase order to confirm correct valuation of the invoice: the completeness assertion would normally be used here.

Finally, many comments related to procedures that either could not be carried out or were simply incorrect.

For example:

- Agreeing details from the purchase invoice to the goods held in the inventory store. There are two problems with this comment: Firstly, goods received notes are normally used to update inventory, not purchase invoices. Secondly, it would be virtually impossible to agree details to the goods held – as the parts, etc. would have been used during the year in the manufacture of the items produced by the company.

- Agreeing individual items of physical inventory to the goods inwards documentation. Again, agreeing physical goods to the goods inwards documentation would be impossible – as noted above, the goods would be included in items manufactured by the company.

- Tracing details of orders to the purchase day book. Orders are normally agreed to the delivery notes, not the purchase day book. The latter is for recording the purchase invoices. So agreeing orders to purchase day book is not possible.

Overall, the standard of the answers for this basic auditing question was disappointing. Candidates and tutors are reminded of the importance of understanding sales, purchases and similar systems and the need to be able to provide clear audit procedures and explanation for those procedures. This will remain a key element of the audit and assurance examination.

Part (b)

Candidates tended to obtain either full marks or zero marks for this question, depending on whether or not they had read the question requirement correctly. The key word in the requirement was "**prior**;" a significant minority of candidates missed reading this word and listed procedures relevant to actually attending the inventory count; these procedures were unfortunately not relevant.

Other common errors and reasons why those errors did not obtain marks included:

- Not stating the procedure in sufficient detail. For example; "contact client" was insufficient for a procedure whereas "contact client to obtain inventory count instructions" was sufficient.

- While not an error as such, many candidates wrote significant amounts of text in providing an answer to this section, in some cases easily exceeding one page of writing. Given that only four procedures had to be **listed**, this amount of writing was clearly inappropriate.

Part (c)

In practice, most candidates provided more than three deficiencies with some explanation and methods of overcoming each deficiency. As the question requirement did not place any cap on the number of deficiencies that could be mentioned in the answer, all valid deficiencies were marked.

For the future, where letter of deficiency type questions are allowed, **a cap will be placed on the number of deficiencies allowed** to provide a clear and transparent guide to candidates.

As already noted, the overall standard of answers to this section was high. The identification of deficiencies and how to respond to those deficiencies had clearly been well learned/taught enabling candidates to provide sound answers. The difficulty for many candidates appeared to be simply when to stop writing as the scenario did include six or seven key deficiencies where marks could be obtained. Following the published guidance from the examiner in this respect in the Examiner's Approach may have helped provide this guidance.

Common errors and reasons why those errors did not obtain marks included:

- Not linking the explanation of the deficiency to the deficiency itself. To obtain the reason marks there had to be a clear link between the deficiency and the reason for that deficiency.

- Not linking the method of overcoming the deficiency with the deficiency itself. To obtain the method of overcoming the deficiency marks there had to be a clear link between the deficiency and the method of alleviating that deficiency.

- Not necessarily thinking about the practicality or realism of the comments being made. For example, stating that the auditor would assign count teams to different areas of the depot. In practice, the auditor is there to observe the inventory count, not organise it.

Overall, the question was well answered, with almost all candidates correctly using the information in the scenario .

Part (d)

This question turned out to be an unusually good discriminator of candidates. Many candidates obtained full marks, clearly demonstrating their knowledge of tests of control and substantive audit procedures. However, a significant minority of candidates either did not attempt the question or scored zero points due to poor and incorrect explanation and examples.

Common errors and reasons why those errors did not obtain marks included:

- Explaining substantive audit procedures as being used when tests of controls were not available or had failed. While the reason for using substantive procedures may have been partly correct, the reason for the procedure in terms of validating balance sheet assertions was not mentioned.

- Explaining tests of controls as substantive test and substantive tests as tests of controls. For example, stating that ensuring all count sheets were signed was a substantive test or agreeing the quantities of inventory to the inventory ledgers. No marks could be awarded because the example was incorrect.

- Providing examples not relevant to the inventory count, for example, confirmation of balances in the suppliers' ledger or other substantive tests on purchasing system. The question requirement clearly stated examples had to be provided from the inventory count, therefore these points were not relevant.

	Marking scheme	
(a)	**Audit procedures procurement and purchases system**	*Marks*
	1 for stating procedure and 1 for the reason for that procedure. Limit marks to 0.5 where the reason is not fully explained. Maximum 2 marks per point.	
	Procedure	
	- E-mails to order database	
	- Order database to delivery note	
	- Orders to inventory database	
	- Paper goods receipt notes to inventory database	
	- Orders database to payables ledger database	
	- Computerised details to record of purchase invoice	
	- Details of purchase invoice database	
	- Purchase invoice record to payables database	
	- CAATs – cast PDB, trace to general ledger	
	- Walk through test	
	- Observing goods being received	12
(b)	**Audit procedures prior to inventory count attendance**	
	0.5 for each procedure	
	Procedures	
	- Review prior year working papers for problems	
	- Contact client to obtain stocktake instructions	
	- Book audit staff to attend the inventory counts	
	- Obtain copy of inventory count instructions from client	
	- Ascertain whether any inventory is held by third parties	
	- Obtain last year's inventory count memo	
	- Prepare audit programme for the count	
	- Obtain prior year management letter	2
(c)	**Deficiencies in counting inventory**	
	1 per deficiency, up to 1.5 for the explanation and up to 1.5 for how to overcome deficiency. 4 max per deficiency.	
	Deficiencies	
	- Inventory sheets stating the quantity of items	
	- Count staff all drawn from the	
	- Count teams allowed to decidewhich areas to count	
	- Count sheets not signed by the staff	
	- Inventory not marked to indicate it has been counted	
	- Recording information on the count sheets in pencil	
	- Manual sheets only numbered when used	12
(d)	1 mark each for:	
	Test of control aim	
	Substantive procedure aim	
	Stating test of control relevant to inventory count	
	Stating substantive procedure relevant to inventory count	4
	Total	**30**

8   FIREFLY TENNIS CLUB *Walk in the footsteps of a top tutor*

Key answer tips

Questions on not for profit entities come up regularly, and completeness of income is a key area. Note the use of analytical review to test membership income; this technique can be used by the auditor as a substantive test and by the entity as a control. The highlighted words are key phrases that markers are looking for.

(a) **Audit tests for completeness of income**

All income

For a sample of paying-in slips during the year, trace amount banked to the bank statements agreeing the total banked.

Agree the total per the paying-in slip to the cash book to confirm that the total has been correctly recorded in the cash book.

Confirm that the analysis on the bank paying-in slips is correctly recorded between membership fees and court hire in the cash book.

Cast the cash book to confirm total income for the year.

Agree total income received and the analysis of membership fees and court hire to the financial statements.

Membership fees

Compare the list of members as at 1 October 2004 to 1 October 2005 to determine how many members did not renew their membership during the year. This is normally approximately 10%.

Confirm total membership fees are correct by analytical review. Membership income should be:

430 members less 10% = 387, 387 × $200 = $77,400, 50 new members at 50% fee = 50 × $100 = $5,000, Total fee income $82,400.

Agree the membership fee income to the financial statements. If the amount is materially different enquire of the treasurer why this is the case.

Court hire fees

Obtain the list of court hires from the clubhouse.

For a number of weeks, determine how many hours courts were hired for. Agree this time to the bank paying-in slip (hours × $5 should equal the amount banked).

Ask the secretary to explain any differences in amounts banked.

(b) **Audit tests on expenditure**

Perform analytical review on expenditure this year compared to last year. Obtain reasons for any unusual amounts, e.g. increased expenditure on tennis balls due to increased number of matches.

For a sample of purchase invoices, ensure recorded in the cash book and that the amount and analysis of expenditure (e.g. lighting, tennis balls, etc) is correct.

Obtain the statements from the debit card used by the club official – trace items from the statements to the cash book to ensure all expenditure has been recorded.

For a sample of entries in the cash book, agree to the bank statements to ensure they represent actual expenditure.

Cast and cross cast the cash book to ensure the book is arithmetically correct.

For totals in the cash book, agree to the trial balance and financial accounts, ensuring that the presentation in the accounts is correct (e.g. stated as tennis balls, line painting, etc).

(c)   **Limitation of internal control testing**

Internal control testing is limited in relatively small audits such as FireFly Tennis Club for the following reasons:

- There is a lack of segregation of duties. The club has only a limited number of staff in responsible positions. This means segregation of duties between, for example, authorising of purchase invoices and paying them, is not possible.

- Lack of authorisation controls. In small organisations, the senior officials tend to be the people 'authorising' transactions and also carrying them out. For example, the treasurer effectively authorises purchase invoices by paying for them rather than a senior official signing the invoice and a more junior clerk paying the invoice.

- Cost. Establishing an internal control system can be expensive. It may therefore not be cost effective for a small entity to establish a detailed internal control system.

- Management override. Even if there was an internal control system in place, senior officials are in a position to override that system. For example, the club treasurer could pay for his own expenses using the club debit card.

9   ATLANTIS STANDARD GOODS (ASG) CO (A)

Key answer tips

This question focuses on the sales system, and hence is reflective of the F8 exam which concentrates on core business areas. In part (a) it is important that you can differentiate between control objectives and control procedures; this question focuses on the former and hence no marks will be earned for a detailed description as to how they are achieved.

Part (b) asks you to tabulate your answer allowing an easy pro forma to differentiate between the test and the reason for its use. Ensure that your tests (approximately fifteen is the ideal) are tailored to the scenario, and that each stands alone without assuming extensive knowledge on behalf of the reader.

Part (c) is book knowledge of inventory count procedures.

(a)   **Aims of controls**

- Ordering of goods.
- Goods are only supplied to authorised customers.
- Orders are recorded correctly regarding price, quantity, item and customer details.
- Despatch and invoicing of goods.
- Orders are despatched to the correct customer.
- All despatches are correctly recorded.
- Despatches only relate to goods ordered and paid for by customers.
- Invoices raised relate to goods supplied by the company.

Audit test	**Reason for test**
Using test data if necessary, access ASG's website and input order details for specific goods. Trace those order details to the orders pending file.	Ensure that order details are completely and accurately recorded by the website software. Ensure that details recorded agree to those input.
For a sample of items in the orders pending file, <ul><li>agree to the orders awaiting despatch file, ensuring that appliance details and quantities are the same</li></ul>	To ensure that details from the website software are completely and accurately transferred to the orders awaiting despatch file.
<ul><li>agree sales details for that customer to the monthly reimbursement from the credit card company, checking amount received is the product price less the appropriate commission charged by the credit card company</li></ul>	To confirm that amounts are received for each appliance sold, and therefore that monies received are complete and accurate.
<ul><li>agree the sales amount to the sales ledger file.</li></ul>	To confirm that the amount of sales is not understated or overstated in the ledger, general ledger or financial statements.
Review goods awaiting despatch file for old items and inquire as to why those items are still on file.	To ensure that reasons for orders not being processed are being obtained. A large number of old items may also indicate problems with the credit card authorisation systems which again will need to be investigated.
For a sample of days, cast the sales ledger file and agree the total sales to the general ledger accounts for that day.	To check the numerical accuracy of the ledger and the accuracy of posting to the general ledger file.
For a sample of items in the goods awaiting despatch file, agree to the despatch information held on the despatch department computer.	To confirm that order details are completely and accurately transferred to the despatch department.
For a sample of items on the despatch department computer <ul><li>agree back to the goods awaiting dispatch file ensuring details of product, quantity and customer agree</li></ul>	To ensure that the despatch information is accurate and that the despatch record itself relates to a valid sale.
<ul><li>agree to the inventory records confirming that the correct appliance record was updated</li></ul>	Ensures that the inventory system correctly records the appliance ordered and that the inventory system remains accurate.
<ul><li>check customer signature is on file agreeing receipt of goods.</li></ul>	To confirm that evidence is available for receipt of goods confirming that goods have been delivered.

Audit test	**Reason for test**
For a sample of items on the despatch department computer, review to see that evidence of delivery to customer is available. Investigate records where no delivery information is available obtaining reasons for this.	To ensure that goods have been received and that procedures for investigating non-despatch or receipt are working.
Review the despatch department computer files for items not flagged 'order complete'. Investigate and obtain reasons for these items.	To ensure that the despatch process is working correctly and that incomplete items are being investigated.

(c)   During the count I should:

- observe the client's staff to see if they are complying with inventory count instructions so as to provide reasonable assurance that count will be accurate

- make test counts of inventory

    – from count sheets to the physical inventory (to test existence)

    – from physical inventory to the count sheets (to test completeness)

- record details of last movements in and out of inventory (which will be used subsequently during cut-off work)

- make photocopies of samples of count sheets and take details of sequence of sheets so that checks can be made later that no changes were made

- observe the condition of inventory to identify damaged, missing, out of date or slow moving inventor and ensure that third party inventory is separately identified

- consider whether management has implemented adequate year end cut-off (that is movements into, within and out of inventory are properly identified and recorded in the correct period).

After the count I would:

- follow up the details of last movements of inventory in and out into the accounting records to ensure sales and purchases are recorded in the correct period

- ensure the finished count sheets are accurate and complete by comparing to photocopied sheets

- follow up the results of test counts, i.e. finish test counts for completeness and existence. I would select a sample from inventory valuation report and agree to count sheets, and I would trace my completeness sample from the inventory count through to the valuation report

- follow up any problems identified at the count and report to management as necessary

- when the count date is not the exact day of the year end, ensure that management has implemented proper procedures to deal with transactions occurring between the two dates, e.g. ensure that if the count takes place one day before the year end that purchases on the last day of the year are added to the inventory figure and that sales are deducted.

10   DECE & CO

Key answer tips

Make sure you give a reason for each test in part (a), otherwise you only get a maximum of half marks. Ensure that you only talk about the value of inventory in part (c) and don't talk about quantities, for example.

(a)

Audit procedure – Physical count	Reason for procedure
Perform an overall review with client staff – ensure that they are following the client's physical count instructions. Specifically ensure that:	Check that client's physical count instructions are being followed as this will help to ensure that the count is complete and accurate.
Inventory is divided into appropriate sections for recording – perhaps by type of jewellery.	Confirms a clear layout of inventory ensuring items are not missed.
Staff are counting in pairs with one person checking the inventory and another recording details.	Prevents collusion and provides a check over security of inventory and that the count sheets are not falsified.
Appropriate checks are in place to ensure that each item of jewellery is only counted once.	Check to ensure that inventory is not double counted.
The shop is closed during the count.	To ensure that there is no confusion regarding which items are sold.
Countsheets are pre-numbered.	To ensure that no count sheets are lost.
Obtain a sample of inventory items already recorded on the inventory sheets and agree to the jewellery inventory.	Check to ensure that inventory recorded on the inventory sheets actually exists.
For a sample of jewellery in the shop, agree to the count sheets.	Check to ensure that all inventory is recorded on the inventory sheets – check for completeness of recording.
Obtain a sample of countsheets, photocopy and place on the audit file.	To check that details on the countsheets are not amended post physical count and for agreement to the final inventory sheets to ensure quantities are recorded correctly.
Check all countsheets are returned after the physical inventory count.	Ensures that all sheets are accounted for and inventory is therefore not understated.
Obtain last inventory receipt note and sales invoice numbers.	To ensure that cut off is correct. Subsequent checking should show that goods received notes post physical count are not included in payables for the year, and sales invoices after the physical inventory count are not included in sales for the year.
Review the condition of the jewellery with the independent valuer. Ensure that there are no reasons why the inventory could be obsolete (e.g. due to changes in fashion) or damaged.	To check that any inventory which is damaged or unsaleable is correctly valued.
Form an opinion regarding the overall accuracy of the physical count.	To confirm that inventory quantities have been correctly recorded.

(b) **Factors to consider when placing reliance on the work of UJ**

DeCe need to confirm that they actually need an expert. It is not clear whether DeCe have the necessary skills in-house. However, given that Rocks Forever is the only client in the diamond industry, then some assistance would be expected as valuing diamonds is difficult.

Check that the specialist has relevant experience in valuing diamond jewellery. Part of the appointment process will include checking the work portfolio of UJ to show that they have valued diamonds in other situations.

Ensure that UJ is a member of an appropriate professional body. This will help ensure that UJ follow the appropriate ethical standards as these will be enforced by their professional body.

Check that UJ cannot be influenced by the client – for example because they are employed by Rocks Forever. Being employed by the client would imply less independence and limit the value of the specialist's report.

Check that the report produced by the specialist regarding the valuation of the diamonds appears to be reasonable. Although DeCe do not have any other clients retailing diamonds, basic price comparisons for a given weight of diamond could still be obtained from other shops or Internet site to prove the accuracy of UJ's figures.

(c) **Audit evidence**

The jewellery inventory should be valued at the lower of cost and net realisable value.

For a sample of jewellery on the final inventory sheets, trace the cost of those items to the original purchase invoice, ensuring that the description of goods on the invoice matches the jewellery.

For jewellery sold after the end of the year, check a sample of sales invoices back to the final inventory sheets ensuring that the sales value exceeds the cost. Where sales value is less than cost, ensure that the jewellery is stated at the realizable value on the inventory sheet.

Review the report of the professional valuer. Ensure that the inventory is genuine. For the items checked by the valuer, agree the valuation to the items of jewellery on the inventory statements. Where there is a difference, for example due to age of the inventory or where it is unlikely to be sold due to changes in fashion, discuss with the client and agree a realistic valuation. In these situations, the value should be that provided by the professional valuer.

Where an item has been in inventory for a long period of time (perhaps over one year), check the valuer's report to find out whether any allowance is required.

11 TRACEY TRANSPORTERS

Key answer tips

Part (a) deals with the audit of the sales figure in the financial statements of a vehicle hire company. Don't be put off by the apparent complexity of the business and by the fact that there are different computer programs involved. Think of the typical tests on the documents in the system and you should come up with a good answer.

Part (b) is similar but deals with the vehicles figure in the statement of financial position. Again the best approach is to think of the numbers and documents involved and how they can be checked.

Your audit work should cover each of the financial statement assertions.

(a)

Audit test	Reason for test
Discuss with booking clerk how orders are recorded from the customer.	The main problem with the sales system in TT is the lack of evidence for the receipt of the telephone order. Checks are therefore required to ensure that orders are completely and accurately recorded in the Vehicle Management System (VMS) where no input document is available.
Discuss with the directors the recruitment and training of booking clerks.	To check on the personnel controls in TT which will be designed to minimise loss of customer orders. To ensure that staff have appropriate skill and training to operate the ordering system without losing customer orders.
With client's permission, attempt to enter orders into the VMS from an input terminal.	To confirm the completeness and accuracy of recording of orders by the computer system.
For a sample of confirmed e-mail orders held in the e-mail program, trace details onto the VMS ensuring that details of vehicle hire regarding time and dates are accurately recorded.	To check for accuracy of transfer of information from the e-mail to the VMS. The method of filing of the e-mails means that completeness of e-mail orders cannot easily be determined. Audit software may be able to re-sort the orders.
Review hard copy customer complaint files and e-mail files on computer for evidence of unfilled orders.	To check for evidence of orders being sent by customers but not entered into TT's sales system.
For a sample of bookings in the VMS, trace details to the list of sales invoices raised maintained in the receivables ledger program.	To check for completeness of transfer of information between the two programs. The test can be carried out manually or using test data. Manual testing may be difficult where there is no obvious audit trail between the two systems.
For a sample of sales invoices in the VMS, agree the rental amount being charged to standard charges held in the receivables ledger file.	To check for accuracy of charging for each individual vehicle hire. Evidence of undercharging would indicate that sales are understated.
Cast the list of invoices in the receivables ledger program for one month. Trace total sales to the general ledger program.	To ensure that the total sales for that month are accurate. Transfer of data to the nominal ledger ensures that the total sales amount is recorded correctly in the ledger.
Cast the monthly sales figures in the general ledger and agree to the financial statements. Investigate any discrepancies.	The final cast and checking ensures that the financial accounts figure is accurate. Casting tests can be carried out manually or using computer audit software.

(b)   **Audit work on vehicles**

- Obtain non-current asset register from client. Cast the cost, depreciation and net book value columns of the register and agree to the financial statements of TT.

For a sample of new additions in the non-current asset register:

- Agree to board minute or similar documentation for evidence of authority to purchase vehicle. (Occurrence assertion).

- Agree to the physical asset to confirm existence of the vehicle. Where the vehicle is on hire during the audit visit, obtain alternative evidence of existence such as payment from customer near year-end for hire. (Existence assertion).

- Check the physical condition of the vehicle to ensure that repairs and renewal expenditure is not being understated. (Existence of repair expenditure).

- Agree details to purchase invoice or similar document for evidence of ownership. (Ownership assertion).

- Test the calculation of depreciation in the non-current asset register, ensuring that the rates used are those disclosed in the financial statements. (Valuation and accuracy assertion).

For a sample of disposals during the year (for occurrence assertion).

- Review profits and losses generated on sale of vehicles and ensure these are not excessive. If they are check the accuracy of the depreciation rates used as this may indicate over or under charge of depreciation. (Valuation and accuracy assertion).

- Compare sales income to sale of similar vehicles with similar mileage and ensure comparable.

- Ensure asset has been removed from the non-current asset register.

- Check calculation of profit or loss on sale.

- Agree receipt on sale to the cash book.

For a sample of vehicles purchased during the year, agree details to purchase invoice and Purchase Day Book (PDB) ensuring details recorded in the correct year (Occurrence assertion).

For a sample of vehicle purchases in the PDB, agree details to the non-current asset register (Completeness assertion).

Agree totals in non-current asset register to the financial statements, ensuring vehicles are disclosed separately in the non-current assets note (material item). (Classification and understandability assertion).

Ensure that the accounting policy for depreciation is clearly stated in the financial statements and is the same as last year. (Classification and understandability assertion).

12   BEARSWORLD (A)

Key answer tips

This is a straightforward question since you should be very familiar with the ISA 500 procedures for gathering audit evidence. You should hope to score very highly on a standard question like this.

Small company audits come up regularly.

(a)   **Audit procedures**

(i)   *Analytical procedures* consist of evaluations of financial information made by a study of plausible relationships among both financial and non-financial data.

Inquiry means to seek relevant information from sources, both financial and non-financial, either inside or outside the company being audited. Evidence may be obtained orally or in writing.

Inspection is the physical review or examination of records, documents and tangible assets. It may include examination of records for evidence of controls in the form of a compliance test.

Observation involves looking at a process or procedure as it is being performed to ensure that the process actually works as documented.

Re-calculation means the checking of the mathematical accuracy of documents or records.

(ii)   *Analytical procedures*

Review of sales income year on year to try to identify whether income has been understated, possibly by cash being taken prior to banking. There is no control over the opening of post so cash could be withdrawn by one assistant, and the deficit made up by a fraud on customers.

Inquiry

Obtain statements from suppliers to check the completeness of liabilities at the end of the year. As there is no control over purchases, invoices could have been misplaced resulting in a lower purchases and trade payables figure.

Inspection

The assets of the company, namely cuddly toys in inventory at the end of the year, can be inspected to ensure all inventory is recorded and that the toys are saleable in their current condition.

Observation

Procedures such as the opening of the post and recording of customer orders can be observed to ensure that the administrator is recording all orders in the sales day book and cash book.

Re-calculation

Checking additions in the cash book to confirm that the total amount of cash recorded is accurate and can be included in the sales figure (cash receipts normally equal sales because there are no receivables).

(b)   **Analytical procedures**

This method of collecting evidence will be useful in BearsWorld because it will help to identify unusual changes in income and expenditure. As BearsWorld is a relatively small company, monitoring gross profit will show relatively small changes in sales margin or purchasing costs. Decisions by Mr Kyto to amend margins can therefore be traced into the actual sales made.

However, the technique may be limited in its application because it will not detect errors or omissions made consistently year on year. If either assistant is defrauding the company (for example by removing cash) each year, then analytical procedures will not detect this.

Enquiry

Enquiry evidence will be very useful in the audit of BearsWorld, especially where this is derived from third parties. Third party evidence is generally more reliable than client originated evidence as there is a decreased likelihood of bias. Trade payables can therefore be verified using supplier statement reconciliations. A review of any customer complaints file (if these letters are kept) will also help to identify any orders that have not been despatched.

External inquiry evidence will be less useful in the audit of sales and receivables because goods are paid for prior to despatch – there are no receivables. Internal evidence will be available from Mr Kyto and the assistant; however the lack of segregation of duties means that this will not be so reliable.

Inspection

Inspection of documents within BearsWorld will be useful, particularly regarding checking whether expenses are bona fide. All purchase invoices, for example, should be addressed to BearsWorld and relate to purchases expected from that company, e.g. cuddly toys for resale, office expenses, etc.

Inspection of documents can take a long time; however, given the poor internal control system within BearsWorld, the auditor may have no choice but to use this method of gathering evidence.

The fact that an invoice is addressed to the company does not confirm completeness of recording so inspection of the cash book for unusual payments verified by checking the purchase invoice will also be required. Additional substantive testing would also be required due to poor controls.

Observation

Observation may be useful because it will show how the assistants check documents. However, no information is provided on any internal controls within BearsWorld so simply viewing how documents are checked without any evidence of checking has limited benefit.

Observation tests will be of limited usefulness because the assistants may act differently when an auditor is present. The same problem will apply to any observation checking carried out by Mr Kyto.

Re-calculation

Re-calculation evidence is very useful for checking additions on invoices, balancing of control accounts, etc. This means that the arithmetical accuracy of the books and records in BearsWorld can be confirmed.

The main weakness of re-calculation checking is that calculations can only be carried out on figures that have been recorded. If there are any omissions then checks cannot be carried out.

(c)   **Features of Small Companies**

Feature	Effect on audit
Concentration of ownership and management in one/few people	There is likely to be more supervision, since the owner will want to protect his investment. But there is an increased risk of fraud by the owner as he may not distinguish between personal/business assets.
Less complicated business activities	Easier for auditor to gain an understanding of the business and assess risk.
Less sophisticated accounting systems	Auditor unlikely to use CAATs
Limited internal controls as less segregation of duties and management can override	Unlikely to reply on controls. Likely to perform extensive substantive testing.
Unlikely to have a qualified accountant	Audit firm is likely to prepare the financial statements prior to the audit. This means they should be prepared with due care, but the auditor must be careful to check just as thoroughly as if the accounts had been prepared by someone else.

RISK AND AUDIT APPROACH

13   LV FONES CO *Walk in the footsteps of a top tutor*

Key answer tips

Part (a) is a straightforward, knowledge based question.

Part (b) requires you to apply your knowledge of ethics to the specific circumstances in the scenario. For that reason you cannot simply "knowledge dump" pre-learnt facts and phrases. Given that the two elements of the question are linked a table format is appropriate for your answer.

Part (c) is a straightforward, knowledge based question.

The highlighted words are key phases that markers are looking for.

(a)   Compliance with ACCA's Code of Ethics and Conduct fundamental principles can be threatened by a number of areas. The five categories of threats, which may impact on ethical risk, are:

- Self-interest
- Self-review
- Advocacy
- Familiarity
- Intimidation.

Examples for each category (Only one example required per threat):

Self-interest

- Undue dependence on fee income from one client
- Close personal or business relationships
- Financial interest in a client
- Incentive fee arrangements
- Concern over employment security
- Commercial pressure from outside the employing organisation
- Inappropriate personal use of corporate assets.

Self-review

- Member of assurance team being or recently having been employed by the client in a position to influence the subject matter being reviewed
- Involvement in implementation of financial system and subsequently reporting on the operation of said system
- Same person reviewing decisions or data that prepared them
- An analyst, or member of a board, audit committee or audit firm being in a position to exert a direct or significant influence over the financial reports
- The discovery of a significant error during a re-evaluation of the work undertaken by the member
- Performing a service for a client that directly affects the subject matter of an assurance engagement.

Advocacy

- Acting as an advocate on behalf of a client in litigation or disputes
- Promoting shares in a listed audit client
- Commenting publicly on future events in particular circumstances
- Where information is incomplete or advocating an argument which is unlawful.

Familiarity

- Long association with a client
- Acceptance of gifts or preferential treatment (significant value)
- Over familiarity with management
- Former partner of firm being employed by client
- A person in a position to influence financial or non-financial reporting or business decisions having an immediate or close family member who is in a position to benefit from that influence.

Intimidation

- Threat of litigation
- Threat of removal as assurance firm
- Dominant personality of client director attempting to influence decisions
- Pressure to reduce inappropriately the extent of work performed in order to reduce fees.

(b)

Ethical threat	Managing risk
The audit team has in previous years been offered a staff discount of 10% on purchasing luxury mobile phones.	The audit firm should ascertain whether the discount is to be offered to staff this year.
This is a familiarity threat. It would need to be confirmed if this discount is to be offered to this year's team as well, as only goods of an insignificant value are allowed to be accepted. A discount of 10% may not appear to be significant, but as these are luxury mobile phones then this may still be a significant value.	If it is then the discount should be reviewed for significance. If it is deemed to be of significant value then the offer of discount should be declined.
An audit senior of Jones & Co has been on secondment as the financial controller of LV Fones and is currently part of the audit team.	The firm should clarify exactly what areas the senior assisted the client on. If he worked on areas not related to the financial statements then he may be able to remain in the audit team.
There is a self-review threat if the senior has prepared records or schedules that support the year end financial statements and he then audits these same documents.	However, it is likely that he has worked on some related schedules and therefore he should be removed from the audit team to ensure that independence is not threatened.
The total fee income from LV Fones is 16% of the total fees for the audit firm. If the fees for audit and recurring work exceed 15% then there is a self-interest threat.	The firm should assess if the recurring fees will exceed 15%. If this is the case then it might need to consider whether the appearance of independence will still be met if the tax and audit work is retained.
The fees for LV Fones include tax and audit that are assumed to be recurring, however the secondment fees would not recur each year.	No further work should be accepted in the current year from the client, and it might be advisable to perform external quality control reviews. It may also become necessary to consider resigning from either the tax or the audit engagement.
The partner and the finance director know each other socially and have holidayed together. Personal relationships between the client and members of the audit team can create a familiarity or self-interest threat.	The personal relationship should be reviewed in line with Jones's ethical policies.
ACCA's *Code of Ethics and Conduct* does not specifically prohibit friendships between the audit client and the team. However, due to the senior positions held by both parties then there is a risk that independence may be perceived to have been threatened.	Consideration should be given to rotating the partner off this engagement and replacing with an alternative partner.

Ethical threat	Managing risk
Last year's audit fee is still outstanding. This amounts to 20% of the total fee and is likely to be a significant value.	Jones & Co should chase the outstanding fees.
A self-interest threat can arise if the fees remain outstanding, as Jones & Co may feel pressure to agree to certain accounting adjustments in order to have the previous year and the current year fee paid.	If they remain outstanding, the firm should discuss with those charged with governance the reasons for the continued non-payment, and ideally agree a payment schedule which will result in the fees being settled before much more work is performed for the current year audit.
In addition outstanding fees could be perceived as a loan to a client, this is strictly prohibited.	

(c)   Prior to accepting

Prior to accepting an audit engagement the firm should consider any issues which might arise which could threaten compliance with ACCA's *Code of Ethics and Conduct* or any local legislation. If issues arise then their significance must be considered.

The firm should consider whether they are competent to perform the work and whether they would have appropriate resources available, as well as any specialist skills or knowledge.

The prospective firm must communicate with the outgoing auditor to assess if there are any ethical or professional reasons why they should not accept appointment.

The prospective firm must obtain permission from the client to contact the existing auditor, if this is not given then the engagement should be refused.

The existing auditor must obtain permission from the client to respond, if not given then the prospective auditor should refuse the engagement.

If given permission to respond, then the existing auditor should reply to the prospective auditor, who should then carefully review the response for any issues that could affect acceptance.

In addition the audit firm should undertake client screening procedures such as considering management integrity and assessing whether any conflict of interest with existing clients would arise.

Further client screening procedures would include assessing the level of audit risk of the client and whether the expected engagement fee would be sufficient for the level of anticipated risk.

ACCA marking scheme

			Marks
(a)	½ mark for each threat and ½ per example of a threat		
	– Self-interest –		
	– Self-review		
	– Advocacy		
	– Familiarity		
	– Intimidation		
		Maximum	5
(b)	Up to 1 mark per ethical threat and up to 1 mark per managing method		
	– Staff discount		
	– Secondment		
	– Total fee income		
	– Finance director and partner good friends		
	– Outstanding fees		
		Maximum for threats	5
		Maximum for methods	5
(c)	Up to 1 mark per step		
	– Compliance with ACCA's Code of Ethics and Conduct		
	– Competent		
	– Write outgoing auditor		
	– Permission to contact old auditor		
	– Old auditor permission to respond		
	– Review response		
	– Client screening procedures		
			5
Total			20

14 SMOOTHBRUSH PAINTS CO *Walk in the footsteps of a top tutor*

Key answer tips

This question appeared on the June 2010 exam paper and is another example of the new examiner's style, namely that she will mix up the topics in question 1, rather than always choosing systems and controls.

Part (b) requires little more than pre-learnt knowledge. The remaining requirements all require you to apply your knowledge to the scenario. There will therefore be little scope to repeat facts and concepts learnt from study texts. Any such attempts will score poorly.

Part (a) requires you to consider which factors from the scenario specifically increase the risk that the auditor offers an inappropriate audit opinion (i.e. there is a material misstatement and the auditor fails to spot it).

Make sure that the controls you recommend in part (c) specifically address the **completeness** and **accuracy** of inventory records. Likewise, the procedures you recommend in part (d) must address **valuation** and **completeness** of inventory and provisions respectively.

The highlighted words are key phases that markers are looking for.

(a)

Identification of risk	Explanation of risk
Smoothbrush supplies 60% of its goods to Homewares at a significantly reduced selling price, hence inventory may be overvalued.	Per IAS 2 *Inventories,* inventory should be stated at the lower of cost and net realisable value (NRV). Therefore, as selling prices are much lower for goods sold to Homewares, there is a risk that the NRV of some inventory items may be lower than cost and hence that inventory could be overvalued.
Recoverability of receivable balances as credit period extended.	Smoothbrush has extended its credit terms to Homewares from one month to four months. Hence there is an increased risk as balances outstanding become older, that they may become irrecoverable.
Valuation of plant and equipment.	The production facility has a large amount of unused plant and equipment. As per IAS 16 *Property, Plant and Equipment* and IAS 36 *Impairment of Assets*, this plant and equipment should be stated at the lower of its carrying value and recoverable amount, which may be at scrap value depending on its age and condition
Cut-off of purchases and inventory may not be accurate.	Smoothbrush imports goods from South Asia and the paint can be in transit for up to two months. The company accounts for goods when they receive them. Therefore at the year end only goods that have been received into the warehouse should be included in the inventory balance and a respective payables balance recognised.
New inventory system introduced in the year. This could result in inventory balances being misstated.	Smoothbrush has introduced a continuous/perpetual inventory counting system in the year. These records will be used for recording inventory at the year end. If the records and new system have not initially been set up correctly then there is a risk that the year end balances may not be fairly stated.
Inventory may be overstated as Smoothbrush no longer has a slow moving provision.	Previously Smoothbrush maintained an inventory provision of 1%, however, this year it has decided to remove this. Unless all slow moving/obsolete items are identified at the year end and their value adjusted, there is a risk that the overall value of inventory may be overstated.

(a)

Identification of risk	Explanation of risk
Provisions/contingent liability disclosures may not be complete.	The company's finance director (FD) has left and is intending to sue Smoothbrush for unfair dismissal. However, the company does not intend to make any provision/disclosures for sums due to the FD. Under IAS 37 *Provisions, Contingent Liabilities and Contingent Assets,* if there is a present obligation, a probable outflow of resources to settle the obligation and a reliable estimate can be made of the obligation then a provision should be recognised. If the obligation is only possible, or if there is a present obligation but it is not recognised as there is not a probable outflow of resources, or the amount of the obligation cannot be measured with sufficient reliability then a contingent liability should be disclosed, unless the likelihood of payment is remote.
Inherent risk is higher due to the changes in the finance department.	The financial controller has been appointed as temporary FD and this lack of experience could result in an increased risk of errors arising in the financial statements. In addition the previous FD is not available to help the finance or audit team.
Inventory may be over or understated if the perpetual inventory counts are not complete and accurate.	The inventory counts are to cover all of the inventory lines. If any areas of the warehouse are not counted then this will need to be done at the year end. In addition inventory adjustments arising from the counts must be verified and updated by an appropriate member of the finance team to ensure that the records are accurate.

(b) ISA 315 *Identifying and Assessing the Risks of Material Misstatement Through Understanding the Entity and Its Environment,* requires auditors 'to identify and assess the risks of material misstatement, whether due to fraud or error, at the financial statement and assertion levels'.

It is vitally important for auditors to assess engagement risks at the planning stage, this will ensure that attention is focused early on the areas most likely to cause material misstatements.

A thorough risk assessment will also help the auditor to fully understand the entity, which is vital for an effective audit. Any unusual transactions or balances would also be identified early, so that these could be addressed in a timely manner.

In addition, as most auditors adopt a risks based audit approach then these risks need to be assessed early in order for the audit strategy and detailed work programmes to be developed.

Assessing risks early should also result in an efficient audit. The team will only focus their time and effort on key areas as opposed to balances or transactions that might be immaterial or unlikely to contain errors.

In addition assessing risk early should ensure that the most appropriate team is selected with more experienced staff allocated to higher risk audits and high risk balances.

A thorough risk analysis should ultimately reduce the risk of an inappropriate audit opinion being given. The audit would have focused on the main risk areas and hence all material misstatements should have been identified, resulting in the correct opinion being given.

It should enable the auditor to have a good understanding of the risks of fraud, money laundering, etc. Assessing risk should enable the auditor to assess whether the client is a going concern.

(c)   Controls over the perpetual/continuous inventory system.

Control	Explanation
The inventory count team should be independent of the warehouse team.	Currently the team includes a warehouse staff member and an internal auditor. There should be segregation of roles between those who have day-to-day responsibility for inventory and those who are checking it. If the same team are responsible for maintaining and checking inventory, then errors and fraud could be hidden.
Timetable of counts should be regularly reviewed to ensure that all areas are counted.	The warehouse has been divided into 12 areas that are each due to be counted once over the year. All inventory is required to be counted once a year, hence if the timetable is not monitored then some areas could be missed out.
Movements of inventory should be stopped from the designated areas during continuous/perpetual inventory counts.	Goods will continue to move in and out of the warehouse during the counts. Inventory records could be under/over stated if product lines are missed or double counted due to movements in the warehouse.
Inventory counting sheets should be pre-printed with a description or item code of the goods, but the quantities per the records should not be pre-recorded.	The inventory sheets produced for the count have the quantities pre-printed, therefore a risk arises that the counting team could just agree with the record quantities, making under counting more likely, rather than counting the inventory lines correctly.
A second independent team should check the counts performed by the inventory count team.	By counting the lines twice this should help to ensure completeness and accuracy of the counts, and hence that any inventory adjustments are appropriate.

Control	Explanation
Inventory checks should be performed from inventory physically present in the warehouse to the records.	Currently the team is comparing the records to the inventory in the warehouse. If the count is performed from the records to the warehouse then this will only ensure existence or overstatement of the records. To ensure completeness is addressed the inventory in the warehouse must be compared to the records as this will identify any goods physically present but not included in the records.
Any damaged or obsolete goods should be moved to a designated area, where a responsible official then inspects it, it should not be removed from the sheets.	Damaged or obsolete goods should be written down or provided against to ensure that they are stated at the lower of cost and NRV. This may not involve fully writing off the inventory item as is currently occurring. This is an assessment that should only be performed by a suitably trained member of the finance team, as opposed to the inventory count team.
After the count, the inventory count sheets should be compared to the inventory records, any adjustments should be investigated and if appropriate the records updated in a prompt manner by an authorised person.	At the year end the inventory of Smoothbrush will be based on the records maintained. Hence the records must be complete, accurate and valid. It is important that only individuals authorised to do so can amend records.
	Senior members of the finance team should regularly review the types and levels of adjustments, as recurring inventory adjustments could indicate possible fraud.

(d)   Substantive procedures to confirm valuation of inventory

- Select a representative sample of goods in inventory at the year end, agree the cost per the records to a recent purchase invoice and ensure that the cost is correctly stated.

- Select a sample of year end goods and review post year end sales invoices to ascertain if NRV is above cost or if an adjustment is required.

- For a sample of manufactured items obtain cost sheets and confirm:

  – raw material costs to recent purchase invoices

  – labour costs to time sheets or wage records

  – overheads allocated are of a production nature.

- Review aged inventory reports and identify any slow moving goods, discuss with management why these items have not been written down.

- Compare the level/value of aged product lines to the total inventory value to assess whether the provision for slow moving goods of 1% should be reinstated.

- Review the inventory records to identify the level of adjustments made throughout the year for damaged/obsolete items. If significant consider whether the year end records require further adjustments and discuss with management whether any further write downs/provision may be required.

- Follow up any damaged/obsolete items noted by the auditor at the inventory counts attended, to ensure that the inventory records have been updated correctly.

- Perform a review of the average inventory days for the current year and compare to prior year inventory days. Discuss any significant variations with management.

- Compare the gross margin for current year with prior year. Fluctuations in gross margin could be due to inventory valuation issues. Discuss significant variations in the margin with management.

Substantive procedures to confirm completeness of provisions or contingent liability

- Discuss with management the nature of the dispute between Smoothbrush and the former finance director (FD), to ensure that a full understanding of the issue is obtained and to assess whether an obligation exists. Review any correspondence with the former FD to assess if a reliable estimate of any potential payments can be made. Write to the company's lawyers to obtain their views as to the probability of the FD's claim being successful.

- Review board minutes and any company correspondence to assess whether there is any evidence to support the former FD's claims of unfair dismissal.

- Obtain a written representation from the directors of Smoothbrush confirming their view that the former FD's chances of a successful claim are remote, and hence no provision or contingent liability is required.

- Credit will be awarded for any substantive procedures which test for additional provisions or contingent liabilities of Smoothbrush.

ACCA marking scheme		
		Marks
(a)	½ mark for each identification of risk and up to 1 per description of the risk	
	– Sole supplier to Homewares, NRV of inventory	
	– Recoverability of receivable as credit period extended	
	– Valuation of plant and equipment – Cut-off	
	– New system	
	– Inventory provision	
	– Provision/contingent liability	
	– Inherent risk increased	
	– Perpetual inventory counts	
	Maximum	10
(b)	Up to 1 mark per valid point	
	– ISA 315 requirement (1/2 mark only for ISA ref)	
	– Early identification of material errors	
	– Understand entity	
	– Identification of unusual transactions/balances –	
	– Efficient audit	
	– Most appropriate team	
	– Reduce risk incorrect opinion	
	– Understanding fraud, money laundering	
	– Assess risk going concern	
	Maximum	4

(c)   ½ mark for each identification of a control and up to 1 mark per well
        explained description of the control
        –   Team independent of warehouse
        –   Timetable of counts
        –   Inventory movements stopped
        –   No pre-printed quantities on count sheets
        –   Second independent team
        –   Direction of counting floor to records
        –   Damaged/obsolete goods to specific area
        –   Records updated by authorised person

                                                        Maximum   10

(d)   Up to 1 mark per substantive procedure
        Inventory:
        –   Cost to purchase invoice
        –   NRV to sales invoice
        –   Manufactured items to invoices/time sheets/production overheads
        –   Review aged inventory reports
        –   Compare aged items to 1% prov
        –   Total level of adjustment over year
        –   Follow up items noted at inventory count
        –   Inventory days
        –   Gross margin

                                                        Maximum   3

        Provisions:
        –   Discuss with management
        –   Review correspondence with FD
        –   Write to lawyers
        –   Review board minutes Obtain written representation
        Marks awarded for tests for additional provisions and contingent liabilities
        of Smoothbrush

                                                        Maximum   3

Total   30

---

15   LETHAM CO *Walk in the footsteps of a top tutor*

Key answer tips

Part (a) requires pre-learnt knowledge from your study text.

Part (b) is typical of a control risk assessment exercise. It is important that you identify **six** control **strengths**. This is obviously different to the more traditional system deficiency style question. Once again it is appropriate to structure your answer as a table.

Part (c) asks you to consider what makes an effective test for the **completeness** of non-current asset records (i.e. that clients have recorded all of their assets in relevant ledgers). Any discussion of tests for valuation and existence will be irrelevant and will not score.

The highlighted words are key phases that markers are looking for.

(a) The auditor obtains an understanding of the entity, its control environment and its detailed internal controls:

   (i) to identify and assess the risks of material misstatements, whether due to fraud or error, at the financial statement and assertion levels. Risks would include inherent risk and control risk. An important objective would be to determine the extent to which the auditor would rely on the internal control system.

   (ii) to provide a basis for designing and implementing responses to the assessed risks of material misstatement in the financial statements. This would involve the design and performance of the audit procedures required to form an opinion on the truth and fairness of the financial statements. An important objective would be to determine the extent and nature of audit procedures to reduce detection risk, and therefore audit risk, to an acceptable level.

   (iii) to set the scene for identifying assertions and collecting sufficient appropriate evidence to prove that the assertions are reasonable.

Tutorial note

Marks would also be available for additional points such as:

- *To assess the adequacy of the accounting system as a basis for preparing financial statements*

- *To assess whether competent to perform the audit*

- *To understand relevant law and regulations impacting the entity*

- *To consider the reliability of various evidence sources.)*

(b) Strong points in the control environment of Letham Co in respect of non-current assets are set out below, together with explanations as to their impact on control risk:

	Strengths	Impact on control risk
(i)	Approval of the five-year and annual budgets by the board of directors	The annual budget is the 'trigger' for placing orders for equipment. Its approval by the board will ensure that only authorised non-current assets are purchased.
(ii)	The budget is updated when the order for new equipment is placed	The company can use the updated budget at any time. to anticipate cash outflows. It will also ensure that there is no duplication of assets purchased.
(iii)	Pre-numbered goods received notes and operational certificates are available to the accounting department for comparison with the purchase invoice.	Only goods that have been received and are operating effectively will be paid for.
(iv)	Informed people in the production department carefully assess the proper operation of the equipment.	This will help to ensure the operational effectiveness of plant and equipment.

	Strengths	Impact on control risk
(v)	The accounting department, independent of the production facility, updates the non-tangible assets register and only the accounting department has access to it.	The potential for fraudulent entries to cover theft/unauthorised purchases will be reduced and the non-current assets register, an important non-current. assets control document, cannot be manipulated by the people who hold the assets.
(vi)	Accounting department personnel, independent of production, perform rolling tests to ensure that the non-current assets register and non-current assets on hand are in agreement with each other.	The risk of theft and loss of plant and equipment is reduced and the likelihood that all items in the register existing increased.
(vii)	The internal audit department tests on a sample basis that recorded non-current assets are in existence, but see (c) below.	The internal auditing department will be more independent than the accounting department and hence will provide further comfort that the non-current assets register is not overstated.
(viii)	Internal audit test the operation of the entire non-current assets recording system. • Pre-numbered goods received notes used to update the budget • Permanent identification numbers recorded on assets • Purchase invoice automatically updates the non-current assets register.	Any controls which are not operating effectively are likely to be identified and rectified before significant errors can occur.

(c) (i) Great care must be taken in selecting the starting point for audit testing. The test that the internal auditors performed, namely, selecting a representative sample of purchase invoices for testing to the non-current assets register and to the updating movements on the annual budget, proves merely that register and budget are in agreement with the purchase invoices issued. It is therefore not a good test to prove the completeness of purchase invoices and therefore of the entries in the register and budget. In addition, the purchase invoices are issued by many different suppliers and there is no common serial number to enable the company to ensure that all purchases are accounted for.

(ii) A more appropriate test would be to make the selection from goods received notes (GRNs), as the issue of a GRN is normally the point at which liability is accepted and is in any event the document used to update the non-current assets budget. In other words, it is important to identify your audit objective and then to decide on what sample will be the most appropriate to aid you in meeting that objective. The GRNs would be traced to the recorded purchase invoices to ensure that the latter were complete and then to the entries in the non-current assets register and to the updating entries in the budget to ensure that these too were complete.

An additional appropriate test would be to select a sample of plant and equipment visible on the shop floor and trace them to the non-current assets register to identify whether they have been:

- included in the register
- noted against the budget as purchased
- paid for by tracing purchase invoice through to payment.

	ACCA marking scheme	Marks
(a)	**Understanding entity and environment**	
	1 mark for each explanation of reason, but maximum 4.	
	Risks of material misstatement	
	Design and performance of audit procedures	
	Identification of assertions	
	Adequacy of accounting system as a basis for preparing financial statements	
	Assessment of competence to perform the audit	
	Understanding relevant law and regulations	
	Consider the reliability of evidence sources	
	Maximum marks	4.0
(b)	**Strengths in control environment**	
	Up to 1 mark for identification of strength and a further 1 mark for impact on control risk, but maximum 12.	
	Approval of budgets	
	Updating of budget	
	Matching operation adequate	
	Assessment of operation of equipment	
	Independent updating and holding of non-current assets register	
	Independent tests on non-current assets register	
	Internal audit tests on existence	
	Internal audit review of whole system	
	Pre numbered goods received notes update budget	
	Permanent identification on assets	
	Automatic update of register with purchase invoice	
	Maximum marks	12.0
(c)	**Test for completeness**	
	Up to 1 mark for what the current test does and a further 1 mark for an adequate explanation.	
	1 mark for identification of a more appropriate test and a further 1 mark for an explanation why it is more appropriate.	
	What the test does	
	Why it is inadequate	
	More appropriate test	
	Why more appropriate	
	Maximum marks	4.0
Total		20.0

16 TIRROL *Walk in the footsteps of a top tutor*

Key answer tips

Part (a) requires both repetition and application of basic knowledge regarding the use of CAAT's. However, the latter carries the majority of the marks and for this reason candidates must refer to the specific information to obtain good quality marks. Simple repetition of learned facts regarding the drawbacks of CAATs will not obtain good marks for this reason.

For each point of explanation relevant to Tirrol you will be awarded 1 mark. Therefore for part (i) you need to make four points of explanatios. For part (ii) you need 5 explained problems and five methods of overcoming those problems.

Part (b) again requires a mix of basic knowledge (i.e. what procedures must be performed before reliance is placed on internal auditors) and application to the facts presented in the scenario.

The highlighted words are key phases that markers are looking for.

(a) (i) **Benefits of using audit software**

Standard systems at client

The same computerised systems and programs as used in all 25 branches of Tirrol Co. This means that the same audit software can be used in each location providing significant time savings compared to the situation where client systems are different in each location.

Use actual computer files not copies or printouts

Use of audit software means that the Tirrol Co's actual inventory files can be tested rather than having to rely on printouts or screen images. The latter could be incorrect, by accident or by deliberate mistake. The audit firm will have more confidence that the 'real' files have been tested.

Test more items

Use of software will mean that more inventory records can be tested – it is possible that all product lines could be tested for obsolescence rather than a sample using manual techniques. The auditor will therefore gain more evidence and have greater confidence that inventory is valued correctly.

Cost

The relative cost of using audit software decreases the more years that software is used. Any cost overruns this year could be offset against the audit fees in future years when the actual expense will be less.

(ii) **Problems on the audit of Tirrol**

Timescale – six week reporting deadline – audit planning

The audit report is due to be signed six weeks after the year end. This means that there will be considerable pressure on the auditor to complete audit work without compromising standards by rushing procedures.

This problem can be overcome by careful planning of the audit, use of experienced staff and ensuring other staff such as second partner reviews are booked well in advance.

Timescale – six week reporting deadline – software issues

The audit report is due to be signed about six weeks after the year end. This means that there is little time to write and test audit software, let alone use the software and evaluate the results of testing.

This problem can be alleviated by careful planning. Access to Tirrol Co's software and data files must be obtained as soon as possible and work commenced on tailoring Cal & Co's software following this. Specialist computer audit staff should be booked as soon as possible to perform this work.

First year audit costs

The relative costs of an audit in the first year at a client tend to be greater due to the additional work of ascertaining client systems. This means that Cal & Co may have a limited budget to document systems including computer systems.

This problem can be alleviated to some extent again by good audit planning. The manager must also monitor the audit process carefully, ensuring that any additional work caused by the client not providing access to systems information including computer systems is identified and added to the total billing cost of the audit.

Staff holidays

Most of the audit work will be carried out in July, which is also the month when many of Cal & Co staff take their annual holiday. This means that there will be a shortage of audit staff, particularly as audit work for Tirrol Co is being booked with little notice.

The problem can be alleviated by booking staff as soon as possible and then identifying any shortages. Where necessary, staff may be borrowed from other offices or even different countries on a secondment basis where shortages are acute.

Non-standard systems

Tirrol Co's computer software is non-standard, having been written specifically for the organisation. This means that more time will be necessary to understand the system than if standard systems were used.

This problem can be alleviated either by obtaining documentation from the client or by approaching the software house (with Tirrol Co's permission) to see if they can assist with provision of information on data structures for the inventory systems. Provision of this information will decrease the time taken to tailor audit software for use in Tirrol Co.

Issues of live testing

Cal & Co has been informed that inventory systems must be tested on a live basis. This increases the risk of accidental amendment or deletion of client data systems compared to testing copy files.

To limit the possibility of damage to client systems, Cal & Co can consider performing inventory testing on days when Tirrol Co is not operating e.g.

weekends. At the worst, backups of data files taken from the previous day can be re-installed when Cal & Co's testing is complete.

Computer systems

The client has 25 locations, with each location maintaining its own computer system. It is possible that computer systems are not common across the client due to amendments made at the branch level.

This problem can be overcome to some extent by asking staff at each branch whether systems have been amended and focusing audit work on material branches.

Usefulness of audit software

The use of audit software at Tirrol Co does appear to have significant problems this year. This means that even if the audit software is ready, there may still be some risk of incorrect conclusions being derived due to lack of testing, etc.

This problem can be alleviated by seriously considering the possibility of using a manual audit this year. The manager may need to investigate whether a manual audit is feasible and if so whether it could be completed within the necessary timescale with minimal audit risk.

(b) **Reliance on internal audit documentation**

There are two issues to consider; the ability of internal audit to produce the documentation and the actual accuracy of the documentation itself.

The ability of the internal audit department to produce the documentation can be determined by:

- Ensuring that the department has staff who have appropriate qualifications. Provision of a relevant qualification e.g. membership of a computer related institute would be appropriate.

- Ensuring that this and similar documentation is produced using a recognised plan and that the documentation is tested prior to use. The use of different staff in the internal audit department to produce and test documentation will increase confidence in its accuracy.

- Ensuring that the documentation is actually used during internal audit work and that problems with documentation are noted and investigated as part of that work. Being given access to internal audit reports on the inventory software will provide appropriate evidence.

Regarding the actual documentation:

- Reviewing the documentation to ensure that it appears logical and that terms and symbols are used consistently throughout. This will provide evidence that the flowcharts, etc should be accurate.

- Comparing the documentation against the 'live' inventory system to ensure it correctly reflects the inventory system. This comparison will include tracing individual transactions through the inventory systems.

- Using part of the documentation to amend Cal & Co's audit software, and then ensuring that the software processes inventory system data accurately. However, this stage may be limited due to the need to use live files at Tirrol Co.

		Marking scheme	
(a)	(i)	**Benefits of audit software** 1 mark per benefit – 0.5 for identifying the benefit and 0.5 for explaining the benefit. • Standard systems • Use actual computer files • Test more items – • Cost	*Marks* 4
	(ii)	**Problems in the audit of Tirrol** 2 marks for each problem. 1 for explaining the problem and 1 for explaining how to alleviate the problem. • Six week reporting deadline • Timescale – software issues • First year audit costs • Staff holidays • Non-standard systems • Live testing • Usefulness of audit software	 10
(b)		Reliance on internal audit documentation 1 mark per point Appropriate qualifications Produced according to plan Problems with use noted Documentation logical Compare to live system Use documentation to amend audit software	 6
		Total	20

Examiner's comments

Part (a)

Most candidates provided sufficient points in their answers; although a minority spent too much time on (ii) by including up to 8 or 9 points; marks in this situation had to be capped at the stated 10.

In part (i), most candidates demonstrated basic knowledge of the use of audit software. A few candidates made some good links to the scenario, for example, explaining how data could be amalgamated to avoid having to visit the 25 branches in the company.

In part (ii), again most candidates provided a range of valid points and obtained decent marks. However, common deficiencies in this section included:

- Not explaining how to overcome the deficiency either by omitting this comment or by making unrealistic comments. E.g. in terms of potential damage to client systems from the use of test data, suggesting the deficiency would be overcome by 'being careful' or in a handful of answers by simply not accepting the audit engagement.

- Suggesting deficiencies that were not mentioned in the scenario. For example, suggesting that inventory valuation would be difficult as experts on car parts were difficult to find, or that the auditor had to attend all 25 locations simultaneously to prevent the client double counting inventory in more than one location.

- Recommending amendments to the client systems for other perceived deficiencies. For example, stating that a distributed processing system was not appropriate for the client and recommending a centralised system instead. Even if this was a recommendation to the client, it would not affect audit planning now and so was not relevant as a current audit problem.

Part (b)

Most candidates obtained a marginal result explaining either how the internal audit department itself could be relied on or the documentation; only a minority of answers mentioned both. Marks were generally obtained from:

- Considering the work of internal audit in areas such as experience in computer systems, and quality of documentation provided, and
- Testing the documentation itself for example, in comparison to the actual system using walk-through or similar testing methods, or obtaining advice from external specialists.

There were relatively few less relevant points in this section. The main area of weakness related to candidates spending too much time explaining the appointment and general work of internal audit rather than placing reliance on this function.

---

17   STARK *Walk in the footsteps of a top tutor*

Key answer tips

This question is a straight forward ethics question. Most of the issues are relatively simple: length of service of partner, accepting gifts, using client's services etc. These should be discussed first. With regard to solutions: whilst in real life there are ways of allowing certain practices to continue through various safeguards, for exam purposes keep things simple by considering the strongest possible solution that entirely eliminates the threat.

Part (b), whilst requiring some basic knowledge repetition about the benefits of internal audit, should be tailored specifically to Stark Co and the issues referred to in the scenario.

The highlighted words are key phases that markers are looking for.

(a)   **Ethical threats**

Ethical threat	**Mitigation of threat**
Mr Son, the engagement partner has been involved with the client for the last nine years. This means he may be too familiar with the client to be able to make objective decisions due to this long association.	Mr Son should be rotated from being engagement partner. He can still contact the client but should not be in the position of signing the audit report.
There is no ethical rule which stops Mr Son recommending Zoe for the audit, or letting Zoe take part in the audit. However, there may be the *impression* of lack of independence as Zoe is related to the engagement partner. Zoe could be tempted not to identify errors in case this prejudiced her father's relationship with the client.	To show complete independence, Zoe should not be part of the audit team. This ruling should still apply even if Mr Son is no longer the engagement partner.
As long as Mr Far paid a full fee to Stark Co for the investment advice, then there is no ethical threat.	Mr Far should be asked not to use the services of Stark Co again unless this is first agreed with the engagement partner.

Ethical threat	Mitigation of threat
However, continued use of client services could imply a lack of independence as Mr Far may not be paying a full fee and therefore receiving a benefit from the client.	
The audit team have been offered a balloon flight at the end of the audit. Acceptance of gifts from a client, unless of an insignificant amount, is not allowed. The fact that the flight costs less than the yacht expense is irrelevant, independence could still be impaired.	The balloon flight should not be accepted. I would investigate why hospitality was accepted in previous years.
Agreeing to accept taxation work on the percentage of the tax saved is essentially accepting a contingent fee. There will be pressure to gain the highest tax refund for the client and this could tempt the audit firm to suggest illegal tax avoidance schemes.	The audit firm must confirm that assistance with taxation work is acceptable, although the fee must be based on time and experience for the job, not the contingent fee.
Representing Stark Co in court could be seen as an advocacy threat – that is the audit firm is promoting the position of the client. Objectivity could be compromised because the audit firm is seen to take the position that the client is correct, affecting judgement on the tax issue.	To remain independent, the audit firm should decline to represent the client in court.

(b)   **Benefits of internal audit**

Regulation

Stark Co operates in a regulated sector and is under the supervision of a regulatory authority. It is very likely that there are regulatory controls and reports that Stark must produce or comply with. Establishing an internal audit department will enable Stark to produce those reports more efficiently and show compliance with the regulatory regime. Even if internal audit is not required now, codes of governance increasingly suggest that it is good practice to have an internal audit department.

Reports to the board

As a financial services provider, Stark Co will be producing various financial reports for their board. The internal audit department will be able to monitor the accuracy of those reports, especially those not audited by the external auditors. This function will help enhance the accuracy and reliability of the reports.

Liaison with external auditors

The internal auditors can liaise with the external auditors, especially where it is possible for the external auditors to place reliance on the work of internal audit. This will decrease the time and cost of the external audit.

Internal audit can also monitor the external audit to ensure they are carrying out an efficient and effective service.

Monitor effectiveness of internal controls

It is likely that Stark has to maintain a strong internal control system as the company is regulated and will be handling significant amounts of client cash. Internal audit can review the effectiveness of those controls and make recommendations to management for improvement where necessary.

Value for Money Audit

Internal audit can carry out value for money audits within Stark Co. For example, a review could be undertaken on the cost-effectiveness of the various control systems or whether investment advice being provided is cost-effective given the nature of products being recommended and the income/commission generated from those products.

Risk assessment

Internal audit could also carry out risk assessments on the portfolios being recommended to clients to ensure the portfolio matched the client's risk profile and Stark Co's risk appetite. Any deficiencies in this area would result in a recommendation to amend investment policies as well as decreasing Stark's exposure to unnecessary risk.

Taxation services

Stark Co require assistance with the preparation of taxation computations and specialist assistance in court regarding a taxation dispute. Internal audit could assist in both areas as long as appropriate specialists were available in the department. Provision of these services would remove any conflict of interest that Stark's auditors have as well as ensuring expertise was available in house when necessary.

	Marking scheme	
		Marks
(a)	1 for each ethical threat and 1 for explanation of how to mitigate that threat = 2 marks per linked points. Part (i) therefore is 6 marks total and part (ii) is 6 marks total Engagement partner – time providing service Engagement partner's daughter takes part in audit Payment for investment advice Gift of balloon flight from client Contingent fee – taxation work Representing client in court	12
(b)	2 marks per well-explained point Regulation Reports to the board Liaison with external auditors Monitor effectiveness of internal controls Value for money audit Risk assessment Taxation services	8
	Total	**20**

Examiner's comments

Part (a)

Most candidates identified up to 6 points although a minority mentioned 7 or more; the lack of a specific number of threats to mention in the requirement meant that candidates could accumulate marks over more than 6 threats.

Common errors included:

- Not explaining the ethical threat (as noted above). Simply stating a threat was "intimidation" for example, tended to be insufficient as an explanation.

- Mentioning non-relevant points. Firstly, in this situation Zoe being part-qualified would not bar her from being on the audit team as this is how auditors obtain "on the job" training. A significant minority of candidates suggested that the entire audit team had to be qualified indicating a lack of practical audit experience. Secondly, the first time audit for the manager was not a threat; staff have to be changed at some stage. Lastly there was insufficient information to correctly determine a fee dependency threat; the contingent fee and fixed fee were sufficient to discuss in this area.

- Not mentioning sufficient points. A small minority of candidates only mentioned say 3 points and spent up to a page explaining each threat. Candidates are reminded again about the need to check the requirement verbs used in a question and how these relate to the number of points expected in an answer.

The standard of answers for this question was satisfactory. As noted above, not providing sufficient points was the main reason for a candidate not achieving a pass standard.

Part (b)

Common errors included:

- Repeating points already made. For example, a significant minority of candidates mentioned internal audit and internal control monitoring more than once; obviously only one mark was allowed for this duplication.

- Explaining the work of an audit committee such as recommending auditor appointment. These points did not meet the question requirement and so were not relevant.

- Explaining the problems of establishing an internal audit department. Again, these points did not meet the question requirement and so were not relevant.

- Explaining the benefits of internal audit rather than outsourcing. These comments did not focus precisely on the question requirement regarding the benefits of internal audit to the company in the scenario.

The overall standard of answers was satisfactory. As noted above, most candidates obtained a pass standard by stating generic points about the benefits of internal audit. It was pleasing the find the odd candidate making use of the scenario and providing valid reasons for an internal audit department from the scenario.

18   ZAK CO

Key answer tips

Part (a) This was a purely knowledge based question, (i) what analtical procdures are, (ii) the types so comparisons should come to mind and   (iii) when we can use them. Mentioning at the planning, testing and final stage will ensure an excellent answer.

Part (b), asks you to identify and explain with reasons for the unusual trends to the Income Statement, therefore analytical procedures are the key technique required here. A sound approach would be to identify the main features as revealed by a comparison between to two years' figures and by identifying key relationships within each year's figures. Ensure you do not focus on the bank, as this is to support the interest figures.

Part (c), the words to focus on is procedures to obtain a bank letter, this is not scenario based so three points should be noted to score well.

(a) (i)   **Explanation of analytical procedures**

Analytical procedures are used in obtaining an understanding of an entity and its environment and in the overall review at the end of the audit.

'Analytical procedures' actually means the evaluation of financial and other information, and the review of plausible relationships in that information. The review also includes identifying fluctuations and relationships that do not appear consistent with other relevant information or results.

(ii)   **Types of analytical procedures**

Analytical procedures can be used as:

–   Comparison of comparable information to prior periods to identify unusual changes or fluctuations in amounts.

–   Comparison of actual or anticipated results of the entity with budgets and/or forecasts, or the expectations of the auditor in order to determine the potential accuracy of those results.

–   Comparison to industry information either for the industry as a whole or by comparison to entities of similar size to the client to determine whether receivable days, for example, are reasonable.

(iii)   **Use of analytical procedures**

Risk assessment procedures

Analytical procedures are used at the beginning of the audit to help the auditor obtain an understanding of the entity and assess the risk of material misstatement. Audit procedures can then be directed to these 'risky' areas.

Analytical procedures as substantive procedures

Analytical procedures can be used as substantive procedures in determining the risk of material misstatement at the assertion level during work on the income statement and statement of financial position (balance sheet).

Analytical procedures in the overall review at the end of the audit

Analytical procedures help the auditor at the end of the audit in forming an overall conclusion as to whether the financial statements as a whole are consistent with the auditor's understanding of the entity.

(b)   **Net profit**

Overall, Zak's result has changed from a net loss to a net profit. Given that sales have only increased by 17% and that expenses, at least administration expenses, appear low, then there is the possibility that expenditure may be understated.

Sales – increase 17%

According to the directors, Zak has had a 'difficult year'. Reasons for the increase in sales income must be ascertained as the change does not conform to the directors' comments. It is possible that the industry as a whole, has been growing allowing Zak to produce this good result.

Cost of sales – fall 17%

A fall in cost of sales is unusual given that sales have increased significantly. This may have been caused by an incorrect inventory valuation and the use of different (cheaper) suppliers which may cause problems with faulty goods in the next year.

Gross profit (GP) – increase 88%

This is a significant increase with the GP% changing from 33% last year to 53% in 2008. Identifying reasons for this change will need to focus initially on the change in sales and cost of sales.

Administration – fall 6%

A fall is unusual given that sales are increasing and so an increase in administration to support those sales would be expected. Expenditure may be understated, or there has been a decrease in the number of administration staff.

Selling and distribution – increase 42%

This increase does not appear to be in line with the increase in sales – selling and distribution would be expected to increase in line with sales. There may be a mis-allocation of expenses from administration or the age of Zak's delivery vans is increasing resulting in additional service costs.

Interest payable – small fall

Given that Zak has a considerable cash surplus this year, continuing to pay interest is surprising. The amount may be overstated – reasons for lack of fall in interest payment e.g. loans that cannot be repaid early, must be determined.

Investment income – new this year

This is expected given cash surplus on the year, although the amount is still very high indicating possible errors in the amount or other income generating assets not disclosed on the balance sheet extract.

(c)   **Obtaining a bank letter**

–   Review the need to obtain a bank letter from the information obtained from the preliminary risk assessment of Zak.

–   Prepare a standard bank letter in the format agreed with banks in your jurisdiction.

- Obtain authorisation on that letter from a director of Zak for the bank to disclose information to the auditor.

- Where Zak has provided their bank with a standing authority to disclose information to the auditors, refer to this authority in the bank letter.

- The auditor sends the letter directly to Zak's bank with a request to send the reply directly back to the auditors.

Examiner's comments

Part (a)

This was a purely knowledge based question providing a relatively lengthy, but hopefully straight-forward introduction to the main application type section of this question.

Most candidates recognised the mark allocation and divided their time accordingly. A minority of candidates tended to repeat the same or very similar points in each section of the answer, but the overall standard was satisfactory.

A "typical" candidate obtained:

- 1 mark for section (i), with the explanation being limited to providing an overview of analytical procedures,

- up to three marks in (ii) where good examples of different procedures were given. The most common list being comparison within one year, comparisons to different industries and "proof of total", and

- between 2 and 3 marks for (iii). The marks obtained in this section depended more on provision of examples of the three sections of the audit rather than actually identifying those sections in the answer.

Other common errors included:

- Explaining different methods of collecting audit evidence such as enquiry, computation, observation, etc. These methods of collection are not analytical procedures and therefore did not obtain any marks (part (ii)).

- Re-iterating examples of collecting evidence in part (iii) of the question. The answer needed to focus on the three stages of the audit.

- Not providing sufficient breadth of examples. A minority of answers listed the same analytical procedures for each section of the balance sheet (fixed assets, debtors, creditors etc.). These answers were generally "capped" regarding the marks awarded as "different types" of procedure per the question requirement were not being provided.

Overall, the standard of answers was reasonable. However some answers did not provide the necessary breadth of comment or simply omitted sections altogether, presumably due to lack of knowledge.

Part (b)

An income statement was provided in the scenario, with what were hopefully some fairly obvious changes that should make an auditor question the accuracy of the figures. The comment that the directors thought the company had had a difficult year, but the results appeared to be good was supposed to elicit this questioning attitude towards the income statement.

Many candidates did question the figures in the statement, as far as considering the possibility of window-dressing or fraudulent activity given the directors' initial comments. However, many candidates made only basic comments such as "sales have increased" which was really self-evident from the scenario. Inadequate answers also typically covered a very limited range of points. Candidates needed to realise that because some very basic information was provided that, finding problems with that information should be relatively straight forward.

While basic calculations were helpful, these should not have taken very long. It was evident that many candidates did not have a calculator although the examiner has noted that questions required basic calculations can be set in this paper.

Other common errors included:

- not understanding basic accounting principles meaning that some explanations were strange or in some cases simply incorrect. For example, simply stating that sales had increased because more goods were being sold on credit compared to cash (debtors may increase due to this mix change, sales would not unless linked to better credit terms being provided). Also, cost of sales falling due to stock being undervalued....

- Lack of structure or format to answers. Very few answers followed the structure of the income statement, but tended to make points in almost any order (e.g. selling costs, cash, cost of sales, etc.). This meant that there were serious omissions from most answers regarding the changes between the two years; following the format of the income statement would have to alleviate this error.

- Providing excessive detail on the cash and bank balances. The question requirement specifically mentioned the income statement; the cash balances were included to demonstrate that the interest paid and receivable may be suspect. Detailed speculation on why the bank balance had improved was therefore not required.

Overall, the standard of answers was unsatisfactory. Many candidates provided very brief answers with little or no explanation for changes in the income statement.

Part (c)

The overall standard was adequate. The main reason for an inadequate answer was a candidate explaining how to perform a bank reconciliation, rather than obtain the bank letter.

Answers from a number of jurisdictions indicated that the auditor would visit the bank to obtain the letter rather than use the postal service. This appeared reasonable as it meant that the letter would go direct to the audit rather than the client.

Overall, the standard of answers was reasonable.

Marking scheme		
(a)	Analytical procedures	*Marks*
	1 mark for each valid, well explained, point	
	(i) – Obtain information on client situation	
	– Evaluation financial information	
	(ii) – Comparison prior periods	
	– Comparison actual/anticipated results	
	– Comparison industry information	
	– Specific procedures for individual account balances (e.g. receivables)	
	– Ratio analysis e.g. GP% year on year	
	– Proof in total e.g. total wages = employees * average wage	
	(iii)– Risk assessment procedures	
	– Substantive procedures	
	– End of audit analytical procedures	
	Maximum marks	8

(b)	Risks – income statement	
	0.5 mark, for identifying unusual changes in income statement. Award up to 1 more mark. Total 1-5 marks per point.	
	– Net profit	
	– Revenue	
	– Cost of sales	
	– Gross profit	
	– Administration	
	– Selling and distribution	
	– Interest payable	
	– Interest receivable (must be linked to the change in bank balance – not enough cash for interest received)	
	– Other relevant points	
	Maximum marks	9
(c)	Bank letter	
	1 mark for each audit procedure	
	– Evaluate need for letter	
	– Prepare bank letter – standard form	
	– Client permission	
	– Refer to standing authority at bank	
	– Letter direct to bank	
	Maximum marks	3
	Total	**20**

19 MATALAS CO

Key answer tips

Note that part (a) is asking you to explain issues that could limit the independence of the internal audit department in a company and then recommend a way of overcoming that issue. To obtain credit, answers have to relate to information presented in the scenario.

In part (b), explain the deficiencies in the petty cash system of Matalas and then recommend a control to overcome that deficiency.

(a) **Factors limiting independence of internal audit**

Reporting system

The chief internal auditor reports to the finance director. This limits the effectiveness of the internal audit reports as the finance director will also be responsible for some of the financial systems that the internal auditor is reporting on. Similarly, the chief internal auditor may soften or limit criticism in reports to avoid confrontation with the finance director.

To ensure independence, the internal auditor should report to an audit committee.

Scope of work

The scope of work of internal audit is decided by the finance director in discussion with the chief internal auditor. This means that the finance director may try and influence the chief internal auditor regarding the areas that the internal audit department is auditing, possibly directing attention away from any contentious areas that the director does not want auditing.

To ensure independence, the scope of work of the internal audit department should be decided by the chief internal auditor, perhaps with the assistance of an audit committee.

Audit work

The chief internal auditor appears to be auditing the controls which were proposed by that department. This limits independence as the auditor is effectively auditing his own work, and may not therefore identify any mistakes.

To ensure independence, the chief internal auditor should not establish control systems in Matalas. However, where controls have already been established, another member of the internal audit should carry out the audit of petty cash to provide some limited independence.

Length of service of internal audit staff

All internal audit staff at Matalas have been employed for at least five years. This may limit their effectiveness as they will be very familiar with the systems being reviewed and therefore may not be sufficiently objective to identify errors in those systems.

To ensure independence, the existing staff should be rotated into different areas of internal audit work and the chief internal auditor independently review the work carried out.

Appointment of chief internal auditor

The chief internal auditor is appointed by the chief executive officer (CEO) of Matalas. Given that the CEO is responsible for the running of the company, it is possible that there will be bias in the appointment of the chief internal auditor; the CEO may appoint someone who he knows will not criticise his work or the company.

To ensure independence, the chief internal auditor should be appointed by an audit committee or at least the appointment agreed by the whole board.

(b) **Internal control deficiencies – petty cash**

<u>Deficiency</u>	<u>Suggested control</u>
The petty cash balance is approximately three months expenditure. This is excessive and will increase the possibility of petty cash being stolen or errors not being identified.	The petty cash balance should be $2,000, being about one month's expenditure.
The petty cash box itself is not secure; it is placed on a bookcase where any member of staff could steal it.	When not in use, the petty cash box should be kept in the branch safe, or at least a locked drawer in the accountant's desk.
Petty cash appears to be used for some larger items of expenditure (up to $500). Vouchers are only authorised after expenditure is incurred indicating that some significant expenditure can take place without authorisation.	A maximum expenditure limit (e.g. $50) should be set before which prior authorisation is required.
Petty cash vouchers are only signed by	All vouchers should be signed by an

the person incurring the expenditure, indicating a lack of authorisation control for that expenditure.	independent official showing that the expenditure has been authorised.
Petty cash only appears to be counted by the accounts clerk, who is also responsible for the petty cash balance. There is no independent check that the petty cash balance is accurate.	The counting of petty cash should be checked by the accountant to ensure that the clerk is not stealing the cash.
When the imprest cheque is signed, only the journal entry for petty cash is reviewed, not the petty cash vouchers. The accountant has no evidence that the journal entry actually relates to the petty cash expenditure incurred.	The petty cash vouchers should be available for review to provide evidence of petty cash expenditure.
Petty cash vouchers are not pre-numbered so it is impossible to check the completeness of vouchers; unauthorised expenditure could be blamed on 'missing' vouchers.	Petty cash vouchers should be pre-numbered and the numbering checked in the petty cash book to confirm completeness of recording of expenditure.

Examiner's comments

Part (a)

Candidates were provided with information in a scenario with specific reference in the question requirement to that information. To obtain credit, answers therefore had to relate to information presented in the scenario.

To obtain the full two marks per point, answers would normally take the format "issue 1 could limit independence in Matalas, because..... This issue can be overcome by...."

However, as the question requirement did not specify the number of points to make, then any number of valid points could be included in the answer. Most candidates included four fairly well explained points in their answer. A minority of candidates provided limited or no explanation of the points made, limiting the marks awarded.

Common errors and reasons why those errors did not obtain marks included:

- Including points in the answer which were not mentioned in the scenario. A minority of candidates mentioned generic reasons why internal audit may not be independent. These points were not relevant and so no marks could be awarded.

- Including points which although could be relevant to the scenario were not necessarily best practice. For example, in many internal audit departments the chief internal auditor is involved in appointing staff because they can identify the skills required and whether that person is suitable to work within the department. These points were not fundamental flaws limiting the independence of the internal audit department.

- Not explaining the reason for the deficiency. For example, a common comment was the chief internal auditor reports to the finance director. While this was correct in relation to the question, the reason in terms of lack of independence of reporting or the finance director suppressing adverse reports on his department was not explained.

- Stating changes to take place within the company without justifying why that change was necessary. For example, stating an audit committee was needed.

- The method of overcoming deficiencies (an audit committee being one) had to be linked to a deficiency identified in the scenario. Simply stating areas of good corporate governance was normally insufficient as the reason for the suggested change was not clear.

- Mentioning that the internal audit department had only six internal auditors limiting their independence. The number of staff may have limited the department's effectiveness, but not necessarily their independence.

Overall, the candidates answered this question well.

Part (b)

To obtain the full two marks per point, answers would normally take the format "issue 1 is a petty cash deficiency in Matalas, because..... . This deficiency can be overcome by...." However, as the question requirement did not specify the number of points to make, then any number of valid points could be included in the answer. Most candidates included up to six fairly well explained points in their answer. Again, a minority of candidates provided limited or no explanation of the points made, limiting the marks awarded.

The most interesting point to mark in this question concerned the location of the petty cash box itself. Almost all candidates recognised that it was inappropriate to maintain the petty cash book in public view on a bookcase, with the reason that the box could be stolen easily. However, controls over this deficiency varied from simply keeping the box in a safe to using CCTV and employing security guards to ensure the box was not stolen. Given the (relatively) small amount of money in the box, some controls did appear excessive. However, they were normally marked as valid as certainly in some jurisdictions the control could well be appropriate.

Common errors and reasons why those errors did not obtain marks included:

- Not explaining the reason for deficiencies identified. For example, many candidates noted that petty cash was counted by the cashier – but not the deficiency that the cashier could report incorrect cash balances and steal some of the money.

- Suggesting deficiencies that were not mentioned in the scenario. The most common weakness in this respect was the comment that petty cash should be computerised. To gain full marks, the deficiency had to be clearly related to the information provided in scenario.

- Suggesting many, and sometimes completely impractical procedures for the control of petty cash. For example, suggesting that all petty cash vouchers had to be signed by the senior accountant or that a voucher should be signed by one person, recorded in the petty cash book by another and then a third person dispensed the actual cash. Awarding marks in these situations was limited because the controls were simply not practical or cost effective for any company.

- A significant number of candidates struggled to provide sufficient reasons. The overall standard was satisfactory which was possibly more an indication that candidates were not always familiar with petty cash systems but that they could identify and comment on deficiencies.

	Marking scheme	Marks
(a)	2 marks for each independence factor. 1 for explaining the issue and 1 for mitigating that factor. – Reporting system – Scope of work – Actual audit work – Length of service of internal audit staff – Appointment of chief internal auditor – External auditor assistance with internal audit? (additional to answer)	8
(b)	2 marks for each control deficiency. 1 for explaining the deficiency and 1 for control over that deficiency. – Size of petty cash balance – Security of petty cash box – High value petty cash expenditure – individual items – Authorisation of petty cash expenditure – Counting of petty cash – No review of petty cash vouchers – signing of imprest cheque – Vouchers not pre-numbered	12
	Total	**20**

20   SPECS4YOU

Key answer tips

Parts (a) and (b) are book knowledge. Part (c) expects you to apply that knowledge to identify deficiencies in a working paper, illustrating that memorising without understanding is insufficient.

(a)   The purposes of audit working papers include:

 –   To assist with the planning and performance of the audit.

 –   To assist in the supervision and review of audit work.

 –   To record the audit evidence resulting from the audit work performed to support the auditor's opinion.

(b)   *Familiarisation*

Documentation	**Information obtained**
Memorandum and articles of association	Details of the objectives of Specs4You, its permitted capital structure and the internal constitution of the company.
Most recent published financial statements	Provide detail on the size of the company, profitability, etc as well as any unusual factors such as loans due for repayment.

Documentation	Information obtained
Most recent management accounts/budgets/cash flow information	Determine the current status of the company including ongoing profitability, ability to meet budget, etc as well as identifying any potential going concern problems.
Organisation chart of Specs4You	To identify the key managers and employees in the company and other people to contact during the audit.
Industry data on spectacle sales	To find out how Specs4You is performing compared to the industry standards. This will help to highlight any areas of concern, for example higher than expected cost of sales, for investigation on the audit.
Financial statements of similar entities	To compare the accounting policies of Specs4You and obtain additional information on industry standards.
Prior year audit file	To establish what problems were encountered in last year's audit, how those problems were resolved and identify any areas of concern for this year's audit.
Search of Internet news sites	To find out whether the company has any significant news stories (good or bad) which may affect the audit approach.

(c) The audit working paper does not meet the standards normally expected in a working paper because:

- The page reference is unclear making it very difficult to either file the working paper in the audit file or locate the working paper should there be queries on it.

- It is not clear what the client year-end date is – the year is missing. The working paper could easily be filed in the wrong year's audit file.

- There is no signature of the person who prepared the working paper. This means it is unclear who to address queries to regarding the preparation or contents of the working paper.

- There is evidence of a reviewer's signature. However, given that the reviewer did not query the lack of preparer's signature or other omissions noted below, the effectiveness of the review must be put in question.

- The test 'objective' is vague – it is not clear what 'correct' means for example, it would be better to state the objective in terms of assertions such as completeness or accuracy.

- The test objective is also stated as an audit assertion. This is not the case as no audit assertions are actually listed here.

- It is not clear how the number for testing was determined. This means it will be very difficult to determine whether sufficient audit evidence was obtained for this test.

- Stating that details of testing can be found on another working paper is insufficient – time will be wasted finding the working paper, if it has, in fact, been included in the audit working paper file.

- Information on the results of the test is unclear – the working paper should clearly state the results of the test without bias. The preparer appears to have used personal judgement which is not appropriate as the opinion should be based on the facts available, not speculation.

- The conclusion provided does not appear to be consistent with the results of the test. Five errors were found therefore it is likely that there are some systems deficiencies.

21   MAL & CO

(a)   Risk assessment procedures

(i)   The main purpose of risk assessment procedures is to help the auditor obtain an understanding of the audit client.

The procedures will provide audit evidence relating to the auditor's risk assessment of a material misstatement in the client's financial statements.

The auditor will also obtain initial evidence regarding the classes of transactions at the client and the operating effectiveness of the client's internal controls.

Finally, the auditor may identify risks in other areas such as being associated with a particular client or not being able to follow ethical guidelines of ACCA.

(ii)   The auditor may obtain evidence from:

- Enquiries of management and others connected with the entity such as external legal counsel or valuation experts

- Analytical procedures including ratio analysis to obtain high level data on the client

- Observation of entity activities and inspection of documents, etc.

(b)   Provide the range of services required – small firm

Serenity requires an enhanced range of services this year including review of and implementation of additional control systems. This service provides the following risks:

Skills necessary

Mal & Co must check whether they can provide these services. Mal & Co is only a seven partner firm and so the company must ensure it has the necessary staff and skills to undertake this work.

Self-review threat

There is a self-review threat. If Mal & Co are to implement new control systems then they may also be auditing those systems as part of the statutory audit. Mal & Co must ensure different staff implement and audit the systems. Preferably different departments in the firm should undertake the work. If insufficient staff are available then Mal & Co must refuse the additional systems work.

Acceptance of non-audit work

There is a possibility that Mal & Co will be breaching ethical or statutory guidelines by accepting the work. In some countries such as the USA, audit firms are barred from undertaking any other work for a client. Mal & Co must ensure this is not the case in their country.

Fee income

Acceptance of additional work will result in additional fee income for Mal & Co. ACCA's Code of Ethics and Conduct states that the amount of fee income derived from any one client should not exceed 15% for non public companies. Mal & Co will need to ensure that total fee income from Serenity does not breach these guidelines.

Client growth

Serenity is growing quickly. The company has poor internal controls providing high risk of financial misstatement. Mal & Co will need to ensure sufficient staff of appropriate experience are available and that enough time is allocated to the audit to complete all audit procedures.

Internal audit

Client expectations regarding the use of internal audit may be difficult to meet. As a new department, it will take time for the internal auditors to understand the systems at Serenity and produce any useful reports. Expectation of reduced fee will have to be managed carefully and checks made to ensure the auditor does not limit work because of fee pressure.

Association threat

Serenity are producing a new mobile telephone. The legal status of the telephone is currently uncertain; it may be illegal. Mal & Co need to determine the likelihood that the telephone is illegal. The audit firm may not wish to be associated with a company producing illegal products.

Report on cash flow

The mobile telephone application also requires a report on Serenity's cash flow forecast. This will be a separate engagement, with risk to Mal & Co because Serenity may attempt to show an unrealistic cash position in the forecast. Serenity must determine exactly what type of report is required (positive or negative) and ensure they have the time and staff with the necessary skills to provide the service.

Possible going concern

It is not clear whether failure to obtain the new mobile telephone licence will result in Serenity no longer being a going concern. Mal & Co will need to review the cash flow forecasts closely to determine the company's status in the future.

(c)   The term negative assurance means that the auditor has carried out work on the cash flow but that the accuracy of the forecast cannot be confirmed. The auditor will report that the cash flow appears to be reasonable, but not that it shows a true and fair view. The auditor is therefore not confirming that the cash flow is correct, rather that there is nothing to indicate it is incorrect.

This type of report is appropriate for a forecast because it relates to the future. It is therefore not possible to state that the forecast is materially correct in terms of truth and fairness because the forecast has not been tested against the future. The actual results are therefore uncertain. It may not be correct simply because future conditions do not agree with those under which the forecast was prepared.

22   WEAR WRAITH CO

(a)   Audit Work on Railway Trucks

- Examine board minutes authorising the purchase of the trucks (authorisation)

- Cast the non-current asset ledger; agree total of railway trucks to the general ledger and financial statements (completeness)

- Ensure that railway trucks are actually stated as such in the non-current asset note. As a material item, separate disclosure of this category is allowed (disclosure)

- Cast the non-current asset note in the financial statements. Ensure the note agrees to the amount disclosed in the balance sheet (disclosure)

- For a sample of assets from the ledger, confirm existence by physically seeing the trucks (existence)

- Identify the supplier of railway trucks from a purchase invoice. Obtain all invoices from this supplier and confirm completeness of recording in the non-current asset register (completeness). Also, during non-current asset inspection, record details of some railway trucks and ensure those trucks are recorded in the non-current asset register

- Examine a sample of purchase invoices to confirm ownership of the trucks (rights and obligations)

- Review company policy for depreciation. As this is a new category of non-current asset, obtain representation letter point regarding accuracy of amount. Confirm with amount charged in similar companies that the depreciation percentage appears to be correct (valuation and allocation)

- Agree depreciation charged in the non-current asset note to the amount on the profit and loss account (valuation and allocation)

- Check a sample of depreciation calculations to ensure that they are accurate and that they conform to company policy (valuation and allocation)

- Ensure that any sales tax has been correctly treated e.g. capitalised where this is non-recoverable (valuation and allocation)

- Current value may also be confirmed using a specialist or appropriate trade journal and compared to the net book value shown in the non-current asset register (valuation and allocation).

(b)   Issues to raise with management

Land and buildings

The depreciation rate has been correctly applied at 2% – given an estimated life for the land and buildings category of 50 years. However, the rate has been applied to the whole balance – that is land and buildings. In most companies, the value of land is not thought to decrease and therefore depreciation is not appropriate.

To allocate depreciation accurately, a split is required between the land and buildings amounts in the financial statements. Buildings will then be depreciated, but not the land.

Plant and machinery

Depreciation has been charged in full in the year of acquisition, but not charged at all in the year of disposal. This appears to be an appropriate accounting policy – charging depreciation in the year of disposal would only amend the profit or loss on sale in that year and so have a neutral effect on the financial statements..

There appears to be an error in the disposals calculation as the depreciation amount exceeds the cost being eliminated There does not appear to be any logical reason for this situation and it should be discussed with the directors to identify the reason, if any, for this treatment.

If an error is found, then the depreciation amount must be decreased (or cost eliminated increased) and the profit or loss on sale amended accordingly.

Motor vehicles – point 1

The depreciation percentage stated in the financial statements is 33%. However, the calculation is either 25% on the year-end balance or about 21% on cost brought forward and additions for the year. To be consistent, the non-current asset disclosure note must agree to the actual calculation in the non-current asset note.

The reason for the difference must be found and either the disclosure note or the depreciation calculation amended If there has been a change in the depreciation rate, then this must also be disclosed in the financial statements. There has not been a change in accounting policy – the policy of depreciation is unchanged, it is only the method of applying that policy that has changed. There is no need to amend the prior year figures.

Motor vehicles – point 2

The cost and depreciation eliminated on sale are the same amount; this is not surprising given that the assets were fully depreciated. However, the depreciation policy for motor vehicles is to depreciate the category over three years. If those vehicles are now being kept for five years, then the depreciation rate may need revising to show the actual useful life of the vehicles.

The depreciation rate needs to be discussed with company management, and if necessary the rate amended to reflect the actual life of the vehicles.

23 MCKAY & CO

Key answer tips

Part (a) is theoretical and requires that you have learned the key ethical aspects of the syllabus. The mark allocation is quite high, but this often implies that the marking guide will be generous so do not be intimidated. Make sure you adhere to the principles of good presentation with each mark-scoring point being clearly separated.

Part (b) provides a wide range of ethical issues to identify, but do not overlook that you are also specifically asked to suggest mitigating factors and this will be worth at least one third of the marks on offer in this section.

(a)   **Confidential information**

General rules

Information obtained during an audit is normally held to be confidential; that is it will not be disclosed to a third party. However, client information may be disclosed where:

- consent has been obtained from the client
- there is a public duty to disclose
- there is a legal or professional right or duty to disclose.

However, these rules are general principles only; more detailed guidance is also available to accountants, as explained below.

ACCA's Code of ethics – obligatory disclosure

As noted above, ACCA's Code of ethics confirms that when a member agrees to work for a client in a professional capacity, it is an implied term of that agreement that the member will not disclose a client's affairs to any other person.

The recognised exceptions to this rule are where a member knows or suspects that his client has committed treason, or is involved in drug trafficking or terrorist offences. In this situation, information must be disclosed to a competent authority. The actual disclosure will depend on the laws of the jurisdiction where the auditor is located.

The auditor may also be obliged to provide information where a court demands disclosure. Refusal to provide information is likely to be considered contempt of court with the auditor being liable for this offence.

ACCA Code of ethics – voluntary disclosure

A member may also disclose client confidential information voluntarily, that is without client permission, in a limited number of situations. Examples include:

- To protect a member's interest, e.g. to allow a member to sue a client for unpaid fees or defend an action for negligence.
- Where there is a public duty to disclose, e.g. the client has committed an action against the public interest such as unauthorised release of toxic chemicals.

(b)   **Independence risks**

Audit partner – time in office

Mr Grace has been the audit partner of Ancients for eight years. His objectivity for the audit may be threatened by the ongoing close relationship with the client. In other words, he may be too friendly with the directors of Ancients. This means he may not be willing or able to take difficult decisions such as issuing a modified audit report for fear of prejudicing his friendship with the directors. Rotating the audit partner would remove this threat.

Unpaid taxation fees

Ancients has not paid the taxation fees for work that took place nearly six months ago. The non-payment of fees can be a threat to objectivity similar to that of an unpaid loan. In effect, McKay is providing Ancients with an interest free loan. The audit partner in McKay may not wish to issue a modified report for fear that the client leaves and the 'loan' is not repaid. The unpaid fee must be discussed with the directors in Ancients and reasons for non-payment obtained. McKay may wish to delay starting the audit work for this year until the fee is paid to remove the potential independence problem. If the fee is not paid at all then McKay may decline to carry out the audit.

Fee income

No details are provided regarding fee income obtained from Ancients. However, the company is growing rapidly and McKay does provide other services besides audit. As a limited liability company, McKay should ensure that no more than 10% of its recurring practice income (including auditing, accountancy and other work combined) is derived from this client. Obtaining more than 10% could indicate undue financial reliance on one client, and impair objectivity regarding the audit report (again fear of issuing a modified report and losing the fee income from the audit client). If the 10% limit is close, McKay may have to limit other services provided so that independence is not impaired. An annual review will be required on clients where the fee is between 5 and 10% to ensure that the fee income rules will not be breached.

Allyson Grace

Allyson Grace is not deemed to be connected to Mr Grace because she is presumably over the age of 18. If she was still a minor, then there would be a connection and it would be inappropriate for Mr Grace to be the audit partner as he could in theory influence Allyson's decisions. However, there may still appear to be an independence problem as Mr Grace may not be objective in making audit decisions. He may not wish to annoy his daughter by having to qualify the financial statements. Appointing another audit partner would remove the perceived independence problem.

Meal

The offer of a meal by Allyson may appear to be a threat to independence; having received an expensive meal, the audit staff may be favourably disposed towards Ancients and be less inclined to investigate potential errors. Audit staff are allowed to receive modest benefits on commercial terms; whether there is a benefit depends on how expensive the meal is. To ensure no independence issues it would appear that the invitation should be declined. One possible option would be for Mr Grace and Allyson to pay personally as a purely social event even though this may be unlikely. However, this does not remove the implied independence issue.

24   TEMPEST (A)

Key answer tips

Book knowledge is required in both parts of this question. In part (a) the answer is entirely knowledge based. In (b) you should use your knowledge of the auditing standard to help you structure the headings for your answer.

(a)   **Importance of audit planning**

According to International Standard on Auditing 300 (Revised), the auditor should plan the audit work so that the engagement will be performed in an effective manner. Specifically, planning is required for the following reasons:

- To help the auditor devote appropriate attention to important areas of the audit;
- To help the auditor identify and resolve potential problems on a timely basis;
- To help the auditor properly organise and manage the audit engagement so that it is performed in an effective and efficient manner;
- To assist in the selection of engagement team members with appropriate levels of capabilities and competence to respond to anticipated risks, and the proper assignment of work to them;
- To facilitate the direction and supervision of engagement team members and the review of their work; and
- To assist, where applicable, in coordination of work done by auditors of components and experts.

(b) **Tempest**

Year-end 31 December 2005

Prepared by: A Manager

Audit Strategy – Tempest Ltd 31.12.05

Characteristics of entity

Tempest requires a normal statutory audit – there are no audit or filing exemptions available.

The financial reporting framework is the International Accounting Standards and there are no industry specific reporting requirements.

Tempest buys and then resells all types of fixtures and fittings for ships from yachts through to large cruise ships. The company has ten warehouses, seven of which are located near to branches of our audit firm.

Key dates

Key dates in the audit timetable are:

- Interim audit.
- Final audit.
- Meeting with Audit committee.
- Financial statements approved by management.

Specific dates are to be confirmed.

Overview of audit approach

The shipping supply industry has grown by 7% during the last year. Tempest's sales increase is 12% indicating that the company continues to perform well with the industry.

There have been no changes to the accounting policies of Tempest during the year.

This is the first year that International Standards on Auditing (ISAs) are relevant to this company. A detailed check will be required to ensure that no changes are required to the audit plan.

The overall audit approach will be to use tests of control where possible. However, the fall in gross profit indicates that sales may be understated or Cost of Sales (COS) overstated, so additional substantive procedures may be required in this area.

Materiality determination

Materiality will initially be set at 0.5% to 1% of revenue as this figure appears to be more accurate than gross profit.

Materiality on the statement of financial position will be based on net asset values.

Identification of risk areas with a higher risk of mis-statement

A review of the draft financial statements for the company shows the following risks:

- Sales have increased by 12% but COS by 19%. There is a risk of COS being overstated.

- Inventory on the statement of financial position is down significantly on last year indicating that there may be valuation or quantity errors.

- Trade receivables have increased by about 50%, significantly more than the increase in sales. This indicates that the company may have debt collection problems. Additional testing may be required on after date cash collections to check for bad debts.

- Non-current assets have fallen by $900k, which is significant given that most non-current assets are land and buildings. The reason for sale must be ascertained.

- Non-current liabilities have also fallen by $1 million. While not necessarily linked to the fall in non-current assets, there is a possibility that non-current assets have been sold to pay off the liabilities.

Audit approach – extent of control testing

Audit testing will focus on the use of compliance testing where possible. However, changes have been made to the inventory system limiting the extent of compliance testing. Client systems have changed in the year with a new computerised inventory control system. Unfortunately, the change was not identified until audit planning started. Three actions are necessary in respect of this system:

- Audit initial installation of the system including transfer of balances. One of the reasons for the low inventory value could be omission of inventory balances on transfer.

- Test count inventory at the year-end and agree to the computerised inventory records (and vice versa) to test their accuracy. Note that the client will not be counting inventory at the year-end but relying on the computerised system.

- Test check bookings into and out of inventory from the purchases and sales systems.

Other risk areas

- The client appears to be a going concern, although the fall in gross profit must be investigated. Cash and profit forecasts for the next 12 months must also be obtained to confirm ongoing profitability and that the fall in cash balances will not continue.

- There is the possibility of related party transactions. One of the directors purchased a yacht during the year. Checks must be made to determine whether company products were purchased, and if so whether these were in the normal course of business.

- A new engagement letter is required in ISA format.

- Assistance may be required on the inventory count; three warehouses are located away from our offices.

25   ROCK

Key answer tips

This question is split into two equal sections and both relate to the scenario about the audit of Rock.   It concentrates on the planning/audit approach and review elements of the audit. Part (a) is relatively straightforward and is testing your knowledge of the procedures you would perform during the planning/risk assessment stage of the audit, methods you would use to decide your audit approach and the information you would obtain and from whom. Part (b) focuses on the review stage and tests your knowledge of audit working papers and their completion. Clearly, you should include details of the different types of audit working papers and their purpose. With this type of question it can often help to put yourself in the position of the reviewer and consider your expectations of a junior.

(a)   **Information and procedures: understanding the entity and its environment and risk assessment for Rock**

(i)   Understanding the entity and risk assessment is likely to involve a review of prior year risk assessments as a starting point and the identification of changes during the year from the information gathered that may alter that assessment.

(ii)   Risk assessment procedures involve enquiries of management and others, analytical procedures and observation and inspection. Members of the engagement team should discuss the susceptibility of the financial statements to material misstatements.

(iii)   Risk assessment also involves obtaining an understanding of the relevant industry, regulatory and other matters including the financial reporting framework, the nature of the entity, the application of accounting policies, the entity's objectives and related business risks, and its financial performance. This may involve:

(1)   a review of prior year working papers noting any particular issues that arose warranting attention in the current year;

(2)   discussions with the audit senior or manager working on Rock in prior years to establish any particular problem areas;

(3)   discussions with Rock (and their other advisors such as banks and lawyers) to establish any particular problem areas;

(4)   review of any third party information on the client such as press reports;

(5)   a review of management accounts, any financial information provided to the stock exchange or draft financial statements that may be available to establish trends in the business;

(6)   a review of any changes in stock exchange requirements;

(7)   a review of systems documentation (either generated by Rock or held by the firm) to see if it needs updating.

(iv)   Auditors should obtain an understanding of the control environment, the entity's process for identifying and dealing with business risk, information systems, control activities and monitoring of contents.

(v) Risks should be assessed at the financial statements level, and at the assertion level, and identify significant risks that require special audit consideration, and risks for which substantive procedures alone do not provide sufficient, appropriate audit evidence.

(vi) Analytical procedures are often used to highlight areas warranting particular audit attention. In the case of Rock, they are likely to focus on inventory which is likely to have a significant effect on profit (there may be slow moving or obsolete inventory that needs to be written down) and on property, plant and equipment which (as a manufacturer and distributor) is likely to be a significant item on the statement of financial position.

(vii) Risk assessment will facilitate the determination of materiality and tolerable error (calculations are normally based on sales, profit and assets) that will be used in determining the sample sizes and in the evaluation of errors.

(b) **Types and features of audit working papers**

(i) *Types of audit working papers include*:

    (1) systems documentation (flowcharts, systems manuals, narrative notes, checklists and questionnaires, etc.);

    (2) constitutional documents;

    (3) agreements with banks and other providers of finance;

    (4) details of other advisors used by the entity such as lawyers;

    (5) regulatory documentation relating to the stock exchange listing;

    (6) audit planning documentation;

    (7) audit work programs;

    (8) working papers showing the work performed;

    (9) lead schedules showing summaries of work performed and conclusions on individual account areas and the amounts to be included in the financial statements;

    (10) trial balances, management accounts and financial statements;

    (11) standard working papers relating to the calculation of sample sizes, for example;

    (12) schedules of unadjusted differences;

    (13) schedules of review points;

    (14) letters of deficiency and management representation letters.

(ii) *Features of audit working papers*:

    (1) All working papers (without exception) should show by whom they were prepared and when, and when they were reviewed and/or updated, and by whom, by means of signatures and dates – these may be electronic in the case of electronic working papers;

    (2) audit planning documentation should include the risk assessment which should be cross referenced to the audit program, and the audit program should be cross referenced to the audit working papers and vice versa;

(3)   working papers showing the work performed should be cross referenced to the audit program and the lead schedule on that particular section of the audit file, and should describe the nature of the work performed, the evidence obtained, and the conclusions reached;

(4)   each section of the audit file should have a lead schedule which should be cross referenced back to the relevant working papers;

(5)   trial balances should be cross referenced back to the relevant section of the audit file, and cross referenced forward to the financial statements;

(6)   the financial statements should be cross referenced to the trial balance;

(7)   schedules of unadjusted differences should be cross referenced to the sections of the file to which they relate;

(8)   schedules of review points should all be 'cleared' to show that all outstanding matters have been dealt with.

26   EXTERNAL AUDIT

Key answer tips

This question focuses on the purpose and role of external audit in part (a), which is a fundamental part of your studies and therefore should not present any problems. Avoid presenting your answer in a long paragraph; where you are making several points it is always helpful to consider the points separately and it can ensure you focus on the question's requirements. Use of bullets/numbering in your answer would improve presentation.

In part (b) you have to demonstrate that you are clear as to the differences between the interim and final audit in terms of the main audit processes and procedures. You are provided with an outline in the question itself as to the main difference in approach and therefore you only need to extend this and provide the relevant detail.

(a)   **Training material: purpose of external audit and its role**

(i)   The external audit has a long history that derives largely from the separation of the ownership and management of assets. Those who own assets wish to ensure that those to whom they have entrusted control are using those assets wisely. This is known as the 'stewardship' function.

(ii)   The requirement for an independent audit helps ensure that financial statements are free of bias and manipulation for the benefit of users of financial information.

(iii)   Companies are owned by shareholders but they are managed by directors (in very small companies, owners and managers are the same, but many such companies are not subject to statutory audit requirements).

(iv)   The requirement for a statutory audit is a public interest issue: the public is invited to invest in enterprises, it is in the interests of the capital markets (and society as a whole) that those investing do so in the knowledge that they will be provided with 'true and fair' information about the enterprise. This should result in the efficient allocation of capital as investors are able to make rational decisions on the basis of transparent financial information.

(v)   The requirement for an audit can help prevent investors from being defrauded, although there is no guarantee of this because the external audit has inherent limitations. Reducing the possibility of false information being provided by managers to owners is achieved by the requirement for external auditors to be independent of the managers upon whose financial statements they are reporting.

(vi)   The purpose of the external audit under International Standards on Auditing is for the auditor to obtain sufficient appropriate audit evidence on which to base the audit opinion. This opinion is on whether the financial statements give a 'true and fair view' (or 'present fairly in all material respects') of the position, performance (and cash flows) of the entity. This opinion is prepared for the benefit of shareholders.

(b)   **Main audit procedures and processes: interim and final audit**

(i)   The interim audit generally involves risk assessment, the testing of internal controls, and certain analytical and other substantive procedures. Many of these procedures are often performed concurrently.

(ii)   Risk assessment involves gathering information about the business, inquiries, analytical procedures and determining the response to assessed risk. In practice it also involves the determination of materiality and tolerable error.

(iii)   Risk assessment also involves evaluating the design of internal controls and determining whether they have been implemented.

(iv)   Final audit procedures also involve a review of the financial statements as a whole to ensure that they are internally consistent, and in accordance with the relevant financial reporting framework and the auditor's knowledge of the business.

(v)   Substantive procedures, which include analytical procedures, are designed to provide evidence that the figures and disclosures in the financial statements are complete, relevant, and accurate. Arriving at the final conclusions often involves the performance of further analytical procedures on the financial statements as a whole.

(vi)   It is common for auditors to provide management with lists of control deficiencies (both structural and operational) together with recommendations for improvement both after the interim and final audits.

(vii)   Auditors are also required to communicate with those charged with governance.

NB: Mention could also be made of management representations, third party confirmations, the review of working papers, and a number of other matters.

27 CLIFF

Key answer tips

This question focuses on internal controls and provides you with a scenario of a small company running a chain of supermarkets. As with all questions of this type you must ensure that you read the data in the question and relate your answer to it – it often helps if you re-read the question at least once while answering it to ensure that your answer does not lose focus! Part (a) asks you to outline problems that you may find as a result of poor internal controls; ensure that your answer is specific and clearly explain the reason why you have listed a particular problem (e.g. poor inventory control results in...). Part (b) asks you to make recommendations to improve internal controls and explain the advantages and disadvantages of each one. You must give all these considerations for each recommendation or you will not gain full marks; be careful not to give a detailed recommendation without advantages and disadvantages.

(a) **Problems expected at Cliff: poor internal control**

(i) I would expect the company to experience some level of over-ordering, leading to reduced profitability as a result of inventory going past its 'best before' date.

(ii) Inventory that is not well-controlled in a supermarket may result in a breach of health and safety regulations which may result in fines or even closure of the supermarkets.

(iii) I would expect there to be stock-outs leading to the potential loss of business to other supermarkets.

(iv) I would expect there to be inefficiencies as a result of a lack of central ordering system resulting from quantity discounts not being obtained.

(v) All of the problems noted above are likely to be exacerbated where local managers or staff are either inexperienced or possibly dishonest – the question states that poorer quality staff have been recruited recently.

(vi) Supermarket inventory is very easily pilfered either by staff or customers even where it is well-controlled. The lack of regular inventory counts in particular means that pilferage is very easy to hide.

(vii) I would expect there to be a lack of understanding in the business as a whole as to the availability of new products, products with high margins or other areas in which profitability might be improved.

(b) **Four recommendations, explanation of advantages and disadvantages: improvements to internal control**

(1) **Recommendation 1**: that an integrated system be introduced across all supermarkets that links sales, purchases and inventory records.

Advantages

This would provide the company with an overall view of what inventory is held at any particular time, enable it to order centrally and reduce the scope for pilferage. It would result in reduced stock-outs and reduced inventory obsolescence.

Disadvantages

This would require considerable capital investment in hardware, software and training. It would also take control away from local managers which would almost certainly cause resentment.

(2) **Recommendation 2**: the imposition of regular, or continuous inventory counting procedures together with the prompt update of inventory records for discrepancies found and investigation of the reason for the discrepancies.

Advantages

This would further reduce the possibility of stock-outs and provide evidence of over-ordering, which would enable purchasing patterns to be refined.

Disadvantages

There are costs in terms of staff time and, again, a certain level of resentment among staff who may feel that they are being 'spied on', or that they are no longer trusted. Training would also be required and additional administrative work would need to be undertaken by local managers.

(3) **Recommendation 3**: that management accounts are produced on at least a quarterly basis, that figures relating to each supermarket are provided to head office on a monthly basis, and that an analysis is undertaken by head office on the performance of individual supermarkets and inventory lines.

Advantages

This would enable the company to determine which supermarkets are performing better than others. It would also enable the company to identify those inventory lines that sell well and those that are profitable.

Disadvantages

The production of more regular and detailed information will be time-consuming. Local managers may feel that they are unable to service the particular needs of their customers if decisions are made on a global basis; customers may feel the same way.

(4) **Recommendation 4**: that sales price decisions are made by head office.

Advantages

This would enable the company to experiment with the use of 'loss leaders', for example, and to impose a degree of consistency across supermarkets to prevent inappropriate pricing decisions being taken by local managers.

Disadvantages

Again, loss of control at a local level is likely to result in resentment and the possible loss of good staff. What sells well in one supermarket may not do so in another. To the extent that head office have less experience of local conditions than local staff, it is possible that inappropriate pricing decisions may be made by head office.

28 TOUREX AND PUDCO

Key answer tips

This is a well structured question which tests professional conduct matters relating to conflicts of interest, the requirements of IAS 37 together with their application to a given set of circumstances and related aspects of the audit report. The marks on this question are evenly spread over the three part requirement – it is therefore important you give a reasonable amount of attention to each of the requirements.

In dealing with part (a) you must make sure you focus on the area of managing possible conflicts of interest.

In part (b) approximately half the available marks are awarded for explaining the accounting rules of IAS 37 – the remaining marks will only be given for relevant application of those principles to the facts given about the companies referred to in the question – make sure you cover all aspects of the question!

Part (c) requires you to exercise judgement based on your knowledge of the audit report categories under the auditing standard. There may be no clear cut answer to this part of the question – you may require more information before you can reach a conclusion. In this type of question, you should make your thinking clear to the examiner by explaining the approach you are taking.

(a)   **Managing conflicts of interest**

    (i)   ACCA's Rules of Professional Conduct state that auditors should avoid conflicts of interest (both conflicts between the firm and clients, and conflicts between clients) wherever possible. In some cases, such as these, they are unavoidable.

    (ii)   Full disclosure is important – both companies should be fully aware that the firm is acting for the other party.

    (iii)   One or both companies may object to the firm acting for the other company and the auditor may be forced to make a decision as to which company to resign from. However, this is not an attractive course of action because the audits may already have commenced and it may be difficult for one of the companies to find a new auditor, quickly.

    (iv)   The auditor should probably not, therefore, resign unless forced to do so – this might be prejudicial to the interests of one of the clients.

    (v)   It is important in such cases that different teams of staff, and different engagement partners work on the respective audits.

    (vi)   Internal procedures within the firm should be set up to prevent confidential information from one client being transferred to the other and the interests of one firm damaging the interests of the other. Such procedures are sometimes known as 'Chinese Walls'.

    (vii)   If two completely separate offices could work on the two engagements, so much the better.

(b)   **Main requirements of IAS 37**

IAS 37	Application
IAS 37 states that a provision is a liability of uncertain timing or amount. It should only be recognised when there is a present obligation (legal or constructive) arising from past events and it is probable that a transfer of economic benefits will be required to settle the obligation and a reliable estimate of the amount can be made.	If the firm can obtain sufficient appropriate audit evidence to show that Tourex and/or Pudco are likely to have to make a payment, and that the amount can be reliably estimated, a constructive obligation seems to exist and provision should be made.
IAS 37 states that a contingent liability is either a possible obligation arising from past events whose existence will be confirmed by uncertain future events outside the control of the entity or, a present obligation arising from past events that is not recognised because a transfer of economic benefits is not probable, or because the amount of the obligation cannot be measured with sufficient certainty.	If Tourex and/or Pudco are uncertain as to whether a payment will have to be made, or if they are certain but the amount cannot be estimated, a contingent liability should be disclosed in the accounts.
IAS 37 states that a contingent asset is a possible asset arising from past events whose existence will be confirmed by uncertain future events outside the control of the entity. Contingent assets can be disclosed when an inflow of economic benefit is probable. When they are virtually certain, a contingency does not exist; the income may be accrued.	This might apply to Tourex in its claim against the food company. It seems unlikely that there is sufficient certainty relating to the claim and therefore no disclosure should be made.
It also states that expected re-imbursements (such as those arising from insurance contracts) should be recognised only where they are virtually certain, and treated as separate assets. The net expense may be recognised in the statement of comprehensive income.	If either Tourex or Pudco hold insurance against such events, and it is probable that the insurance claim will be met, a contingent asset may need to be disclosed. If there is any uncertainty, there should be no disclosure. If it is virtually certain that the claim will be met, a separate asset should be recognised.
A brief description of the nature of each class of contingent liability should be made unless the possibility of the transfer of benefits is remote. Where practical, an estimate of the financial effect, an indication of the relevant uncertainties, and the possibility of any reimbursement should be disclosed. Similar rules apply to contingent assets.	

(c)   **Sufficient audit evidence and audit reports**

(i)   The main problem for the auditors will be gaining sufficient evidence to determine whether any amounts should be provided for and/or disclosed in the financial statements of the two companies.

(ii)   The lawyers refuse to provide anything other than informal evidence and this will almost certainly not be sufficient to form an audit opinion.

(iii)   Unless audit evidence can be obtained elsewhere – a qualified ('except for') opinion, on the basis of being unable to obtain sufficient appropriate evidence, may be needed for both companies as the amounts involved are material.

(iv)   However, it may be possible to take the view that there is a significant uncertainty, and that an explanatory paragraph referring to this significant uncertainty is therefore appropriate, rather than a qualification to the auditors' opinion, provided that the matter is adequately disclosed in the financial statements.

(v)   It may be possible for the auditors to suggest to the companies that it would be very helpful for the lawyers to provide some indication as to their view of the likely outcome and the amounts involved, in order to avoid a modified opinion.

(vi)   The auditors should also take note of the progress of any legal proceedings and any proceedings that may be instigated by the public health authorities as such authorities might impose significant fines, and they might even close the businesses down, which has implications for the going concern status of both.

SPECIALISED AUDIT AREAS

29   BRAMPTON CO *Walk in the footsteps of a top tutor*

Key answer tips

This question is unusual in that it focuses entirely on more peripheral topics on the syllabus. For that reason it provides a reasonable challenge, particularly to those candidates who have not revised broadly.

In order to answer this successfully you need to have reviewed sections in your text on planning, ISA 610 Using the Work of Internal Auditors, review engagements and reasonable vs limited assurance.

The highlighted words are key phases that markers are looking for.

(a)   The interim audit, as its name suggests, is that part of the whole audit that takes place before the year-end. The auditor uses the interim audit to carry out procedures that would be difficult to perform at the year-end because of time pressure. The final audit, on the other hand, will take place after the year-end and concludes with the auditor forming and expressing an opinion on the financial statements for the whole year subject to audit. It is important to note that the final opinion takes account of conclusions formed at both the interim and final audit.

Typical work carried out at the interim audit includes:

- consideration of inherent risks facing the company.
- recording the system of internal control.
- carrying out tests of control on the company's internal control system and evaluating its effectiveness to determine the level of control risk.
- performing sufficient substantive testing of transactions and balances to be satisfied that the books and records are a reliable basis for the preparation of financial statements.
- identification of potential problems that may affect the final audit work. A basic aim is to ensure as far as possible that there are no undetected problems at the year-end.

Typical work carried out at the final examination includes:

- Follow up of items noted at the inventory count.
- Obtaining confirmations from third parties, such as bankers and lawyers.
- Analytical reviews of figures in the financial statements.
- Reviews of events after the reporting period.
- Consideration of the going concern status of the organisation.

(b) The external auditors would normally be able to use the work of the internal auditors provided that:

- they are independent (in this case, of the accounting department and finance director to whom the accounting department reports). It appears that they have reported to the whole board, which would be a factor increasing their independence. It would be even better if they had strong links with the audit committee (if applicable).
- they are competent. Your firm would have formed a view in past years of their reliability by considering the background (including qualifications and experience, particularly as regards forecasting) of the internal audit staff and by examining their reports and working papers. You may also have reviewed some aspects of their work in the current year to the same end.
- effective communication, whether there is likely to be effective communication between the internal auditors and the external auditor.
- they have exercised due professional care, the work would need to have been properly planned including detailed work programmes, supervised, documented and reviewed.
- the company is experiencing difficulties due to the economic down turn and it requires the loan in order to expand. Management might place pressure upon the internal auditors to present the cash flow forecast in a more favourable light. This would impact the independence of the internal auditors.

You would still take full responsibility for any report that you issue.

(c) Audit procedures adopted in the examination of the cash flow forecast would include:

(1) Check that the opening balance of the cash forecast is in agreement with the closing balance of the cash book, to ensure the opening balance of the forecast is accurate.

(2)   Consider how accurate company forecasts have been in the past by comparing past forecasts with actual outcomes. If forecasts have been reasonably accurate in the past, this would make it more likely that the current forecast is reliable.

(3)   Determine the assumptions that have been made in the preparation of the cash flow forecast. For example, the company is experiencing a poor economic climate, so you would not expect cash flows from sales and realisation of receivables to increase, but either to decrease or remain stable. You are also aware that costs are rising so you would expect cost increases to be reflected in the cash forecasts.

(4)   Examine the sales department detailed budgets for the two years ahead and, in particular, discuss with them the outlets that they will be targeting. This would help the auditor determine whether the cash derived from sales is soundly based.

(5)   Examine the production department's assessment of the non-current assets required to increase the production of white bread to the level required by the sales projections. Obtain an assessment of estimated cost of non-current assets, reviewing bids from suppliers, if available. This would provide evidence on material cash outflows.

(6)   Consider the adequacy of the increased working capital that will be required as a result of the expansion. Increased working capital would result in cash outflows and it would be important to establish its adequacy.

(7)   If relevant review the post year end period to compare the actual performance against the forecast figures.

(8)   Recalculate and cast the cash flow forecast balances.

(9)   Review board minutes for any other relevant issues which should be included within the forecast.

(10)   Review the work of the internal audit department in preparing the cash flow forecast.

(d)   You would inform management that it would not be possible to give a report on the accuracy of the cash flow forecast. The forecast is an assessment of cash flows in the future which is uncertain, particularly in the second year.

The bank should be informed that the kind of report that you could give is a limited assurance or negative assurance report. You would be able to state in your report the kind of work you had carried out, the assumptions that management had made and then to give a negative form of assurance in which you would state, among other things, that nothing had come to your attention that would cause you to believe that the assumptions do not provide a reasonable basis for the cash forecast. You could then go on to say that the forecast has been properly prepared on the basis of the assumptions.

This is assuming that this kind of opinion is appropriate in the light of the work you have performed.

	ACCA marking scheme	
		Marks
(a)	**Difference between interim audit and final audit**	
	Up to 1 mark for each relevant explanation and maximum of 2 marks for examples of procedures at interim and final audit, but overall maximum 4.	
	Interim audit and final audit parts of whole audit	
	Interim audit performed during year but final audit at or after the year-end	
	Interim audit performs procedures that cannot be performed at the final audit	
	Interim audit forms interim conclusion, but final audit results in audit opinion	
	Typical work at interim audit	
	Typical work at final audit	
	Maximum marks	4.0
(b)	**Work of internal audit**	
	½ mark for identification of each factor and up to 1 mark for full explanation, but maximum 6.	
	Independence – to whom report; links to audit committee	
	Competence – qualifications and experience	
	Effective communication – between internal and external auditors	
	Professional care – properly planned and performed	
	Management pressure to present favourable cash flow forecast	
	Maximum marks	6.0
(c)	**Examination of forecast**	
	Up to 1 mark for identification of a relevant procedure and a further 1 mark if adequately described, but maximum 6.	
	Opening balance	
	Accuracy of past forecasts	
	Assumptions	
	Sales budgets	
	Non-current assets required	
	Increased working capital required	
	Review post year end period	
	Recalculate and cast the cash flow forecast	
	Review board minutes	
	Review the work of the internal audit department	
	Maximum marks	6.0
(d)	**Kind of assurance**	
	1 mark for each relevant point, but maximum 4.	
	Not possible to give a report on accuracy and why	
	Limited assurance or negative assurance	
	What this kind of assurance means	
	Testing assumptions and reporting on validity	
	Forecast properly prepared on basis of assumptions	
	Maximum marks	4.0
Total		20.0

30 **CONOY** *Walk in the footsteps of a top tutor*

Key answer tips

The question begins with some basic knowledge recall. However, it is vital to compare and contrast internal and external audit services, as the marking guide splits the award of marks in this way. The examiner is looking for four balanced remarks, with 1 mark going to the discussion of internal audit and 1 mark to the discussion of external audit.

With the second part of the question it is vital to apply knowledge to the specific information given. Simple repetition of rote learned facts from study texts will probably not provide sufficient marks to achieve a good pass. For this part you should try and make six points. 1 mark will be awarded for identifying the basic benefit and 1 for applying it to Conoy.

The highlighted words are key phases that markers are looking for.

(a) **Role of internal and external auditors – differences**

Objectives

The main objective of internal audit is to improve a company's operations, primarily in terms of validating the efficiency and effectiveness of the internal control systems of a company.

The main objective of the external auditor is to express an opinion on the truth and fairness of the financial statements, and other jurisdiction specific requirements such as confirming that the financial statements comply with the reporting requirements included in legislation.

Reporting

Internal audit reports are normally addressed to the board of directors, or other people charged with governance such as the audit committee. Those reports are not publicly available, being confidential between the internal auditor and the recipient.

External audit reports are provided to the shareholders of a company. The report is attached to the annual financial statements of the company and is therefore publicly available to the shareholders and any reader of the financial statements.

Scope of work

The work of the internal auditor normally relates to the operations of the organisation, including the transaction processing systems and the systems to produce the annual financial statements. The internal auditor may also provide other reports to management, such as value for money audits which external auditors rarely become involved with.

The work of the external auditor relates only to the financial statements of the organisation. However, the internal control systems of the organisation will be tested as these provide evidence on the completeness and accuracy of the financial statements.

Relationship with company

In most organisations, the internal auditor is an employee of the organisation, which may have an impact on the auditor's independence. However, in some organisations the internal audit function is outsourced.

The external auditor is appointed by the shareholders of an organisation, providing some degree of independence from the company and management.

(b)   **Benefits of audit committee in Conoy Co**

Assistance with financial reporting (no finance expertise)

The executive directors of Conoy Co do not appear to have any specific financial skills – as the financial director has recently left the company and has not yet been replaced. This may mean that financial reporting in Conoy Co is limited or that the other non-financial directors spend a significant amount of time keeping up to date on financial reporting issues.

An audit committee will assist Conoy Co by providing specialist knowledge of financial reporting on a temporary basis – at least one of the new appointees should have relevant and recent financial reporting experience under codes of corporate governance. This will allow the executive directors to focus on running Conoy Co.

Enhance internal control systems

The board of Conoy Co do not necessarily understand the work of the internal auditor, or the need for control systems. This means that internal control within Conoy Co may be inadequate or that employees may not recognise the importance of internal control systems within an organisation.

The audit committee can raise awareness of the need for good internal control systems simply by being present in Conoy Co and by educating the board on the need for sound controls. Improving the internal control 'climate' will ensure the need for internal controls is understood and reduce control errors.

Reliance on external auditors

Conoy Co's internal auditors currently report to the board of Conoy Co. As previously noted, the lack of financial and control expertise on the board will mean that external auditor reports and advice will not necessarily be understood – and the board may rely too much on external auditors.

If Conoy Co report to an audit committee this will decrease the dependence of the board on the external auditors. The audit committee can take time to understand the external auditor's comments, and then via the non-executive director, ensure that the board take action on those comments.

Appointment of external auditors

At present, the board of Conoy Co appoint the external auditors. This raises issues of independence as the board may become too familiar with the external auditors and so appoint on this friendship rather than merit.

If an audit committee is established, then this committee can recommend the appointment of the external auditors. The committee will have the time and expertise to review the quality of service provided by the external auditors, removing the independence issue.

Corporate governance requirements – best practice

Conoy Co do not need to follow corporate governance requirements (the company is not listed). However, not following those requirements may start to have adverse effects on Conoy. For example, Conoy Co's bank is already concerned about the lack of transparency in reporting.

Establishing an audit committee will show that the board of Conoy Co are committed to maintaining appropriate internal systems in the company and providing the standard of reporting expected by large companies. Obtaining the new bank loan should also be easier as the bank will be satisfied with financial reporting standards.

Given no non-executives – independent advice to board

Currently Conoy Co does not have any non-executive directors. This means that the decisions of the executive directors are not being challenged by other directors independent of the company and with little or no financial interest in the company.

The appointment of an audit committee with one non-executive director on the board of Conoy Co will start to provide some non-executive input to board meetings. While not sufficient in terms of corporate governance requirements (about equal numbers of executive and non-executive directors are expected) it does show the board of Conoy Co are attempting to establish appropriate governance systems.

Advice on risk management

Finally, there are other general areas where Conoy Co would benefit from an audit committee. For example, lack of corporate governance structures probably means Conoy Co does not have a risk management committee. The audit committee can also provide advice on risk management, helping to decrease the risk exposure of the company.

	Marking scheme	Marks
(a)	**Difference – internal and external audit** 2 marks for each point. 1 for point in relation to internal audit and 1 for explaining the point in relation to external audit. Objectives Reporting Scope of work Relationship with company	8
(b)	**Benefits of audit committee** Up to 2 marks for each point. 1 for the benefit and 1 for applying that 1 mark only where point stated in general terms Assistance with financial reporting Enhance internal control systems Reliance on external auditors Appointment of external auditors Best practice – corporate governance Independent advice to board Advice on risk management Other valid points e.g. may be cost benefits over time.	12
	Total	**20**

Examiner's comments

Part (a)

A significant number of candidates obtained full marks for this question. Inadequate answers tended not to provide a clear contrast between the two sets of auditors or be presented as a one long paragraph making individual points difficult and sometimes impossible to identify.

Common errors included:

- Including points which did not appear to be relevant to the role of internal or external auditors. For example, the appointment of the auditor did not appear to affect what the auditor did, although the person the auditor reported to was relevant as this determined the format of report.

- In some situations, not explaining the points made. For example, stating that both sets of auditors were responsible for detecting fraud, without then going on to explain that the main responsibility rests with internal audit while external audit is concerned with material fraud only.

Part (b)

In some answers, the marking guide was recognised and some satisfactory answers showing how an audit committee could assist the company in the scenario were produced. Many answers, however, tended to list the benefits of an audit committee with little or no reference to the detail in the scenario. These answers still obtained 1 mark per point for identifying and explaining the benefit and obviously needed double the number of points to obtain full marks.

The main weakness in many answers was explaining the constitution of the audit committee or the work of other committees rather than the benefit of an audit committee. Overall, this question was answered well. The question obviously benefited those candidates who could apply knowledge to a scenario and those who had good knowledge.

---

31   EUKARE *Walk in the footsteps of a top tutor*

Key answer tips

The question begins with some basic knowledge repetition regarding audit risk. It then continues by requesting that the student applies their knowledge of audit risk (inherent risk in particular) to the scenario. Whilst it should be expected that this nature of question will be frequently examined students need to be aware in this instance of the unique scenario regarding the charity EuKaRe. Students must keep in mind that charities are 'not-for-profit-organisations' and that they face different pressures (internal and external) to private, profit making enterprises.

The highlighted words are key phases that markers are looking for.

(a)   **Audit risk**

Audit risk is the risk that an auditor gives an incorrect opinion on the financial statements being audited.

Inherent risk is the susceptibility of an assertion to a misstatement that could be material individually or when aggregated with misstatements, assuming that there are no related controls. The risk of such misstatement is greater for some assertions and related classes of transactions, account balances, and disclosures than for others.

Control risk is the risk that a material error could occur in an assertion that could be material, individually or when aggregated with other misstatements, will not be prevented or detected on a timely basis by the company's internal control systems.

Detection risk is the risk that the auditors' procedures will not detect a misstatement that exists in an assertion that could be material, individually or when aggregated with other misstatements.

(b)   **Inherent risks in charity**

Area of inherent risk	Effect on audit approach
Income is from voluntary donations only.	It is difficult to estimate that income in the future will be sufficient to meet the expenditure of the charity. Audit of the going concern concept will therefore be quite difficult.
Completeness of income – where there are no controls to ensure income is complete for example sales invoices are not raised to obtain donations.	Audit tests are unlikely to be effective to meet the assertion of completeness. The audit report may need to be modified to explain the lack of evidence stating that completeness of income cannot be confirmed.
Funds can only be spent in accordance with the aims of the charity.	Careful review of expenditure will be necessary to ensure that expenditure is not '*ultra vires*' the objectives of the charity. The auditor will need to review the constitution of the EuKaRe charity carefully in this respect.
Taxation rules relevant to charities.	The auditor will need to ensure that staff familiar with the taxation rules affecting the charity are on the audit team. There is a danger that taxation rules are not followed reflecting adversely on the audit firm.
Requirement to report expenditure in accordance with the constitution – administration expenditure can be no more than 10% of total income.	The trustees may attempt to hide 'excessive' expenditure on administration under other expense headings. As the auditor has to report on the accuracy of expenditure then audit procedures must focus on the accuracy of recording of expenditure.
Donations to charity for specific activities for example provision of sports equipment.	Documentation for any donation will need to be obtained and then expenditure agreed to the terms of the documentation. Any discrepancies will have to be reported to management.

(c)   **Weak control environment**

Lack of segregation of duties

There is normally a limited number of staff working in the charity meaning that a full system of internal control including segregation of duties cannot be implemented.

Volunteer staff

Many staff are volunteers and so will only work at the charity on an occasional basis. Controls will be performed by different staff on different days making the system unreliable.

Lack of qualified staff

Selection of staff is limited – people tend to volunteer for work when they have time – and so they are unlikely to have professional qualifications or experience to implement or maintain good control systems.

No internal audit department

Any control system will not be monitored effectively, mainly due to the lack of any internal audit department. The charity will not have the funds or experience to establish internal audit.

Attitude of the trustees

It is not clear how the charity's trustees view risk. However, where trustees are not professionally trained or have little time to devote to the charity, then there may be an impression that controls are not important. The overall control environment may therefore be weak as other charity workers do not see the importance of maintaining good controls.

	Marking scheme	Marks
(a)	1 mark for explanation of each term Audit risk Inherent risk Control risk Detection risk	4
(b)	1 mark for each area of inherent risk and 1 mark for explaining the effect on the audit approach = 2 marks per linked points Income voluntary only Completeness of income Funds spent in accordance with charity objectives Taxation rules Reporting of expenditure Donation for specific activities	12
(c)	1 mark for each point on weak control environment Lack of segregation of duties Volunteer staff Lack of qualified staff No internal audit Attitude of trustees	4
	Total	20

Examiner's comments

Part (a)

Candidates were required to explain the term audit risk and then the three elements of risk that contribute to total audit risk. Many candidates were uncertain of these concepts and did not manage to obtain the marks on offer.

Common errors included:

- Explaining audit risk in terms of errors in the financial statements rather than inappropriate audit reports.
- Omitting to explain that inherent risk is linked to the nature of the entity.

- Stating that control risk was the problem of not identifying the risk, rather than the error or fraud because the control system was inadequate.
- Explaining detection risk as the only risk that the auditor can amend rather than the auditor not detecting errors in the books, records, financial statements, etc.

The overall standard was therefore inadequate. Certainly an area to visit again at some stage.

Part (b)

Candidates were expected to identify areas of inherent risk in the charity scenario provided and then to explain the effect of each risk on the audit approach.

The standard of answer varied considerably. It appeared that the use of a charity was marginally concerning, although this was within the bounds of the study and followed the style of the examiner from previous diets.

Common errors included:

- Not being able to state a clear and logical effect on the audit approach for inherent risks identified.
- Explaining control risks such as lack of segregation of duties.
- Stating the effect on the audit approach in very general terms e.g. for each point stating that "additional substantive procedures will be required." More focused comments were expected.
- In many situations, simply not stating the obvious. For example, the scenario stated that the taxation of charities was complicated in this specific jurisdiction. Many candidates explained the effect on the audit approach in terms of verifying income and expenditure to source documents, ensuring that the tax liability was paid, or even recommending the appointment of a qualified accountant at the charity to prepare the taxation computation. The obvious thing to do though was simply have a charity taxation specialist on the audit team.

Overall, this was a question that required some thinking but also use of common sense. As the last bullet point above suggested, stating the obvious for the deficiencies mentioned in the scenario would have provided some benefit to many candidates. The standard was therefore inadequate.

Part (c)

The aim of the question was to try and get candidates to think about the bigger "control environment" issues within the entity. The relatively low mark allocation was to recognise that the question was actually quite difficult as candidates are more used to looking for detailed control deficiencies.

Common errors included:

- Re-stating points from part (b) as also relevant to part (c).
- Omitting the question completely from the candidate's answer.

The standard of answers for this question was inadequate. In any similar question in the future, candidates are recommended to "think big", that is to see the larger picture of the control system rather than the detailed points such as lack of cash receipts which relate more to control components.

32   MONTEHODGE CO

Key answer tips

Part (a), Internal audit is an important part of the syllabus therefore you should be prepared for the advantages and disadvantages of outsourcing the internal audit department this is standard bookwork.

Part (b) asked for reason for and against having an IA department outsourced, to gain good solid marks here you have to back relate to the scenario. From a marking allocation point of view the 12 marks need to be split to ensure a balance in your answer.

(a)   **Outsourcing internal audit**

Advantages of outsourcing internal audit

Staff recruitment

There will be no need to recruit staff for the internal audit department; the outsourcing company will provide all staff and ensure staff are of the appropriate quality.

Skills

The outsourcing company will have a large pool of staff available to provide the internal audit service. This will provide access to specialist skills that the company may not be able to afford if the internal audit department was run internally.

Set up time

The department can be set up in a few weeks rather than taking months to advertise and recruit appropriate staff.

Costs

Costs for the service will be agreed in advance. This makes budgeting easier for the recipient company as the cost and standard of service expected are fixed.

Flexibility (staffing arrangements)

Staff can be hired to suit the workloads and requirements of the recipient company rather than full-time staff being idle for some parts of the year.

Disadvantages of outsourcing internal audit

Staff turnover

The internal audit staff allocated to one company may change frequently; this means that company systems may not always be fully understood, decreasing the quality of the service provided.

External auditors

Where external auditors provide the internal audit service there may be a conflict of interest (self-review threat), where internal audit work is then relied upon by external auditors.

Cost

The cost of the outsourced service may be too high for the company, which means that an internal audit department is not established at all. There may be an assumption that internal provision would be even more expensive.

Confidentiality

Knowledge of company systems and confidential data will be available to a third party. Although the service agreement should provide confidentiality clauses, this may not stop breaches of confidentiality e.g. individuals selling data fraudulently.

Control

Where internal audit is provided in-house, the company will have more control over the activities of the department; there is less need to discuss work patterns or suggest areas of work to the internal audit department.

(b) **Need for internal audit**

For establishing an internal audit department

Value for money (VFM) audits

MonteHodge has some relatively complex systems such as the stock market monitoring systems. Internal audit may be able to offer VFM services or review potential upgrades to these systems checking again whether value for money is provided.

Accounting system

While not complex, accounting systems must provide accurate information. Internal audit can audit these systems in detail ensuring that fee calculations, for example, are correct.

Computer systems

Maintenance of computer systems is critical to MonteHodge's business. Without computers, the company cannot operate. Internal audit could review the effectiveness of backup and disaster recovery arrangements.

Internal control systems

Internal control systems appear to be limited. Internal audit could check whether basic control systems are needed, recommending implementation of controls where appropriate.

Effect on audit fee

Provision of internal audit may decrease the audit fee where external auditors can place reliance on the work of internal audit. This is unlikely to happen during the first year of internal audit due to lack of experience.

Image to clients

Provision of internal audit will enable MonteHodge Co to provide a better 'image' to its clients. Good controls imply client monies are safe with MonteHodge.

Corporate governance

Although MonteHodge does not need to comply with corporate governance regulations, internal audit could still recommend policies for good corporate governance. For example, suggesting that the chairman and chief executive officer roles are split.

Compliance with regulations

MonteHodge is in the financial services industry. In most jurisdictions, this industry has a significant amount of regulation. An internal audit department could help ensure compliance with those regulations, especially as additional regulations are expected in the future.

Assistance to financial accountant

The financial accountant in MonteHodge is not qualified. Internal audit could therefore provide assistance in compliance with financial reporting standards, etc as well as recommending control systems.

Against establishing of internal audit department

No statutory requirement

As there is no statutory requirement, the directors may see internal audit as a waste of time and money and therefore not consider establishing the department.

Accounting systems

Many accounting systems are not necessarily complex so the directors may not see the need for another department to review their operations, check integrity, etc.

Family business

MonteHodge is owned by a few shareholders in the same family. There is therefore not the need to provide assurance to other shareholders on the effectiveness of controls, accuracy of financial accounting systems, etc.

Potential cost

There would be a cost of establishing and maintaining the internal audit department. Given that the directors consider focus on profit and trusting employees to be important, then it is unlikely that they would consider the additional cost of establishing internal audit.

Review threat

Some directors may feel challenged by an internal audit department reviewing their work (especially the financial accountant). They are likely therefore not to want to establish an internal audit department.

Examiner's comments

Part (a)

This was a knowledge based question; there was no scenario, so candidates were expected to using their knowledge of internal audit and outsourcing to write their answer. The requirement verb "discuss" indicated that points had to be identified and then explained in the context of outsourcing. Many candidates recognised this requirement and provide eight well explained points. However, many other candidates did not link their comments to outsourcing, which limited the number of marks which could be awarded.

Common errors included:

- Not linking the points made to outsourcing internal audit. Many comments made were generic; that is they could apply to any internal audit department. To gain full credit, comments had to relate to outsourcing.
- Not fully explaining the points made.

Part (b)

The scenario contained many "clues" as to why an internal audit department would be useful (or not) and candidates were expected to identify those points and make specific reference to them in their answers.

The question was worth 12 marks. The requirement verb discuss indicated that some comment was needed to show why the points made were relevant. The marking scheme allowed one mark for mentioning the specific area and a second mark for applying this to the scenario. Many candidates recognised this requirement and provided six well-explained comments to obtain 12 marks. Other candidates did not relate their comments to the scenario at all, which limited the number of marks obtainable per point to 1.

Common errors included:

- Not linking the points made to the scenario. As mentioned above, this limited the number of marks available per point to 1.

- Not fully explaining the points made. Brief comments such as "internal audit would be expensive" only attracted ½ of a mark.

	Marking scheme	Marks
(a)	1 mark for each well-explained point	
	For outsourcing internal audit	
	– Staff recruitment	
	– Skills	
	– Set up time	
	– Costs	
	– Flexibility of staffing arrangements	
	– Independence of external firm	
	Against outsourcing internal audit	
	– Staff turnover	
	– External auditors	
	– Cost	
	– Confidentiality	
	– Control	
	– Independence (where services provided by same firm	
	Maximum marks	8
(b)	Up to 2 marks for each well-explained point	
	For internal audit	
	– VFM audits	
	– Accounting system	
	– Computer systems	
	– Internal control systems	
	– Effect on audit fee	
	– Image to clients	
	– Corporate governance	
	– Lack of control	
	– Law change	
	– Assistance to financial accountant	
	– Nature of industry (financial services)	
	Against internal audit	
	– No statutory requirement	
	– Family business	
	– Potential cost	
	– Review threat	
	Maximum marks	12
	Total	**20**

33   DELPHIC

Key answer tips

This question requires a sound knowledge of audit software, which in conjunction with CAATs is a popular question in F8. Therefore it is vital that you know the sorts of procedures possible with audit software, in particular, who they can be applied to the audit of receivables.

In part (b) it is vital to apply your understanding of the drawbacks of using audit software to the specific information given in the scenario. Points of a general nature will, at best, score limited marks and may not even be relevant at all.

(a)   **Audit procedures using audit software**

Procedure	Reason for procedure
Cast the receivables ledger to ensure it agrees with the total on the receivables control account.	To ensure the completeness and accuracy of recording of items in the receivables ledger and control account.
Compare the balance on each receivable account with its credit limit to ensure this has not been exceeded.	To check for violation of system rules.
Review the balances in the receivables ledger to ensure no balance exceeds total sales to that customer.	To check for unreasonable items in the ledger.
Calculate receivables days for each month end to monitor control of receivables over the year.	To obtaining new/relevant statistical information.
Stratify receivables balances to show all material items and select appropriate sample for testing.	To select items for audit testing.
Produce an aged receivables analysis to assist with the identification of irrecoverable receivables.	To assist with receivables valuation testing.

(b)   **Problems of using audit software**

Cost

There may be substantial setup costs to use the software, especially where the computer systems of the client have not been fully documented, as is the situation in Delphic Co. A cost benefit analysis from the audit point-of-view should be carried out prior to deciding to use audit software.

Lack of software documentation

The computer audit department at Delphic cannot confirm that all system documentation is available, especially for the older 'legacy' systems currently in use. This again confirms the view that use of audit software should be deferred until next year to avoid extensive setup costs which cannot be recouped due to system changes.

Change to clients' systems

Changes to clients' computer systems can result in costly amendments to the audit software. Given that Delphic's systems will change next year, this is almost certain to result in amendments to the software. Starting to use audit software this year is therefore not advisable.

Outputs obtained

The audit manager needs to be clear exactly what audit assertions are to be tested with the audit software and what outputs are expected. Starting testing just to obtain knowledge of the system is inappropriate as testing may be too detailed and output produced that is not required, increasing the cost for the client.

Use of copy files

The use of copy files means that the auditor will not be certain that these are the actual files being used within Delphic's computer systems, especially as the provenance of those files will not be checked. To ensure that the files are genuine either the auditor should supervise the copying or the 'live' files on Delphic's computer systems should be used.

(c)   **Auditing around the computer**

This term means that the 'internal' software of the computer is not documented or audited by the auditor, but that the inputs to the computer are agreed to the expected outputs from the computer.

This method of auditing increases audit risk because:

- The actual computer files and programs are not tested; the auditor has no direct evidence that the programs are working as documented.

- Where errors are found in reconciling inputs to outputs, it may be difficult or even impossible to determine why those errors occurred. Constructive amendments to clients' systems cannot be made and there is an increased likelihood of audit qualifications.

Marking scheme		
(a)	1 for the procedure and 1 for the explanation.	*Marks*
	– Cast receivables ledger	
	– Compare ledger balance to credit limit	
	– Review balances, ensure not excessive	
	– Calculation of receivables days	
	– Stratification of balances/audit sample	
	– Verify items in ledger	
	– Aged receivables analysis	9
(b)	1 for explaining the problem and 1 for resolution. Allow half marks if not related to scenario.	
	– Cost	
	– Lack of software documentation	
	– Change in client's system next year	
	– Outputs obtained	
	– Use of copy files	
	– Old system	
	– File compatibility	8
(c)	Explanation of auditing around computer = 1 mark	
	1 mark for max two problems	
	– Actual computer files not tested	
	– Difficult to track errors	3
	Total	**20**

34 KLE CO

(a) Purpose of three Es

A value for money audit is concerned with obtaining the best possible combination of services for the least resources. It is therefore the pursuit of 'Economy', 'Efficiency' and 'Effectiveness' – sometimes referred to as the three 'Es'.

Economy relates to least cost. The systems in an organisation should operate at a minimum cost associated with an acceptable level of risk.

Efficiency relates to the best use of resources. The goals and objectives of an organisation should be accomplished accurately and on a timely basis with the least use of resources.

Effectiveness provides assurance that organisational objectives will be achieved.

(b) (i) Internal control deficiencies and recommendations

Internal control deficiency	Recommendation
Transfer of information from purchase requisition to order form	
Details of the goods to be ordered are transferred onto the order form after the chief buyer has authorised the initial order requisition. This means that there is no check on the transfer of order information onto the form; clerks could easily make an error or even complete an order form for which there is no valid requisition.	The order form should be signed for authority to purchase and to show that details have been agreed to the requisition.
Purchase requisition	
The purchase requisition is destroyed after goods have been ordered. This means that there is no audit trail to show who ordered the goods or whether the order form has been completed correctly.	The requisition should be filed in the ordering department as audit evidence of goods being ordered.
Order form	
Only the original and one copy of the order form are available – one is sent to the supplier and the second to accounts. This means that there is no record of goods ordered in the ordering department. There are risks that goods could be ordered twice and that late deliveries cannot be identified and queried with suppliers.	The order document is in three copies, with the additional copy being kept in the ordering department.
No copy order to goods inwards department	
A copy of the order form is not available in the goods inwards department. This means that the department does not know what goods to expect and may therefore receive goods that the organisation has not ordered.	A copy of the order is sent to goods inwards. Deliveries are only accepted where they relate to an authorised order.

Internal control deficiency	Recommendation
Goods Received Notes (GRNs) filed in order of goods reference number	
GRNs are filed in order of the reference numbers for the goods being ordered. Filing GRNs in this way provides an internal control deficiency because a numeric sequence check on the completeness of the filing system cannot be performed. GRNs may be missing meaning that the organisation cannot necessarily prove that goods have been received.	GRNs are filed in numeric sequence.

(ii) **Additional deficiencies Issue efficiency – orders authorised by the chief buyer**

All orders are signed by the chief buyer. While this provides good control over the ordering process, the chief buyer does not necessarily need to authorise all orders; orders below a certain limit could be authorised by a junior buyer. This allows the chief buyer more time to concentrate on larger orders and monitor the running of the department.

Issue economy – individual items ordered – no economy of scale

Ordering clerks place orders for goods from each individual order received. However, orders can relate to the same items being ordered from different departments. Orders based on each order do not take into account any volume discounts obtainable from combining orders.

Orders should be combined on a daily or even weekly basis to obtain appropriate economies.

Issue efficiency – routing of GRN

The top copy of the GRN is sent to the accounts department via the ordering department. There does not appear to be any reason for sending the GRN via the ordering department; sending the GRN via this department delays the process of checking the GRN to the order.

To provide an earlier check on whether goods received relate to *bona fide* orders either goods should be checked to the copy order in the goods inwards department, or a copy of the GRN sent directly to accounts.

Issue efficiency – filing GRNs in part number order

This filing system may hinder retrieving a GRN. This gives rise to an efficiency problem that in most situations the GRN number will be known (for example, as a cross reference from the invoice) rather than individual part numbers. Filing in GRN number order will help find GRNs quicker.

35   WALSH

Key answer tips

Your answer to Part (a) should use the question data and give precisely the information which the examiner requires. Note that the answer below is presented in a tabular form. This part is worth half the marks of the question and clearly requires at least five deficiencies and corresponding improvements.

You must expect questions on the paper to be set in a computer environment – this becomes relevant in Part (b) here. The question covers points on both main aspects of computer auditing – controls and computer assisted audit techniques (test data here). As far as access controls are concerned, remember that you are dealing with payroll – these controls are very important here because of the sensitive nature of the data.

Note that in Part (b) the second requirement to recommend test data is worth more marks than the first which requires recommendations on access and program controls.

(a)   **Use of Computer-Assisted Audit Techniques (CAATs)**

Testing programmed controls

–   Reliance on CAATs will force the auditor to rely on programmed controls during an audit; in fact using CAATs may be the only way to test controls within a computer system. Use of the CAAT enables the auditor to meet the auditing standard requirement of obtaining appropriate audit evidence.

–   For example, in Walsh Co, an overtime report is generated by the computer, although this can also be overridden by the accountant. Test data can be used to check that the overtime report is being created correctly and audit software can monitor that only the accountant's password can be used to override the overtime payment.

Test larger number of items

–   Using CAATs enables the auditor to test a larger number of items quickly and accurately, meeting the auditing standard requirement of obtaining sufficient audit evidence.

–   Using audit software, the auditor can check the deduction and net pay calculations of a significant proportion of wages calculations – or all of them if necessary. Checking each calculation manually would take a long time.

Test actual accounting records

–   Using CAATs enables the auditor to test the actual accounting records (the electronic version) rather than relying on printouts or other copies of the data. It is always appropriate for the auditor to test original documentation where possible.

–   In the case of Walsh, the actual wages will be tested rather than any paper copies.

Cost

- After initial set-up costs, using CAATs is likely to be cost effective; the same audit software programs can be run each year as long as the client does not change the accounting systems.

- In Walsh Co, the system has just been implemented. Hopefully the wages system will be used for a number of years, making the use of CAATs cost-effective for the audit firm.

(b) **Examples of the use of audit software**

- Calculation checks. For example, re-calculation of net pay for a number of employees to ensure the mathematical calculation is correct.

- Reviewing the list of employees paid each week/month and printing a list of employees, who have not be been paid, for further investigation.

- Detecting unreasonable items. Reviewing the list of net wages for large or negative payments.

- Detecting violation of system rules. For example, where other people besides the accountant have been overriding overtime payments or employees amending their own gross wages.

- Conducting new analysis as part of the analytical review of wages. For example, calculating total wages for the year from the number of employees and average wages paid.

- Completeness checks – ensuring there is an electronic record of all employees who 'clocked in' for a day's work and 'clocked out' again.

(c) **Audit test data consists of data submitted by the auditor for processing on the client's computer-based accounting systems**.

The data can be processed during a normal processing run (a 'live' testing situation) or in a special run outside of the normal processing cycle (a 'dead' testing situation).

In Walsh, the auditor can create a 'dummy employee' record on the wages master file, and then use a magnetic card to mimic that employee working a certain number of hours in the company over the course of, for example, one week.

Knowing how many hours has been input into the wages system; the auditor can calculate the expected net pay and then compare this to the actual net pay produced by the computer system.

If the amounts agree then this provides appropriate audit evidence of the accuracy of recording and processing of the wages software.

The problems of using this audit technique include:

- The possibility that the client's computer system will be damaged by the testing being undertaken by the auditor. For example, by errors being caused by entering data that the client's software cannot process.

- The need to reverse or remove any transactions input by the auditor. The transactions may be incorrectly or incompletely removed leaving dummy data in the client's live computer system.

- Use of test data can be expensive – the auditor needs to ensure that the benefit gained from the test outweighs the expense.

- In this situation, it will take a long time to input employee details and there may be more efficient audit tests available.

36   JAYNE

Key answer tips

Questions on different types of confirmations come up frequently, so make sure you can discuss them. You also need, as always, a good knowledge of the financial statement assertions.

The procedures to get a bank letter are book knowledge and should present no problem.

(a)   (i)   Four examples of external confirmations are:

1   Accounts receivable letter

2   Solicitor letter

3   Bank report letter

4   Inventory held by third parties.

(ii)   Note one example of each assertion only required.

Accounts receivable letter

This letter provides evidence of the existence of the receivable when a reply is returned from that receivable direct to the auditor.

The letter provides evidence on cut-off because sales or cash receipts recorded in the incorrect accounting period will have to be reconciled to the balance provided by the receivable.

The letter does not provide evidence of completeness of the receivables balance because receivables may not query balances which are understated.

The letter does not provide evidence of the valuation of the receivables balance because the receivable cannot be expected to list all outstanding balances and confirmation of the debt does not mean it will be paid.

Solicitor letter

A solicitor letter provides evidence as to the existence of claims at the period-end as the solicitor will confirm specific claims.

However, the letter does not necessarily confirm the valuation of claims due to uncertainty about the future or the completeness of any legal claims as solicitors do not normally provide a list of all claims – they prefer to comment only on claims they are actually asked about.

Bank report letter

A bank confirmation letter provides good evidence on the existence of the company's bank accounts as the bank has confirmed this information in writing.

A bank letter cannot necessarily be relied on to provide complete or accurate information. Most banks place a disclaimer on the letter of 'errors and omissions excepted' indicating that the auditor must review this evidence against other cash and bank evidence obtained.

Inventory held by third parties

A letter from the third party holding the inventory will provide evidence of the existence of that inventory because the third party has confirmed this in writing.

However, the letter does not provide evidence regarding the valuation of the inventory; confirming something exists does not necessarily mean it is in good condition.

(b)   (i)   Procedure for obtaining a bank letter

The auditor should consider if a bank letter is required. For the audit of Jayne Co the letter is required as the company has significant cash transactions and a loan from the bank.

The auditor will produce a confirmation letter in accordance with local audit regulations and practices.

The letter will be sent to the client to sign and authorise disclosure and then it will be forwarded on to Jayne's bank.

Alternatively, the client may already have provided a standard authority for the bank to respond to a bank letter each year. In this case separate authority would not be required.

Ideally the letter should be sent before the end of the accounting period to enable the bank to complete it on a timely basis, e.g. at the year-end.

The bank will complete the letter and send it back directly to the auditor.

Audit procedures on the bank letter include:

–   Agree the balances for each bank account to the relevant bank reconciliation and the year-end balance in the financial statements.

–   Agree total interest charges on the letter to the interest expense account in the general ledger.

–   For any details of loans, ensure repayment terms are correctly disclosed in the financial statements between current and non-current liabilities.

(ii)   Substantive procedures for the audit of bank balances.

(1)   Obtain a copy of the year-end trial balance.

Agree the bank balance on the trial balance to

–   the year-end bank balance on the computer system

–   the balance on the financial statements.

(2)   Obtain a copy of Jayne Co's bank reconciliation.

–   Cast the reconciliation

–   Agree the bank balance to the trial balance.

–   Agree the bank statement balance to the year-end bank statement.

–   Agree any unpresented lodgements to the bank statement after the end of the year

–   Agree any unpresented cheques or similar expenses to the cash book before the end of the year and the bank statements after the end of the year.

37   TELA & CO   *Walk in the footsteps of a top tutor*

Key answer tips

Corporate governance has become an established exam topic due to its significance for listed companies as they attempt to shake off the shadow of high profile frauds such as Enron. The issues are easy to identify as the volume of information provided is modest, but ensure your answer contains specific recommendations and explanations as it is easy to waffle without providing clear mark scoring points! The highlighted words are key phrases that markers are looking for.

Memo

From: A Manager, Tela & Co
To: Jumper & Co
Subject: Corporate Governance in the SGCC Company
Date: 13 June 2006

As requested, I write to explain where your client SGCC does not appear to be following appropriate corporate governance codes and to recommend changes to ensure that the principles of good corporate governance are being followed.

Chief Executive Officer (CEO) and Chairman

Mr Sheppard is both CEO and chairman of SGCC. Corporate governance indicates that the person responsible for running the company (the CEO) and the person responsible for controlling the board (the chairman) should be different people. This is to ensure that no one individual has unrestricted powers of decision.

I recommend that Mr Sheppard is either the CEO or the chairman and that a second individual is appointed to the other post to ensure that Mr Sheppard does not have too much power in SGCC.

Composition of board

The current board ratio of executive to non-executive directors is 5:2. This means that the executive directors can dominate the board proceedings. Corporate governance codes suggest that there should be a balance of executive and non-executive directors so this cannot happen. A minimum of three non-executive directors are also normally recommended, although reports such as Cadbury note this may be difficult to achieve.

I recommend that the number of executive and non-executive directors is equal to help ensure no one group dominates the board. This will mean appointing more non-executive directors to SGCC.

Director appointment

At present, Mr Sheppard appoints directors to the board, giving him absolute authority over who is appointed. This makes the appointment procedure and qualities directors are being appointed against difficult to determine. Corporate governance suggests that appointment procedures should be transparent so that the suitability of directors for board positions can be clearly seen.

I recommend that an appointments committee is established comprising three non-executive directors to ensure there is no bias in board appointments. Formal job descriptions should also be published making the appointment process more transparent.

Review of board performance

It is correct that the performance of senior managers is reviewed, but this principle should also be applied to the board. While Mr Sheppard may undertake some review, this is not transparent and it is not clear what targets the board either met or did not meet.

I recommend that performance targets are set for each director and actual performance assessed against these on a regular basis. Reasons for underperformance should also be ascertained and where appropriate, changes made to the composition of the board.

Board pay

At present, board members' pay is set by Mr Sheppard. This process breaches principles of good governance because the remuneration structure is not transparent and Mr Sheppard sets his own pay. Mr Sheppard could easily be setting remuneration levels based on his own judgements without any objective criteria.

I recommend that a remuneration committee is established comprising three non-executive directors. They will set remuneration levels for the board, taking into account current salary levels and the performance of board members. Remuneration should also be linked to performance, to encourage a high standard of work.

Internal control

The system of internal control in SGCC does not appear to be reviewed correctly. While external auditors will review the control system, this review is based on their audit requirement and cannot be relied on to test the overall effectiveness of the system.

I recommend that some more formal review of internal control is carried out, perhaps by establishing an internal audit department, as noted below. The relationship with the company's auditors must also be reviewed so that the work of the board and the auditors regarding internal control is understood by both parties.

Internal audit

SGCC does not have an internal audit department. Given the lack of formal review of internal control in the company, this is surprising. Good corporate governance implies that the control system is monitored and that an internal audit department is established to carry out this task.

I recommend that an internal audit department is established, reporting initially to the audit committee who will monitor internal control and then summarise reports for the board.

Financial statements

There appears to be acceptable disclosure in the financial statements regarding the past results of the company. However, the board should also provide an indication of how the company will perform in the future, by a forecast review of operations or similar statement. This is partly to enable investors to assess the value of their investment in the company.

I therefore recommend that the annual accounts of SGCC include some indication of the future operations of the company.

Audit committee

There is no mention in the report of an audit committee. Good corporate governance implies that there is some formal method of monitoring external auditors as well as checking that the reports from the external auditors are given appropriate attention in the company.

I recommend that an audit committee is established – made up from non-executive directors. The committee will receive reports from the external and internal auditors (as mentioned above) and ensure that the board takes appropriate action on these reports.

I hope this information is useful. Please contact me again if you require any further assistance.

Sincerely
Ann C. Outent

38   ZPM

Key answer tips

Part (a) is a 'bread and butter', i.e. standard, requirement. Remember that internal audit questions are now a regular feature of the exam.

Part (b) focuses on the differing roles of internal and external audit, and the interaction between them. The internal audit department is fundamentally an internal control established by management, and will have to be assessed if reliance is to be placed upon them.

(a)   Factors to consider when evaluating and testing the work of the internal auditor include:

*   A check that the work is performed by persons having adequate technical training and proficiency as internal auditors, by ensuring appropriate training programmes are in place and the auditor has appropriate qualifications.

*   Ensuring that the work of assistants is properly supervised, reviewed and documented by reviewing the procedure manuals of the internal audit and the audit working papers produced.

*   Determining that sufficient and appropriate audit evidence is obtained to afford a reasonable basis for the conclusions reached, again by reviewing the internal auditor's working papers.

*   Checking that the conclusions reached are appropriate in the circumstances and that any reports prepared are consistent with the results of the work performed by reviewing the work performed and the reports produced.

*   Ensuring any exceptions or unusual matters disclosed by internal audit are properly resolved by the external auditor and management.

(b)   (i)   **Objectives of internal audit**

Year-end inventory count

The main aim of the year-end inventory count is to ensure that the figure for inventory in the financial statements is accurate. The objective of the internal audit department is to check the accuracy of the inventory count to ensure that the physical goods inventory is correctly stated on the inventory sheets. This objective is achieved by checking the control system over counting inventory. Internal audit work will involve ensuring that all inventory is counted, teams of two people are counting inventory, and then performing test counts to determine the accuracy of the test counts.

Internal controls over procurement systems

The internal auditor will be ensuring that the procurement system is achieving its key objectives and operating according to company guidelines. Specific aims will include:

- Ensuring purchases are authorised.
- Quantity discounts are obtained.
- Inventory received is recorded on goods received notes or similar.

Reviewing operations of the marketing department

The internal auditor will review the work of the marketing department with aims such as ensuring that the process is being managed effectively and information is available to the marketing manager as required. Where deficiencies in the information provided are noted, then an internal audit report will highlight those deficiencies and make recommendations for improvement to the information systems. The objectives of internal audit in this case are more to ensuring the efficiency of operations rather than any specific financial objective.

(ii) **Objectives of the external auditor**

Year-end inventory count

The external auditor also needs to ensure that the figure for inventory is materially correct in the financial statements. Part of the work of the external auditor is to attend the physical inventory count to ensure that the quantities and condition of inventory is correctly recorded. Given that ZPM does not appear to have any perishable inventory, the main objective will be to ensure correct recording of inventory quantity.

Internal controls over procurement systems

The external auditor will test the procurement system with the overall objective of determining that the purchases and payables figures in the financial statements are correct. The objectives of testing will be to ensure that the control system over procurement is operating efficiently, and ensure complete and accurate recording of purchases and payables liabilities. If errors are found then this implies that the financial statements could also contain errors.

Reviewing operations of the marketing department

As the operations of the marketing department do not normally impact on the financial statements, the external auditor may not actually review this function.

(iii) **Reliance by the external auditor**

Year-end inventory count

ZPM has 103 stores – which is likely to mean that the external auditor will not be able to attend the inventory count in all stores, simply due to lack of staff.

However, if inventory count procedures are the same at all stores, then reliance can be placed on the internal auditor to attend some stores and check that the internal control systems are being correctly applied in those stores. This reliance does not mean that the external auditor does not carry out any work; the external auditor will compare results from stores tested with those of the internal auditor. Results should be about the same; any differences in terms of errors found will be investigated, and reasons for those differences obtained.

Internal controls over procurement systems

The external auditor may rely on the work of the internal auditor regarding the procurement systems, where the work of the internal auditor is relevant to the financial statements. Some areas such as ensuring quantity discounts are obtained are less important than ensuring completeness of recording of liabilities. Again, the external auditor must perform some work on the procurement systems; the presence of an internal auditor simply means that the work can be reduced.

Reviewing operations of the marketing department

Given that the external auditor does not need to review the operations of the marketing department then no formal reliance is needed on the work of the internal auditor. However, internal audit reports may be reviewed to determine, for example, the effectiveness of advertising spend etc to help determine the going concern situation of the company. In the case of ZPM, the effectiveness of advertising new stores could be reviewed.

39   OCTBALL

Key answer tips

There are no tricks in this question, but you do have to make sure you read the requirements carefully, as the question is not quite what you'd expect. In particular you must ensure that in part (a) you don't discuss the advantages and disadvantages of outsourcing, as that's not what's being asked. In part (c) ensure that the controls you mention are those that may be operated by the client.

(a)   **Benefits of outsourcing to NFA**

Expertise available

The NFA partnership will be able to provide the necessary expertise for internal audit work. They may be able to provide a broader range of expertise as they serve many different clients therefore staff may be available for specialist work that Octball could not afford to employ.

Buy-in skills as necessary

If internal audit is only required for specific functions or particular jobs each year then the expertise can be purchased as required. Taking this approach will minimise in-house costs.

Independence/Qualifications

No information is provided on the qualification of staff in NFA, although as an independent firm it is likely that care will be taken that staff do remain independent and have the appropriate qualifications in order that they can provide an appropriate high level of service.

Audit techniques – training

Outsourcing will remove the need for training internal staff. Effectively training will be provided for 'free' as the outsourcing firm will be responsible for keeping staff up-to-date with new auditing techniques and processes.

Problems with outsourcing to NFA

Fee pressure

NFA may experience some fee pressure, but only in respect of maintaining cost effectiveness of the internal audit department. The relationship needs to be managed carefully to ensure that NFA do not decrease the quality of their work due to insufficient fees.

Knowledge

The NFA partnership will not have any prior knowledge of Octball. This will be a disadvantage as this will mean the partnership will need time to ascertain the accounting systems and controls etc in Octball before commencing work. However, provision of an independent view may identify control deficiencies etc that the current internal audit department have missed.

Location

The NFA partnership may not be able to provide this service to Octball as they are a local firm and therefore the issue of travel and working away from home would remain.

Continuity of service – staffing

As provision of audit services is the NFA partnership's main activity, they should also be able to budget for client requirements although this cannot be guaranteed as staff may still leave. However, as a larger internal auditing firm, they will be able to offer staff better career progression which should assist staff retention.

(b) **Items to be considered by T&M**

Independence

T&M need to ensure that independence can be maintained in a number of areas:

- Independence regarding recommending systems or preparing working papers and subsequent checking of those systems or working papers. While the internal audit department may need to carry out these functions, T&M must ensure that separate staff are used to provide the internal and external audit functions.

- Staff from T&M will be expected to follow the ethical guidance of ACCA which means that steps will be taken to avoid conflicts of interest or other independence issues such as close personal relationships building up with staff in Octball. Any real or perceived threats to independence will lower the overall trust that can be placed on internal audit reports produced by T&M.

Training

As a firm of auditors, T&M will automatically provide training for its staff as part of the in-house compliance with association regulations (e.g. compulsory CPD was introduced from January 2005). T&M will need to ensure that staff providing the internal audit function to Octball are aware of relevant guidance for internal auditors.

Skills

T&M must ensure that they have staff with the necessary skills and sufficient time to undertake the internal audit work in Octball. Skills may not be an issue because staff in T&M will already understand audit procedures.

Fee pressure

There may be fee pressure on T&M, either to maintain the cost effectiveness of the internal audit department, or to maintain the competitiveness of the audit fee itself in order to keep the internal audit work.

Knowledge

As external auditors, T&M will already have knowledge of Octball. This will assist in establishing the internal audit department as systems documentation will already be available and the audit firm will already be aware of potential deficiencies in the control systems.

(c) **Controls to maintain the standard of the internal audit department**

- If T&M are appointed, ensure that the internal and external audit is managed by different departments in the firm.

- Setting and review of performance measures such as cost, areas reviewed, etc with explanations obtained for any significant variances.

- Use of appropriate audit methodology, including clear documentation of audit work carried out, adequate review, and appropriate conclusions drawn.

- Review of working papers by myself, ensuring adherence to International Standards on Auditing where appropriate and any in-house standards on auditing.

- The work plan for internal audit is agreed prior to work commencing and this is followed by the outsourcing company.

COMPLETION AND REPORTING

40 **MEDIMADE CO (A)** *Walk in the footsteps of a top tutor*

Key answer tips

This is a good example of how a question combines an understanding of underlying accounting concepts and how they are audited.

Part (a) requires a simple definition of going concern.

Part (b) asks you to provide examples of why Medimade may not be a going concern. Whilst this requires little more than common business sense you must make sure your responses are relevant to the scenario and not from a pre-learnt list of indicators.

Part (c) then introduces the auditing aspect and asks you what procedures you would perform during the audit of Medimade. Again, whilst there are general procedures, try and make your answers specific to the audit of Medimade (i.e. your procedures should be relevant to the concerns you identified in b).

Part (d) is the most difficult section. Remember; when discussing the audit report there are two ways it can be modified: by modifying the wording of your opinion or by adding an additional paragraph. The latter is never used to explain the opinion and it has no affect on it.

The highlighted words are key phases that markers are looking for.

(a) The going concern assumption means that management believes the company will continue in business for the foreseeable future. Foreseeable future is not defined in ISA 570 *Going Concern*. However under IAS 1 *Presentation of Financial Statements*, this period is a minimum of 12 months after the year end.

IAS 1 *Presentation of Financial Statements* requires that management automatically prepare financial statements on a going concern basis unless they believe that the company will soon cease trading.

(b)

Indicator	Why could impact going concern
Medimade has seen a significant decline in demand for its products.	If the company is not able to increase demand for its products then it will struggle to generate sufficient operating cash flows leading to going concern difficulties.
Medimade generates 90% of its revenue through sales of just two products, and this market has now become very competitive.	As the market is very competitive and Medimade has only two products then it is very dependent on these and must ensure that it makes sufficient sales as otherwise it may face difficulties in meeting all expenses.
Lack of investment in future product development	As current products reach the end of their life-cycle they will bring in diminishing cash flows. Without new products to generate future income

Indicator	Why could impact going concern
	operating cash flows will be strained.
The company is struggling to recruit suitably trained scientific staff to develop new products.	The company has decided that it needs to develop new products, however, this is a highly specialised area and therefore it needs sufficiently trained staff. If it cannot recruit enough staff then it could hold up the product development and stop the company from increasing revenue.
Medimade was unable to obtain suitable funding for its $2m investment in plant and machinery.	If Medimade was unable to obtain finance for its investment, then this could indicate that the banks deem the company to be too risky to lend money to. They may be concerned that Medimade is unable to meet its loan payments, suggesting cash flow problems.
Some trade payables have been paid much later than their due dates.	Failing to make payments to suppliers on time could ultimately lead to some of them refusing to supply Medimade. Therefore the company may need to find alternative suppliers and they could be more expensive which will decrease operating cash flows and profits.
Some suppliers have withdrawn credit terms from Medimade resulting in cash on delivery payments.	As Medimade must now make cash on delivery payments, then it puts additional pressure on the company's overdraft, which has already grown substantially. This is because the company has to pay for goods in advance but it may not receive cash from its receivables for some time later.
The overdraft facility has increased substantially and is due for renewal next month.	Medimade's overdraft has grown significantly and it is heavily dependent on it to pay its expenses. If the bank does not renew the overdraft and the company is unable to obtain alternative finance then it may not be able to continue to trade.
The cash flow forecast has shown a significantly worsening position.	The future cash outflows are greater than the inflows and this position is worsening rather than improving. If Medimade cannot start to reverse this position, then it may have difficulties in funding its operating activities.

(c) Obtain the company's cash flow forecast and review the cash in and out flows. Assess the assumptions for reasonableness and discuss the findings with management to understand if the company will have sufficient cash flows.

Perform a sensitivity analysis on the cash flows to understand the margin of safety the company has in terms of its net cash in/out flow.

Review any current agreements with the bank to determine whether any key ratios have been breached. Review any bank correspondence to assess the likelihood of the bank renewing the overdraft facility.

Discuss with the directors whether they have contacted any alternative banks for finance to assess whether they have any other means of repaying the bank overdraft.

Review the company's post year end sales and order book to assess if the levels of trade are likely to increase and if the revenue figures in the cash flow forecast are reasonable.

Review post year end correspondence with suppliers to identify if any further restrictions in credit have arisen, and if so ensure that the cash flow forecast reflects an immediate payment for trade payables.

Enquire of the lawyers of Medimade as to the existence of litigation and claims, if any exist then consider their materiality and impact on the going concern basis.

Perform audit tests in relation to subsequent events to identify any items that might indicate or mitigate the risk of going concern not being appropriate.

Review the post year end board minutes to identify any other issues that might indicate financial difficulties for the company. Review post year end management accounts to assess if in line with cash flow forecast.

Consider whether any additional disclosures as required by IAS 1 *Presentation of Financial Statements* in relation to material uncertainties over going concern should be made in the financial statements.

Obtain a written representation confirming the director's view that Medimade is a going concern.

(d) The directors of Medimade have agreed to make going concern disclosures, however, the impact on the audit report will be dependent on the adequacy of these disclosures. If the disclosures are adequate, then the audit report will be unmodified. However, an emphasis of matter paragraph would be required.

This will state that the audit report is not modified, identify that there is a material uncertainty and will cross reference to the disclosure note made by management, this paragraph would be included after the opinion paragraph.

If the disclosures made by management are not adequate the audit report will need to be modified. A material misstatement modification will be required, depending on the materiality of the issue this will be either qualified or an adverse opinion.

A paragraph describing the matter giving rise to the modification will be included just before the opinion paragraph and this will clearly identify the going concern uncertainty. The opinion paragraph will be amended to state 'except for' or the accounts are not fairly presented.

ACCA marking scheme		
		Marks
(a)	Up to 1 mark per point	
	– Continue to trade for foreseeable future	
	– Foreseeable future not defined ISA 570, but IAS 1 states minimum 12 months after year end	
	– IAS 1 *Accounts* automatically ongoing concern basis	
		———
	Maximum	2
(b)	½ mark per indicator and up to 1 mark per description of why this could indicate going concern problems for Medimade:	
	– Decline in demand	
	– Dependent on two products	
	– Lack of investment in future product development	
	– Unable to recruit staff	
	– Inability to obtain funding	
	– Failing to pay payables on time	
	– Withdrawal of credit terms	
	– Overdraft facility due for renewal	
	– Cash flow forecast shows worsening position	
		———
	Maximum	8

ACCA marking scheme		
		Marks
(c)	Up to 1 mark per well explained point – If the procedure does not clearly explain how this will help the auditor to consider going concern then a 1/2 mark only should be awarded:	
	– Review cash flow forecasts	
	– Sensitivity analysis	
	– Review bank agreements, breach of key ratios	
	– Review bank correspondence	
	– Discuss if alternative finance obtained	
	– Review post year end sales and order book	
	– Review suppliers correspondence	
	– Inquire lawyers any litigation	
	– Subsequent events	
	– Board minutes	
	– Management accounts	
	– Consider additional disclosures under IAS 1	
	– Written representation	
	Maximum	6
(d)	Up to 1 mark per point	
	– Depends on adequacy of disclosures	
	– Adequately disclosed – unmodified	
	– Emphasis of matter para – after opinion	
	– Not adequately disclosed – modified	
	– Material misstatement	
	– Add paragraph before opinion and impact on opinion paragraph	
		4
Total		20

41 HAVE A BITE CO (A) *Walk in the footsteps of a top tutor*

Key answer tips

Parts (a) and (b) of the question are unusual in question 5 because systems and controls usually feature elsewhere in the exam. The new examiner has stated that in the future this question will usually incorporate concepts of audit completion, review and reporting.

Parts (c) and (d) are more typical of question 5 in that they contain a contentious issue that could have an impact on the audit report. Part (c) should not pose too many problems but it is vital that you identify the evidence you would seek **and** explain its use to the auditor. Remember; in part (d) you have to consider whether the audit report needs to be modified, either by modifying the opinion or by adding an additional paragraph. If you believe it is the former then also remember the opinion can only be modified due to a material misstatement or a lack of evidence. The wording of the opinion then depends upon whether the matter is simply material or whether it is also pervasive.

The highlighted words are key phases that markers are looking for.

(a) As regards accounts payable there are many different assertions that have to be addressed. Some relevant assertions are set out below:

(i) Rights and obligations – Accounts payable represent amounts actually due by the company, that is, there is an obligation, taking into account:

- the actual performance of services for the company; or
- transfer of title in goods transferred to the company; and
- cash payments or other genuine debit entry.

(ii) Valuation and allocation – Accounts payable have been correctly valued taking into account original transaction amounts and such matters as trade discounts and local sales tax.

(iii) Existence – The original transaction amounts are valid and the liability exists.

(iv) Completeness – All accounts payable are recorded in the accounting records.

(b) Controls that the company has in place to reduce the risk associated with purchases of food and its preparation in the kitchen, together with relevant audit procedures on controls testing, would include the following:

Tutorial note

For a restaurant it is important that food quality is good and in particular that it does not present any danger to the customer arising from deterioration or poor practices in its preparation.

	Controls	**Audit Procedures**
(i)	Overall authority for food purchasing should be in the hands of a designated person to ensure that the food purchased is of the desired quality. This is often in the hands of the head chef.	Review the company's organisation chart and identify the person with overall responsibility for food purchasing. Discuss with management his or her background and. expertise.
(ii)	There should be a list of approved suppliers to ensure that the food comes from sources known for their quality.	Examine the list of approved suppliers of food and check that there are no purchases of food from other parties.
(iii)	On receipt of food, whether meat, fish, or vegetables and fruit, it should be carefully inspected by informed people, including those responsible for food preparation. This would be to ensure that it was of the desired quality(as well as quantity). A goods received note (GRN) should be signed to provide evidence of receipt and inspection.	Examine a sample of GRNs to ensure that all bear an approved signature indicating that food has been inspected for quality on receipt.

	Controls	Audit Procedures
(iv)	Food purchased should be kept in a clean place and refrigerated, if necessary. This would be to ensure that. it has kept its quality.	Examine the food storage areas, including refrigerators, on a surprise basis to ensure they are clean and tidy. Ensure that the refrigerators are maintained at the correct temperature. Another test in this area might be to examine reports of local authority and other inspectors to ensure they were happy that the food was being properly stored.
(v)	Strict adherence to use-by dates to ensure that no poor quality food is prepared. *(Tutorial note: Marks would also be available for additional controls such as:* • Staff training on basic food hygiene. disposed of. • Rotation of inventory. • Recording temperatures of cooked/reheated food.)*	Check that there is no food on the premises which is past its use-by date. Discuss with management what happens to food which is past its use-by date, that is, how it is disposed of.

(c) Evidence collected by the auditor to enable a conclusion to be formed on the likelihood of the claim being successful (that is, whether a provision would be necessary according to IAS 37 Provisions, Contingent Liabilities and Contingent Assets) includes:

	Evidence	Explanation
(i)	Obtain the written claim by the customer.	This would tell you the reason why the claim was being made and provide other relevant details, such as whether the customer dined in the restaurant or purchased carry-out food, and the date when the alleged food poisoning took place.
(ii)	Review the controls in force over purchases and food preparation (see (b) above).	This would be to ensure that the company controls appeared to be effective.
(iii)	Obtain written reports concerning any inspections that had been carried out by company staff or third parties in the food store and food preparation areas	This would provide evidence about any problems that had arisen affecting food quality. Discuss with management the actions that were taken to correct any problems that had arisen.
(iv)	Discuss the matter with the company's lawyers to obtain their view on the likelihood of the claim being successful.	This would provide evidence from a professional third party as to the likelihood of the claim succeeding and the reasons why the lawyers had reached their conclusion.

	Evidence	Explanation
(v)	Obtain management representations regarding the likelihood of the claim succeeding. • Review of board minutes to assess management's view of the likelihood of the claim succeeding • Discussions with management about any previous claims and their outcome.	This is internal evidence and should be approached with professional scepticism, but it would provide the auditor with the views of an informed group of people.

(d) As you have concluded that the likelihood of the claim being successful is only possible, it would be appropriate for the company to explain the contingent liability by way of note as required by IAS 37, giving a description of the nature of the contingent liability, an estimate of its financial effect, an indication of the uncertainties relating to the amount and timing and the possibility of any reimbursement.

If the company includes a note of this nature, there would be no need to modify your audit opinion, however if the litigation is viewed to be exceptional then an emphasis of matter paragraph might be appropriate. However, if the contingency is not disclosed, the auditor would modify the audit opinion on the grounds of a material but not pervasive misstatement. Therefore a qualified opinion would be given and the details of the contingent liability disclosed in the basis of opinion paragraph. The auditor should try to persuade management to include the disclosure before issuing the modified opinion.

Tutorial note

A qualified opinion would be appropriate as the contingent loss is material but not pervasive, i.e. it does not render the accounts unreliable as a whole. The financial figures disclose in the various accounts and notes and not affected and would – assuming no other misstatements – provide a reliable basis for making decisions.

	ACCA marking scheme	
		Marks
(a)	**Accounts payable assertions** ½ mark for identification of assertion and up to 1 mark for each explanation of assertion, maximum 6. Rights and obligation Valuation and allocation Existence Completeness Maximum marks	6.0
(b)	**Control risk and audit procedures** Up to 1 mark for each control identified, but maximum 2. Up to 1 mark for each audit procedure, but maximum 2. Overall authority Approved suppliers Inspection on receipt Storage of food Use-by dates Basic food hygiene training Rotation of inventory Recording temperatures of cooked/reheated food Maximum marks	4.0
(c)	**Evidence on claim** 1 mark for identification of each item of evidence and up to a further 1 mark for explanation. Written claim Review controls Inspection reports View of lawyer Management representations Review of board minutes Discussions with management about previous claims Maximum marks	6.0
(d)	**Reporting in financial statements** Up to 1 mark for assessing meaning of probable and possible and a further mark for showing how the matter should be disclosed, but maximum 2. Meaning of possibility Therefore contingent liability Note disclosure Audit reporting Up to 1 mark for each relevant point, but maximum 2. If contingent liability correctly included then unmodified opinion Emphasis of matter paragraph if litigation exceptional Material matter if not disclosed Therefore qualified opinion Disclosures in audit report Maximum marks	4.0
Total		20.0

42 TYE *Walk in the footsteps of a top tutor*

Key answer tips

This question was set on the back of an examiner's article regarding ISA 240 *Fraud and Error*. Therefore a question regarding some form of fraudulent accounting was expected.

However, it can be clearly seen in the question that the practice chosen by the directors contravenes financial reporting standards. So the error, and the intention of directors, is quite clear.

It is also vital to note that audit work has been **completed**! This point was so important that the examiner wrote it twice in the question. However, many candidates missed this key point.

Once you have clarified those points during your reading of the scenario the remainder of the question becomes somewhat more straightforward. In fact many marks can be gained through simple repetition of facts from the article mentioned above.

The highlighted words are key phases that markers are looking for.

(a)   **Valuation of aviation inventory**

- Review GAAP to ensure that there are no exceptions for aviation fuel or inventory held for emergency purposes which would suggest a market valuation should be used.

- Calculate the difference in valuation. The error in inventory valuation is $105 * 6,000 barrels or $630k, which is a material amount compared to profit.

- Review prior year working papers to determine whether a similar situation occurred last year and ascertain the outcome at that stage.

- Discuss the matter with the directors to obtain reasons why they believe that market value should be used for the inventory this year.

- Warn the directors that in your opinion, aviation fuel should be valued at the lower of cost or net realisable value (that is $15/barrel) and that using market value will result in a modification to the audit report.

- If the directors now amend the financial statements to show inventory valued at cost, then consider mentioning the issue in the deficiency letter and do not modify the audit report in respect of this matter.

- If the directors will not amend the financial statements, quantify the effect of the disagreement in the valuation method

- the sum of $630,000 is material to the financial statements as Tye Co's income statement figure is decreased from a small loss to a loss of $130,000 although net assets decrease by only about 0.3%.

- Obtain a written representation letter from the directors of Tye Co confirming that market value is to be used for the emergency inventory of aviation fuel.

- If the directors will not amend the financial statements, draft the relevant sections of the audit report showing a qualification on the grounds that the financial statements are not free from material misstatement.

(b) (i) **External auditor responsibilities regarding detection of fraud**

Overall responsibility of auditor

The external auditor is primarily responsible for the audit opinion on the financial statements following the international auditing standards (ISAs). ISA 240 (Redrafted) *The Auditor's Responsibilities Relating to Fraud in an Audit of Financial Statements* is relevant to audit work regarding fraud.

The main focus of audit work is therefore to ensure that the financial statements show a true and fair view. The detection of fraud is therefore not the main focus of the external auditor's work. An auditor is responsible for obtaining reasonable assurance that the financial statements as a whole are free from material misstatement, whether caused by fraud or error.

The auditor is responsible for maintaining an attitude of professional scepticism throughout the audit, considering the potential for management override of controls and recognising the fact that audit procedures that are effective for detecting error may not be effective for detecting fraud.

Materiality

ISA 240 states that the auditor should reduce audit risk to an acceptably low level.

Therefore, in reaching the audit opinion and performing audit work, the external auditor takes into account the concept of materiality. In other words, the external auditor is not responsible for checking all the transactions. Audit procedures are planned to have a reasonable likelihood of identifying material fraud.

Discussion among the audit team

A discussion is required among the engagement team placing particular emphasis on how and where the entity's financial statements may be susceptible to material misstatement due to faud, including how fraud might occur.

Identification of fraud

In situations where the external auditor does detect fraud, then the auditor will need to consider the implications for the entire audit. In other words, the external auditor has a responsibility to extend testing into other areas because the risk of providing an incorrect audit opinion will have increased.

(ii) **Groups to report fraud to**

Report to audit committee

Disclose the situation to the audit committee as they are charged with maintaining a high standard of governance in the company.

The committee should be able to discuss the situation with the directors and recommend that they take appropriate action e.g. amend the financial statements.

Report to government

As Tye Co is acting under a government contract, and the over-statement of inventory will mean Tye Co breaches that contract (the reported profit becoming a loss), then the auditor may have to report the situation directly to the government. The auditor of Tye Co needs to review the contract to confirm the reporting required under that contract.

Report to members

If the financial statements do not show a true and fair view then the auditor needs to report this fact to the members of Tye Co. The audit report will be modified by the inclusion of a qualified or an adverse opinion (depending on materiality) and information concerning the reason for the material misstatement. In this case the auditor is likely to state factually the problem of inventory quantities being incorrect, rather than stating or implying that the directors are involved in fraud.

Report to professional body

If the auditor is uncertain as to the correct course of action, advice may be obtained from the auditor's professional body. Depending on the advice received, the auditor may simply report to the members in the audit report, although resignation and the convening of a general meeting is another reporting option.

(iii) **Intimidation threat – safeguards**

In response to the implied threat of dismissal if the audit report is modified regarding the potential fraud/error, the following safeguards are available to the auditor.

Discuss with audit committee

The situation can be discussed with the audit committee. As the audit committee should comprise non-executive directors, they will be able to discuss the situation with the finance director and point out clearly the auditor's opinion. They can also remind the directors as a whole that the appointment of the auditor rests with the members on the recommendation of the audit committee. If the recommendation of the audit committee is rejected by the board, good corporate governance requires disclosure of the reason for rejection.

Obtain second partner review

The engagement partner can ask a second partner to review the working papers and other evidence relating to the issue of possible fraud. While this action does not resolve the issue, it does provide additional assurance that the findings and actions of the engagement partner are valid.

Resignation

If the matter is serious, then the auditor can consider resignation rather than not being re-appointed. Resignation has the additional safeguard that the auditor can normally require the directors to convene a general meeting to consider the circumstances of the resignation.

Marking scheme			
(a)	**Aviation fuel inventory**		*Marks*
	1 mark each for each valid procedure or action:		
	Any alternative treatments in GAAP		
	Materiality calculation		
	Review prior year working papers		
	Discuss with directors		
	Warn directors possible qualification		
	Quantify amount		
	Management representation		
	Draft audit report		6
(b)	(i)	**Auditor and fraud**	
		1 mark each for each valid responsibility:	
		• Overall responsibility	
		• Materiality	
		• Approach to audit	
		• Identification of fraud	4
	(ii)	**Reporting options regarding fraud**	
		Up to 2 marks each for each valid explained option – 0.5 for each body – then up to 2 if good reasons given for reporting to that body.	
		• Audit committee	
		• Government	
		• Members	
		• Professional body	6
	(iii)	Safeguards	
		Up to 2 marks per valid point. 1 for explaining the safeguard and 1 for the effectiveness of the safeguard	
		• Audit committee	
		• Second partner review	
		• Resignation	4
	Total		20

Examiner's comments

Part (a)

This question proved to be a fairly good discriminator with many candidates struggling to obtain more than 3 marks overall. The majority of answers explained the need to discuss the matter with the directors, the effect on materiality and the need to modify the audit opinion to obtain these marks. Some answers went on to mention other points such as representation letters and reviewing the proposed policy against GAAP to see if it actually was valid.

The main weakness in many answers concerned the apparent need to go back and audit inventory from the beginning of the audit, even though the question requirement clearly stated that audit was complete apart from this issue. Audit procedures regarding existence (seeing the inventory), obtaining the government contract to determine the need to hold 6,000 barrels of oil, etc were therefore not relevant to the answer. A minority of candidates also treated the issue as an event after the reporting period and moved on to discussing the going concern status of the company. As no inventory had actually been destroyed, these comments were again treated as not relevant.

Other common errors included:

- Considering resignation if the directors refuse to amend the inventory value; this was normally considered too extreme in this situation; a qualification of the audit report being sufficient,

- Provision of every possible type of audit report modification/qualification without clearly explaining first that the directors' amendments needed to be reviewed and then the appropriate report produced dependent on those amendments.

The overall standard of answer was inadequate. As in previous examinations, candidates need to consider carefully the time positioning of the question and not go back and repeat audit produces that should, by the end of the audit, already be complete.

Part (b)

In part (i), candidates were required to state the responsibilities of the external auditor regarding fraud. Given revisions to ISA 240 this was a relatively topical question. Many candidates managed to state 3 or sometimes 4 responsibilities to obtain a clear pass standard.

Common deficiencies in this section included:

- Talking around the main issue. For example, many candidates explained the responsibilities of management, internal audit and even the audit committee without managing to bring external auditors into their answers.

- Providing comments that were not quite correct. For example, stating that external auditors were responsible to detect all fraud, or in some cases that they had no responsibility at all.

- Providing lengthy explanations of actual watch-dogs and blood-hounds rather than auditor responsibilities.

Overall, the question was fairly well answered.

In part (ii), candidates were required to discuss groups who could be informed regarding the fictitious inventory. 6 marks were available with up to 2 marks for each group discussed.

There were two key issues that limited the marks obtained from this question;

- Firstly, identifying the appropriate groups. The directors appear to have entrenched their view that the inventory is to be revalued; reporting back to the directors appears therefore to be inappropriate. Other reporting options are also limited by confidentiality issues; hence reporting to the bank or payables is probably not acceptable.

- Secondly, discussing why each group was being reported to. Almost all candidates found this discussion element of the question difficult. For example, candidates did mention that reporting to the audit committee was appropriate, but not that the committee was formed by independent NEDs.

Most candidates therefore obtained marks for identifying groups, but few marks were obtained for stating why those groups were being reported.

In part (iii), candidates were required to discuss the safeguards protecting the auditor from the intimidation threat of being removed from office for qualifying the audit report. Most candidates managed to mention key safeguards of resignation and qualifying the audit report anyway. However, other points such as discussion with the audit committee, discussion with the auditors professional body, etc were not always mentioned.

Common errors included:

- Suggesting safeguards that did not appear to be effective such as referring directors to the engagement letter.
- Stating that the auditor should convene a shareholders' meeting. This point was only valid when linked to resignation as otherwise the auditor could not ask for a meeting to be convened.
- Suggesting that the auditor should speak at the annual general meeting. This would not be immediately effective and would only be helpful when linked to resignation or removal.

Overall, the standard of answers could have been better given a little thought about the effectiveness of the safeguard being mentioned in the answers.

43 ZEEDIEM (A) *Walk in the footsteps of a top tutor*

Key answer tips

This question requires an understanding of how financial reporting guidance for a certain complex area of accounting (namely *IAS 10 Events After the Reporting Period*) interacts with auditing guidance in the same area (*IAS 560 Subsequent Events*). Students need to know the basic principles of both sets of guidance and must also be able to identify relevant tests that can be carried out with regard to events identified in the scenario.

The highlighted words are key phases that markers are looking for.

(a) **Event 1**

(i) The problem with the mattress inventory provides additional evidence of conditions existing at the end of the reporting period as the inventory was in existence and the faulty springs were included in the inventory at this time.

The value of the inventory is overstated and should be reduced to the lower of cost and net realisable value in accordance with IAS 2 *Inventories*.

An adjustment for this decrease in value must be made in the financial statements.

The mattresses should therefore be valued at $225,000 being the net realisable value.

(ii) The decrease in value of inventory took place after the end of the reporting period but before the financial statements and the audit report were signed.

The auditor is therefore still responsible for identifying material events that affect the financial statements.

Audit procedures are therefore required to determine the net book value of the inventory and check that the $225,000 is the sales value of the mattresses.

Audit procedures will include:

- Obtain documentation from the insurers confirming their estimate of the value of the mattresses and that no further insurance claim can be made for the loss in value.

- If payment has already been received from the sale of the mattresses, agree this amount to the remittance advice, bank paying-in slip and bank statement. Alternatively, obtain the remittance advice and agree the amount to the bank statement online.

- Obtain the amended financial statements and ensure that the directors have included $225,000 as at the end of the reporting period.

- Ensure that the year-end value of inventory has been decreased to $225,000 on the statement of financial position, statement of financial position note and the income statement.

- Review inventory lists to ensure that the defective springs were not used in any other mattresses and that further adjustments are not required to any other inventory.

- Obtain an additional written representations confirming the accuracy of the amounts written-off and confirming that no other items of inventory are affected.

Event 2

(i) The release of dye occurred after the end of the reporting period, so this is indicative of conditions existing after the end of the reporting period – the event could not be foreseen at the end of the reporting period.

In this case, no adjustment to the financial statements appears to be necessary.

However, the investigation by the Environmental Agency could result in a legal claim against the company for illegal pollution so as a material event it will need disclosure in the financial statements.

(ii) As with event 1, the event takes place before the signing of the audit report, therefore the auditors have a duty to identify material events affecting the financial statements.

Audit procedures will include:

- Obtain any documentation on the event, for example board minutes, copies of environmental legislation and possibly interim reports from the Environmental Agency to determine the extent of the damage.

- Inquire of the directors whether they will disclose the event in the financial statements.

- If the directors plan to make disclosure of the event, ensure that disclosure appears appropriate.

- If the directors do not plan to make any disclosure, consider whether disclosure is necessary and inform the directors accordingly.

- Where disclosure is not made and the auditor considers disclosure is necessary, modify the audit opinion on the grounds that the financial statements contain material misstatement and explain the reason for the qualification in the report. This will be for lack of disclosure (not provision) even though the amount cannot yet be determined.

- Alternatively, if the auditor believes the release of dye and subsequent fine will affect ZeeDiem's ability to continue as a going concern, draw the members' attention to this in an emphasis of matter paragraph.

(b) The notification of a fine has taken place after the audit report has been signed. Audit procedures will include:

- Discuss the matter with the directors to determine their course of action.

- Where the directors decide to amend the financial statements, audit the amendment and then re-draft and re-date the audit report as appropriate. Where the amendment is to revise the financial statements to make provision for the fine, and this is adequately disclosed, then an unmodified audit report can be issued.

- Where the directors decide not to amend the financial statements, the auditor can consider other methods of contacting the members. For example, the auditor can speak in the upcoming general meeting to inform the members of the event.

- Other options such as resignation seem inappropriate due to the proximity of the annual general meeting (AGM). Resignation would allow the auditor to ask the directors to convene an extraordinary general meeting, but this could not take place before the AGM so the auditor should speak at the AGM instead.

	Marking scheme	Marks
(a)	**(i) Explanation of whether events adjusting or not.** 2 marks for each event Destruction of inventory Release of dye	**4**
	(ii) 1 mark for each point regarding auditor responsibility and for each valid audit procedure. Maximum 6 marks for each event **Destruction of inventory** Audit must identify material events post reporting period Need to check value of $225,000 is receivable Documentation from insurers Payment from third party Disclosure in financial statements Total inventory value end of year Other inventory affected? Management representation point **Release of dye** Ensure that material event is disclosed appropriately in financial statements Documentation of event Extent of disclosure in financial statements Action if disagree with amount of disclosure Possibility of modified audit report Management representation letter	**12**
(b)	1 mark for each audit procedure Discuss with directors Audit any amendment to financial statements Produce revised audit report Inform members in other methods – speak at meeting Resignation? Note not effective	**4**
	Total	**20**

Examiner's comments

Part (a)

In part (i) candidates normally recognised which event was adjusting and which was not, although a small minority did swap the events around. Candidates were not always clear regarding the reason for the events being adjusting or not, and frequently mentioned non-adjusting events as simply taking place after the end of the reporting period, without reference to the event affecting conditions at that date.

In part (ii), well prepared candidates gave comprehensive answers including many actions that the auditor could take. Less well-prepared candidates tended to focus on making general comments on subsequent events and in many cases providing significant details on the going concern review.

Other common errors included:

- Listing lots of general procedures for subsequent events rather than linking those procedures to the scenario. For example, stating that a lawyer's letter would be obtained but not stating that the lawyer's opinion was needed on the likelihood of being sued for environmental damage.

- Explaining the going concern review in detail. While event 2 could potentially impact on going concern and mention of this was worth a mark, stating 5 or 6 going concern procedures was clearly inappropriate.

- Provision of every possible type of audit report modification/qualification without clearly explaining first that the directors' amendments needed to be reviewed and then the appropriate report produced dependent on those amendments.

In summary there were two distinct types of answer to this section. Firstly, the well-prepared candidate who provided relevant actions that the auditor could take. The less well-prepared candidate who either spent far too much time explaining general points about subsequent events or in a few cases simply ran out of time to make any useful comments.

Part (b)

Most candidates provided some relevant and useful procedures such as obtaining revised letters of representation and contacting lawyers for additional advice. The main area that was not fully considered was that the audit report had already been signed; many candidates simply assumed that the auditor would issue a new report and management would accept this. Some candidates recognised the problem of attempting to recall the report and went on to suggest that the auditor speak at the upcoming AGM. Only a minority suggested resignation, which would not have been appropriate anyway given the proximity of the AGM.

Common errors included:

- Suggesting that the auditor would amend the financial statements

- Suggesting that the financial statements needed to include a monetary provision for this non-adjusting event.

- Considering every possible type of audit report without any reference to managements' actions.

The standard of answers for this section was therefore adequate.

44 SMITHSON CO (A)

Key answer tips

This question requires an understanding of how financial reporting guidance for a certain complex area of accounting (namely elements of IAS 1 relevant to *going concern*) interacts with auditing guidance in the same area (*IAS 570 Going Concern*).

Students need to know the basic principles of both sets of guidance and must also be able to identify relevant tests that can be carried out with regard to events identified in the scenario. This, along with subsequent events, is one of the key review processes and for that reason will be a common exam topic.

On the whole the question requires little more than basic knowledge recall, with some application.

(a) **Going concern**

Going concern means that the enterprise will continue in operational existence for the foreseeable future without the intention or necessity of liquidation or otherwise ceasing trade. It is one of the fundamental accounting concepts used by auditors and stated in IAS 1 *Presentation of Financial Statements*.

The auditor's responsibility in respect of going concern is explained in ISA 570 *Going Concern*. The ISA states that 'the auditor's responsibility is to obtain sufficient appropriate evidence about the appropriateness of management's use of the going concern assumption in the preparation and presentation of the financial statements and to conclude whether there is a material uncertainty about the entity's ability to continue as a going concern.'

The auditor's responsibility therefore falls into three areas:

(i) To carry out appropriate audit procedures that will identify whether or not an organisation can continue as a going concern.

(ii) To ensure that the organisation's management have been realistic in their use of the going concern assumption when preparing the financial statements.

(iii) To report to the members where they consider that the going concern assumption has been used inappropriately, for example, when the financial statements indicate that the organisation is a going concern, but audit procedures indicate this may not be the case.

(b) **Audit procedures regarding going concern**

– Obtain a copy of the cash flow forecast and discuss the results of this with the directors.

– Discuss with the directors their view on whether Smithson can continue as a going concern. Ask for their reasons and try and determine whether these are accurate.

– Enquire of the directors whether they have considered any other forms of finance for Smithson to make up the cash shortfall identified in the cash flow forecast.

– Obtain a copy of any interim financial statements of Smithson to determine the level of sales/income after the year-end and whether this matches the cash flow forecast.

– Enquire about the possible lack of capital investment within Smithson identified by the employee leaving. Review current levels of non-current assets with similar companies and review purchase policy with the directors.

– Consider the extent to which Smithson relied on the senior employee who recently left the company. Ask the human resources department whether the employee will be replaced and if so how soon.

– Obtain a solicitor's letter and review to identify any legal claims against Smithson related to below standard services being provided to clients. Where possible, consider the financial impact on Smithson and whether insurance is available to mitigate any claims.

– Review Smithson's order book and client lists to try and determine the value of future orders compared to previous years.

– Review the bank letter to determine the extent of any bank loans and whether repayments due in the next 12 months can be made without further borrowing.

– Review other events after the end of the financial year and determine whether these have an impact on Smithson.

– Obtain a letter of representation point confirming the directors' opinion that Smithson is a going concern.

(c) **Audit procedures if Smithson is not considered to be a going concern**

– Discuss the situation again with the directors. Consider whether additional disclosures are required in the financial statements or whether the financial statements should be prepared on a 'break up' basis.

– Explain to the directors that if additional disclosure or restatement of the financial statements is not made then the auditor will have to modify the audit report.

– Consider how the audit report should be modified. Where the directors provide adequate disclosure of the going concern situation of Smithson, then an emphasis of matter paragraph is likely to be appropriate to draw attention to the going concern disclosures.

– Where the directors do not make adequate disclosure of the going concern situation then modify the audit report making reference to the going concern problem. The modification will be a qualification or an adverse opinion depending on the auditor's opinion of the situation.

(d) **Negative assurance**

Negative assurance means that nothing has come to the attention of an auditor which indicates that the cash flow forecast contains any material errors. The assurance is therefore given on the absence of any indication to the contrary.

In contrast, the audit report on statutory financial statements provides positive or reasonable assurance; that is the financial statements do show a true and fair view.

Using negative assurance, the auditor is warning users that the cash flow forecast may be inaccurate. Less reliance can therefore be placed on the forecast than the financial statements, where the positive assurance was given.

With negative assurance, the auditor is also warning that there were limited audit procedures that could be used; the cash flow relates to the future and therefore the auditor cannot obtain all the evidence to guarantee its accuracy. Financial statements relate to the past, and so the auditor should be able to obtain the information to confirm they are correct; hence the use of positive assurance.

	Marking scheme	Marks
(a)	Going concern meaning 1 mark each for: – Definition – ISA 570 explanation (don't need the ISA number) – Audit procedures – Realistic use of assumption – Report to members – Report to audit committee and/or directors – Discussion with management on going concern	4
(b)	Audit procedures on going concern 1 mark per procedure (0.5 if brief or unclear e.g. 'check the cash flow') – Cash flow – Directors' view going concern – Other finance – Interim financial statements – Lack of non-current assets – Reliance on senior employee – Solicitor's letter – Review order book – Review bank letter – Review other events after the reporting period – Management representation	8
(c)	Audit procedures company may not be a going concern 1 mark per action (0.5 if brief or unclear e.g. 'discuss with directors') – Discuss with directors – Need to modify audit report – Possible emphasis of matter – Possible qualification – Letter of representation	4
(d)	Negative assurance 1 mark per action (0.5 if brief or unclear e.g. 'warning cash flow may be inaccurate') – Definition – Audit report = positive assurance – Level of reliance – Limited audit procedures	4
	Total	**20**

Examiner's comments

Part (a)

Very few candidates mentioned responsibilities such as reporting to members or discussing the going concern concept with the directors.

Other common errors included:

- Stating lots of audit procedures that the auditor could carry out. While the auditor is responsible for reviewing the going concern assumption, how the auditor obtains evidence to meet that responsibility is a different issue and therefore not relevant to this particular question.

- Stating that it was the auditor's responsibility to prepare financial statements on the going concern basis!!!

Overall, the standard for this question was average only due to the lack of explanation of auditor responsibilities.

Part (b)

A significant minority lost time in their answer by providing lengthy introductions to the work of the auditor.

Audit procedures mentioned in the answer could be relevant to the scenario – various factors were mentioned to provide "clues" again to the relevant points to make an answer. However, many going concern procedures are generic to all companies, and candidates could still obtain easy marks by mentioning these e.g. reviewing cash flow forecasts or obtaining representations from the directors.

Common errors included:

- Providing a list of going concern indicators rather than audit procedures.

- Not providing sufficient detail on each procedure. For example, the procedure "review board minutes" is insufficient for a full mark because it is not clear why the minutes are being reviewed or when the review takes place.

- Listing audit work on the financial statements. This is a very common error with going concern questions – candidates repeat the audit work already carried out rather than looking for procedures relevant to the future of the company.

A minority of candidates provided eight relevant procedures and obtained full marks from this question. However, many other answers did not state the procedures clearly or simply mentioned only two or three procedures. Many candidates therefore did not answer this question well.

Part (c)

This question proved to be difficult for many candidates. Many comments made were repeats of the audit work already carried out in part (b) of the answer, while others attempted to explain every possible type of audit report that could be produced. While the latter approach had some merit, few candidates mentioned the basic procedures of discussing the situation with directors or obtaining a letter of representation point.

The standard of answers was therefore unsatisfactory for this section. The standard of answers again demonstrates that candidates do not like making decisions at the end of the audit (a weakness common to questions on events after the balance sheet date).

Part (d)

Many candidates managed to produce a basic definition of negative assurance although there remained some confusion regarding the difference between this and assurance given on an audit report. The main weakness was using the term true and fair view in the context of an assurance engagement with only a minority of candidates recognising that truth and fairness relate to statutory audit. A significant minority of candidates did not attempt this question, presumably due to time allocation problems at the end of the examination.

45   JONARC & CO (A)

Key answer tips

Part (a) requires you to explain how you would attempt to resolve an outstanding issue at the end of the audit. Audit procedures" and "actions" is what you need to focus on to gain a soild mark here.

Part (b) Candidates were required to explain the meaning and purpose of five different extracts from an audit report. Therefore the answer needs to be split in two, describe the meaning and then the purpose.

Part (c) The short scenario presented two situations; the answer is looking for the effect on the audit report because of them.

(a)   **Audit procedures regarding non-depreciation of buildings**

- Review audit file to ensure that sufficient appropriate audit evidence has been collected in respect of this matter.
- Ensure that GAAP does apply to the specific buildings owned by Galartha Co and that a departure from GAAP is not needed in order for the financial statements to show a true and fair view.
- Meet with the directors to confirm their reasons for not depreciating buildings.
- Warn the directors that in your opinion buildings should be depreciated and that failure to provide depreciation will result in a modified audit report.
- Determine the effect of the misstatement on the audit report in terms of the modified opinion being material or of pervasive materiality to the financial statements.
- Draft the appropriate sections of the modified audit report.
- Obtain a letter of representation from the directors confirming that depreciation will not be charged on buildings.

(b)   **Audit report extracts**

Extract 1

The meaning of the extract. It confirms that audit work has been carried out in accordance with external Auditing Standards – not arbitrary standards made up by the audit firm and that audit planning was carried out to detect material errors.

The purpose of the extract. It provides the readers of the financial statements with that the auditor can be trusted to carry out the audit because the auditor has followed the ISAs and the ethical standards of the ACCA.

Extract 2

The meaning of the extract. It states that the auditor has compared the normal accounting treatment for depreciation (in the IAS) to that used by the directors and found the directors' method to be different to the standard.

The purpose of the extract. It informs readers that the company is not following the IAS in this particular matter and so the financial statements may be incorrect in this respect.

Extract 3

The meaning of the extract. It shows how the IAS would normally be applied to non-current tangible assets – in this case a standard 5% depreciation rate has been used.

The purpose of the extract. Enables the reader of the financial statements to quantify the impact of the IAS non-compliance – in this case $420,000.

Extract 4

The meaning of the extract. It shows the overall impact of non-compliance with the IAS – with specific focus on the overstatement on non-current assets of $1,200,000.

The purpose of the extract. It enables the reader to see the overall quantified impact on the financial statements – that is non-current assets and profit are both overstated. The members' perception of the 'value' of their company may therefore be altered.

Extract 5

The meaning of the extract. That the auditor believes that the accounts are materially misstated due to the depreciation figure provided by the directors – the auditor's calculation of depreciation is materially different from this hence the auditor's disagreement with the financial statements figure. However, this is the only material misstatement that the auditor has identified.

The purpose of the extract. To communicate to the members that that auditor does not believe that the financial statements show a true and fair view in respect of depreciation.

(c) **Other reporting options**

(i)
- The auditor would still conclude that the financial statements were materially misstated due to the lack of depreciation on non-current assets so a modified opinion would be required.

- Due to the profit becoming a large loss the auditor may conclude that the misstatement is both material and pervasive to the financial statements and issue an adverse opinion (rather than a qualified opinion).

(ii)
- The auditors normally attend the inventory count to confirm the existence of inventory. As the count was not attended, the existence of inventory cannot be confirmed.

- The auditor will be unable to obtain sufficient appropriate evidence regarding the existence and valuation of inventory. A qualified audit opinion will be issued noting that adjustments may be necessary to the inventory value.

Examiner's comments

Part (a)

The question requirement included the terms "audit procedures" and "actions" to elicit comments such as discussing the matter with the directors, which may not be seen as a clear procedure.

The requirement verb for this section was "state". In other words, this was a difficult question and the examiner was looking for valid procedures and actions without any detailed explanation as to why those procedures were being carried out. Providing six valid procedures/actions would therefore enable a candidate to obtain full marks. Obviously, the procedure/action had to be relevant to the scenario.

The short scenario also included the phrase "the audit work has been completed, but there is one outstanding matter" to indicate that audit work was literally complete apart from this matter. The focus of answers had therefore to be on resolving this matter, not on reperforming earlier audit work.

Most candidates focused their answers on the additional audit work. A minority did re-audit buildings in their entirety and normally failed to address at the end of each answer the issue of lack of depreciation.

Common errors and reasons why those errors did not obtain marks included:

- Explaining in detail how to audit buildings, including procedures such as verifying title and determining existence by seeing the buildings. The focus of the question was on the issue of lack of depreciation, and not the general audit work on buildings.

- Not providing sufficient breadth of comments. Most candidates mentioned the need to communicate with the directors and amend the audit report in some way. However, other points such as comparing the proposed accounting treatment to GAAP were mentioned only in a minority of answers.

- Confusion regarding the type of audit report to be provided. In this section, as in part (b), it was obvious that audit reports and specifically modifications/qualifications had not been taught or understood. The range of comments was considerable ranging from a "qualified report – except for", which was a possibility, to an "adverse report, not modified with an emphasis of matter".

- Considering resignation from the audit assignment before other procedures/actions had been attempted. Given the question stated that there was only one matter outstanding, resigning prior to attempting to remedy the issue was taken as inappropriate.

- Stating procedures/actions that could not be performed e.g. arranging a meeting of members. These actions showed a lack of knowledge of appropriate law or auditors rights.

- Providing significant amounts of detail on the accounting treatment of depreciation. While comments of this nature were factually correct, this is an auditing examination. Detailed explanation of how to apply accounting standards are therefore not required. Comments of this type are relevant to papers F3 and F7.

The overall standard for this section was satisfactory. The majority of candidates did obtain marks for contacting the directors, determining the materiality of the situation and considering the effect on the audit report.

Part (b)

To be clear, the distinction between meaning and purpose should be as follows; "meaning" related to explaining the extract while "purpose" to stating why the extract was in an audit report. Many candidates struggled to explain why the extracts were included in an audit report.

Common errors and reasons why those errors did not obtain marks included:

- Taking each audit report extract as a separate opinion paragraph and explaining it in terms of "emphasis of matter", or different types of qualification. This was inappropriate; the question stated these were extracts from an audit report (singular), not separate reports.

- Explaining paragraph 5 was an unmodified audit report. This was not the case; an explanation of the report in terms the modification made was needed.

- For various paragraphs, stating that the report was produced for the benefit of the management.

- Not explaining the meaning of each report extract. Answers tended to focus on explaining the purpose of each paragraph.

The overall standard for this section was satisfactory. However, along with question 2a, the question also identified a lack of basic knowledge. Candidates and tutors are again reminded of the importance of being able to explain audit reports clearly in the context of this examination.

Part (c)

For part (i), candidates were expected to recognise that lack of depreciation, turning a profit into a significant loss, had a significant impact on the audit report. An adverse report was expected for a pervasive situation.

For part (ii), candidates were expected to recognise that not attending the inventory count resulted in uncertainty, but inventory was only material to the financial statements. An "except for" qualification was therefore expected.

Common errors and reasons why those errors did not obtain marks included:

- Not stating the effect on the audit report.

- Confusion regarding the terminology of the effect on the audit report. As in part (b) extract 5, there were some interesting and varied comments regarding the type of audit report to produce. The most common mistake was to qualify with an emphasis of matter closely followed by the unmodified adverse report.

Marking scheme		
(a)	1 mark each for:	*Marks*
	– Review of audit file	
	– Ensure true and fair override not required	
	– Meet with directors	
	– Warn directors about qualification	
	– Material or pervasive?	
	– Draft report	
	– Letter of representation	
	– Assets may not need depreciation	
	– Discuss with audit committee	**6**
(b)	1 mark per point	
	Work in accordance with external standards	
	Work to identify material misstatements	
	May be other material misstatements	
	Shows auditor disagrees with directors	
	Shows auditor view based on standards	
	Quantifies effect of non-compliance	
	Shows what depreciation policy normally is	
	Confirms quantification of financial effect	
	So members can see total effect	
	'Except for' = material qualified opinion	**10**

(c)	1 mark per point	
	(i) Still disagree – modify report (+ reason) Qualification = 'fundamental'	
	(ii) Uncertainty on one item only = modify report	
	Qualification = material 'except for adjustments that may be necessary'	4
	Total	**20**

46   GREEN CO (A)

Key answer tips

This question should be straightforward for a well-prepared student with a good understanding of ethics and going concern.

(a)   **Ethical threats**

Self review threat

If Lime & Co provides audit and other professional services to Green Co, then they will be preparing the financial statements and also auditing those financial statements. This will provide a self-review threat to Lime & Co as they will be auditing their own work. Lime & Co would be advised to tender only for the audit work.

Self interest threat

If Lime & Co prepare the financial statements of Green Co and then also audit those financial statements, they may be less inclined to report any errors. Reporting of errors may result in loss of work in the future as the managers of Green Co may stop using the services of Lime & Co. Again Lime & Co should only tender for the audit.

Management threat

There is a risk that Lime & Co will make decisions that the managers of Green Co should make (for example which accounting policies should apply to the financial statements). It is possible that these type of decisions have been made before, on an informal basis, as the partner in Lime & Co already knows and gives advice to the managers of Green Co.

Advocacy threat

This threat arises because Lime & Co may be asked to present details of Green Co's financial statements and profit forecasts in court to support its application to stop Black Co growing genetically modified (GM) crops. Lime & Co may be seen to support their client in court, which may limit their independence in relation to the audit work.

Familiarity threat

You have been friends with the managers of Green Co for some time. This means that you may not question the decisions of the managers due to this close personal relationship. As a partner in Lime & Co, you will in effect not be independent from your client.

Fee income

Acceptance of audit and professional services work from Green Co, will result in an increase in fee income. To retain independence, Lime & Co need to ensure that total fees generated from Green Co do not exceed 15% of the total practice income.

Association threat

The managers of Green Co, while not being criminals, appear to lack integrity in their business affairs. The partners in Lime & Co need to decide whether they want to be professionally associated with Green Co; any criminal activity in the future may have an adverse effect on Lime & Co's reputation and image. Specifically Lime & Co will not want to be seen to be associated with or advising a firm which is breaking the law.

Cease trading – payment of fees

The farm may lose organic certification if the genetically modified crops continue to be grown next to Green Co's farm. There is a risk that Lime & Co may not be paid for services provided should Green Co cease trading.

(b)   (i)   **Going concern**

IAS 1 defines the going concern concept as the assumption that the enterprise will continue in operational existence for the foreseeable future.

The farm may lose organic certification if the genetically modified crops continue to be grown next to Green Co's farm.

This means that Green Co may not be a going concern.

An entity will normally use the going concern basis unless:

–   It is being liquidated or has ceased trading, or

–   The directors have no realistic alternative than to liquidate the company or to cease trading.

(ii)   **Responsibilities**

IAS 1 requires the directors to assess the entity's ability to continue as a going concern, and make appropriate disclosures in the financial statements based upon this assessment. Their assessment involves making a judgement about inherently uncertain future outcomes of events or conditions.

The auditor's responsibility in respect of going concern is explained in ISA 570 *Going Concern*. It states that 'the auditor's responsibility is to obtain sufficient appropriate evidence about the appropriateness of management's use of the going concern assumption in the preparation and presentation of the financial statements and to conclude whether there is a material uncertainty about the entity's ability to continue as a going concern.'

(c)   **Audit procedures**

In the case of Green Co, audit procedures on going concern will include:

–   Obtaining cash and profit forecasts from the directors. Ensure that these have been properly prepared (for example are arithmetically correct) and show that Green will continue trading. Appropriate adjustments should have been made for the decrease in sales resulting from contamination of Green Co's farm.

–   Review the order books for Green Co to determine the level of future sales.

– Contacting Green Co's lawyers to determine the progress, if any, on the court case against Black Co.

– Review the financial status of Green Co during the audit to identify other indicators of a going concern problem such as failure to repay loans or decrease in sales.

– Review correspondence, if any, with the organic certification authority to determine whether Green Co's organic status has been withdrawn.

– Contacting Green Co's bank to ascertain whether any loan or overdraft agreements are due for renewal and whether these will be renewed.

– Obtaining written representation from the directors confirming that they are not aware of any circumstances other than those evaluated by the auditor, so they expect Green Co to continue as a going concern.

47 MSV

Key answer tips

Part (a) requires a reasonable knowledge of the content of the audit report. This is book knowledge and should present no problems.

Part (b) requires you to apply your knowledge and state how you would investigate potential misstatements and the impact on your audit report.

(a)

Audit report element	Reason for that element
Title of 'independent auditor'	To identify this as an audit report and distinguish it from other reports on financial statements that might be issued by others, directors, etc.
Addressee	To identify the person(s) who may use or rely on the report.
Opening or introductory paragraph identifying – the financial statements audited and – responsibilities of entity's management and auditors	To make it clear which pages of an annual report have been audited. To make clear that the directors prepare the financial statements and the auditors audit them.
Scope paragraph describing the nature of the audit in terms of International Standards on Auditing (ISAs) followed and the work performed by the auditor	To explain the scope of the audit so the standard of the auditors work is clear and other factors such as limitation of audit testing (for example, not tested all items) is known.
Opinion paragraph referring to the financial reporting framework followed and expressing the auditor's opinion.	To provide the auditor's opinion on the financial statements in terms of true and fair view, to assure the reader that the audit has been carried out in accordance with established principles and practices.

Audit report element	Reason for that element
Date of the report	To inform the reader that the auditor has considered effects of transactions that the auditor became aware of on the financial statements up to that date.
Auditor's address	This is normally the address where the auditor responsible for the audit is located so he/she can be contacted, if necessary.
Auditor's signature	This is normally the signature of the audit firm as the firm assumes responsibility for the audit, not the individual engagement partner.

(b)   **Issue one – Understatement of sales income**

(i)   –   If possible, conduct day-by-day analytical review to determine the extent of the misappropriation.

–   Discuss the situation with the other directors to ascertain their knowledge of the situation.

–   Ask the other directors what action they will take regarding the director who appears to have misappropriated money from the company.

–   Recommend in the management letter that strict numeric sequence is maintained over sales invoices and that two directors are always on duty to prevent misappropriation of income.

–   Obtain a letter of representation to confirm the directors' estimate of the extent of the fraud and confirm that the directors are not aware of any other instances of fraud.

(ii)   The misappropriation is material, being about 5% of income for the year. Therefore:

–   Modify the auditor's report with a qualification due to the auditor being unable to obtain sufficient appropriate evidence to conclude on sales income.

–   Explain the reason for the understatement of income in the basis of opinion paragraph above the opinion paragraph.

Issue two – Director's use of yacht

(i)   –   Ask the director why the yacht is located at his house.

–   Ask the director whether any payment was made for the yacht – confirm payment to the cash book and company bank statements.

–   If the yacht is for private use only, check that disclosure of the benefit has been made in the directors' emoluments note in the financial statements.

–   Ensure the company has provided relevant information to the benefit authority and accrued any penalty for nondisclosure.

–   Consider additional audit work to determine whether or not any other company assets have been used in a similar fashion.

(ii)   Assuming that disclosure of the benefit has not been shown in the financial statements then:

–   Modify the auditor's report with a qualification due to a material misstatement in the financial statements.

48   TAM (A)

Key answer tips

Questions based on audit sampling ((part a) here) are rarely 'popular' with students. This is perceived to be one of the more technically advanced aspects of auditing and tends to be associated with 'maths' in the mind of students.

However, you should take the question at its face value. Very often, as is the case here, the examiner makes it very clear what you are expected to do and almost 'leads you through the answer'.

Part (a) is testing your knowledge of the main determinants of sample size in the context both of tests of controls and of substantive testing procedures. This is where a knowledge of the technical language of statistical sampling will score you marks here.

Part (b) is dealing with an area that most students may find more to their liking – general controls in a computer based accounting system. This topic should be part of your basic bank of knowledge on the computer auditing area.

(a)   **Sampling risk**

Sampling risk is the possibility that the auditor's conclusion, based on a sample, may be different from the conclusion reached if the entire population were subjected to the audit procedure.

The auditor may conclude from the results of testing that either material misstatements exist, when they do not, or that material misstatements do not exist when in fact they do.

Sampling risk is controlled by the audit firm ensuring that it is using a valid method of selecting items from a population and/or increasing the sample size.

Non-sampling risk

Non-sampling risk arises from any factor that causes an auditor to reach an incorrect conclusion that is not related to the size of the sample.

Examples of non-sampling risk include the use of inappropriate procedures, misinterpretation of evidence or the auditor simply 'missing' an error.

Non-sampling risk is controlled by providing appropriate training for staff so they know which audit techniques to use and will recognise an error when one occurs.

(b)   The audit manager suggests checking all invoices, effectively ignoring any statistical sampling; in other words this is not statistical sampling. Audit tests will be applied to all of the sales invoices. This approach may be appropriate for the audit of Tam because:

> – The population is relatively small and it is likely to be quicker to test all the items than spend time constructing a sample.
>
> – All the transactions are not large but could be considered material in their own right, e.g. compared to project. As all the transactions are material, then they all need to be tested.

The audit senior suggests using statistical sampling. This will mean selecting a limited number of sales invoices from the population using probability theory ensuring a random selection of the sample and then applying audit tests to those invoices only. This approach may be appropriate because:

> – The population consists of similar items (i.e. it is homogeneous) and there are no indications of the control system failing or changing during the year. There is the query about how long it will take to determine and produce a sample, which may make statistical sampling inappropriate in this situation.

The audit junior suggests using 'random' sampling, which the junior auditor appears to understand as manually choosing which invoices to look at. The approach therefore involves an element of bias and is not statistical or true 'random' sampling.

While this approach appears to save time, it is not appropriate because:

> – The sample selected will not be chosen 'randomly' but on the whim of the auditor. Human nature will tend to avoid difficult items for testing.
>
> – Also, as invoices will not have been chosen using statistical sampling, no valid conclusion can be drawn from the results of the test. If an error is found it will be difficult extrapolating that error on to the population.

(c) Misstatements, including omissions, are considered to be material if they, individually or in aggregate, could reasonably be expected to influence the economic decisions of users taken on the basis of the financial statements.

Judgements about materiality are made in light of surrounding circumstances, and are affected by the size and nature of a misstatement, or a combination of both; and

Judgements about matters that are considered material to users of the financial statements are based on a consideration of the common financial information needs of users as a group.

It is important that the auditors of Tam ensure that the financial statements are free from material error for the following reasons:

> – There is a legal requirement to audit financial statements and present an opinion on those financial statements. If the auditors do not detect a material error then their opinion on the financial statements could be incorrect.
>
> – There are only two owner/directors who will be the initial users of the financial statements. While the owners/directors maintain the accounting records, the directors will want to know if there are material errors resulting from any mistakes they may have made; the auditor has a responsibility to the members to ensure that the financial statements are materially correct.
>
> – There are also other users of the financial statements who will include the taxation authorities and the bank who have made a loan to the company. They will want to see 'true and fair' accounts. The auditors must therefore ensure that the financial statements are free from material misstatement to avoid any legal liability to third parties if they audit the financial statements negligently.

49   LALD

Key answer tips

Part (a) and (b) are unusual, in that you are asked what you would do having discovered misstatements. Go through this answer very carefully as the examiner has indicated that he will examine this again.

(a)   Audit procedures for underpayment of sales tax

- Discuss the underpayment with the head of the accounting department to ascertain whether the error was known, and if so why no action had been taken to correct the error.

- Evaluate the results of testing to determine the amount of the underpayment. Where necessary perform additional substantive tests checking from the tax declared on sales invoices issued during August to the sales tax calculation.

- Summarise the results of testing, providing an estimate of the amount of sales tax underpaid.

- Discuss the situation with the directors to obtain an understanding of how the error occurred and determine what actions the directors will take.

- Include the deficiency in the management letter noting, if possible, the reason for the error and the action that must be taken to correct the error.

- Inform the directors that non-payment of sales tax to the government is a breach of specific law of their country.

- Ask for a formal response from the directors, clearly indicating what action they propose to take regarding the underpayment.

- Where the amount due has been paid to the government, audit the payment and ensure it is sufficient given the extent of underpayment already detected.

- Where the amount due is not paid, consider informing the appropriate authorities where legislation requires this.

- Consider and ask the directors to provide for any late penalties that will need to be paid to the government with regards to the late payment.

(b)   Audit procedures for under-provision of depreciation

- Review the results of the audit working papers to check that an error did occur.

- Extend substantive testing for this particular class of non-current assets to try and determine the extent of the error.

- Calculate the new depreciation provision based on the results of your testing.

- Compare your estimate of depreciation to the amount calculated by the client to determine whether the difference is material. .

- Discuss the underprovision with the head of the accounting department to ascertain whether the error was known, and if so why no action had been taken to correct the error.

- Discuss the situation with the directors to ascertain what action the directors will take. If the difference is material then an amendment to the financial statements would be expected.

- Include the deficiency in the management letter noting, if possible, the reason for the error and the action that must be taken to correct the error.

- If the difference is material and the directors do not amend the financial statements, consider the need to modify the auditor's report.

(c)   To remove the auditor from office before their term of office has expired, the directors of LALD must proceed as follows:

- Arrange for a meeting of the shareholders of the company.

- Write to the shareholders providing notice of the meeting and the agenda. The notice must also be sent to the auditor.

- Attend the meeting and organise a counting of votes at the meeting on the resolution to remove the auditor from office. In most situations, a simple majority of the shareholders is required to confirm the resolution.

- Auditors are sometimes given the right to make written representations and to speak at the meeting.

- If the auditor is removed, where necessary, obtain a statement of circumstances from the auditor. If there are no circumstances that need to be brought to the attention of the shareholders then a statement of no circumstances is required. Where required by specific country legislation, deposit this statement along with notice of removal of auditor, with the appropriate authorities.

- Make arrangements to appoint another auditor as companies are normally required to have auditors.

50   CRIGHTON-WARD (A) *Walk in the footsteps of a top tutor*

Key answer tips

This is a standard question on management representation letters that should cause you few problems. Make your five separate points in part (a) to earn the five marks available.

In part (b) it is very likely that one of the items will be appropriate for inclusion in the letter, while the other will not. The requirement to 'discuss' each situation means that you must justify your decision.

Part (c) is again standard bookwork on what to do if the directors are unwilling to sign the representation letter. Try to solve the problem by discussion; qualifying the audit report is always the last resort if alternative approaches have failed. The highlighted words are key phrases that markers are looking for.

(a)   Written representations are a form of audit evidence. They are contained in a letter, written by the company's directors and sent to the auditor, just prior to the completion of audit work and before the audit report is signed.

Representations are required for two reasons:

First, so the directors can acknowledge their collective responsibility for the preparation of the financial statements and to confirm that they have approved those statements.

Second, to confirm any matters, which are material to the financial statements where representations are crucial to obtaining sufficient and appropriate audit evidence.

In the latter situation, other forms of audit evidence are normally unavailable because knowledge of the facts is confined to management and the matter is one of judgement or opinion.

Obtaining representations does not mean that other evidence does not have to be obtained. Audit evidence will still be collected and the representation will support that evidence. Any contradiction between sources of evidence should, as always, be investigated.

(b)   **Lion's Roar**

The amount of the claim is material being 50% of profit before taxation.

There is also a lack of definitive supporting evidence for the claim. The two main pieces of evidence available are the claim from Lion's Roar itself and the legal advice from Crighton Ward's solicitors. However, any claim amount cannot be accurately determined because the dispute has not been settled.

The directors have stated that they believe the claim not to be justified, which is one possible outcome of the dispute. However, in order to obtain sufficient evidence to show how the treatment of the potential claim was decided for the financial statements, the auditor must obtain this opinion in writing. Reference must therefore be made to the claim in the representation letter.

Paragraph for inclusion in representation letter.

'A legal claim against Crighton-Ward by Lion's Roar has been estimated at $4 million by Lion's Roar. However, the directors are of the opinion that the claim is not justified on the grounds of breach of product specification. No provision has been made in the financial statements, although disclosure of the situation is adequate. No similar claims have been received or are expected to be received.'

Depreciation

This matter is unlikely to be included in the letter of representation because the auditor appears to have obtained sufficient evidence to confirm the accounting treatment. The lack of profit or loss on sale confirms that the depreciation charge is appropriate – large profits would indicate over-depreciation and large losses, under-depreciation. The amount also meets industry standards confirming that Crighton-Ward's accounting policy is acceptable. Including the point in the representation letter is inappropriate because the matter is not crucial and does not appear to be based on judgment or opinion. The only opinion here appears to be that of the auditor – unless the 'feelings' can be turned into some appropriate audit evidence, the matter should be closed.

(c)   **Lack of representation letter**

The auditor may take the following actions:

Discuss the situation with the directors to try and resolve the issue that the directors have raised. The auditor will need to explain the need for the representation letter again (and note that the signing of the letter was mentioned in the engagement letter). Ascertain exact reasons why the directors will not sign the letter. Consider whether amendments can be made to the letter to incorporate the directors' concerns that will still provide the auditor with appropriate and sufficient audit evidence.

The discussion must clearly explain the fact that if the auditor does not receive sufficient and appropriate audit evidence, then the audit report will have to be modified.

The reason for the modification will be the auditor's inability to obtain sufficient appropriate evidence regarding the amounts and disclosures in the financial statements. An 'except for' qualification for the material uncertainty is likely, although a disclaimer may be required, especially if the legal claim is thought to require a provision.

Even if the letter is subsequently signed, the auditor must still evaluate the reliability of the evidence. If, in the auditor's opinion, the letter no longer provides sufficient or reliable evidence, then a qualification may still be required.

ISAs AND OTHER KEY AREAS

51   ASSURANCE/ISA 320 *Walk in the footsteps of a top tutor*

Key answer tips

This is a straightforward knowledge based question. Note that in part (a) you are asked to "list" and "explain." Assuming ½ for each adjective you need to identify five elements of an assurance assignment.

With part (b) you will score 1 mark for the definition, meaning you need to make four other valid points to secure maximum marks.

The highlighted words are key phases that markers are looking for.

(a)   An assurance engagement will involve three separate parties;

- The intended user who is the person who requires the assurance report.
- The responsible party, which is the organisation responsible for preparing the subject matter to be reviewed.
- The practitioner (i.e. an accountant) who is the professional who will review the subject matter and provide the assurance.

A second element is a suitable subject matter. The subject matter is the data that the responsible party has prepared and which requires verification.

Suitable criteria are required in an assurance engagement. The subject matter is compared to the criteria in order for it to be assessed and an opinion provided.

Appropriate evidence has to be obtained by the practitioner in order to give the required level of assurance.

An assurance report is the opinion that is given by the practitioner to the intended user and the responsible party.

(b)   Materiality is defined as follows:

'Misstatements, including omissions, are considered to be material if they, individually or in the aggregate, could reasonably be expected to influence the economic decisions of users taken on the basis of the financial statements.'

In assessing the level of materiality there are a number of areas that should be considered. Firstly the auditor must consider both the amount (quantity) and the nature (quality) of any misstatements, or a combination of both. The quantity of the misstatement refers to the relative size of it and the quality refers to an amount that might be low in value but due to its prominence could influence the user's decision, for example, directors' transactions.

In assessing materiality the auditor must consider that a number of errors each with a low value may when aggregated amount to a material misstatement.

The assessment of what is material is ultimately a matter of the auditors' professional judgement, and it is affected by the auditor's perception of the financial information needs of users of the financial statements.

In calculating materiality the auditor should also consider setting the performance materiality level. This is the amount set by the auditor, it is below materiality, and is used for particular transactions, account balances and disclosures.

As per ISA 320 materiality is often calculated using benchmarks such as 5% of profit before tax or 1% of gross revenue. These values are useful as a starting point for assessing materiality.

ACCA marking scheme		
		Marks
(a)	Up to 1 mark per description of element: – Intended user – Responsible party – Practitioner – Suitable criteria – Subject matter – Appropriate evidence – Assurance report	
	Maximum	5
(b)	Up to 1 mark per valid point: – ISA 320 (½ mark only for ISA ref) – Definition – Amount – Nature, or both – Small errors aggregated – Judgement, needs of users – Performance materiality – 5% profit before tax or 1% revenue	
	Maximum	5
Total		10

52   ISA 500/260 *Walk in the footsteps of a top tutor*

Key answer tips

This question requires little more than pre-learnt knowledge. Take care to offer the appropriate number of responses requested in the question.

The highlighted words are key phases that markers are looking for.

(a) The following five factors that influence the reliability of audit evidence are taken from ISA 500 Audit Evidence:

(i) Audit evidence is more reliable when it is obtained from independent sources outside the entity.

(ii) Audit evidence that is generated internally is more reliable when the related controls imposed by the entity are effective.

(iii) Audit evidence obtained directly by the auditor (for example, observation of the application of a control) is more reliable than audit evidence obtained indirectly or by inference (for example, inquiry about the application of a control).

(iv) Audit evidence is more reliable when it exists in documentary form, whether paper, electronic, or other medium. (For example, a contemporaneously written record of a meeting is more reliable than a subsequent oral representation of the matters discussed.)

(v) Audit evidence provided by original documents is more reliable than audit evidence provided by photocopies or facsimiles.

Other examples are:

(vi) Evidence created in the normal course of business is better than evidence specially created to satisfy the auditor.

(vii) The best-informed source of audit evidence will normally be management of the company (although management's lack of independence may reduce its value as a source of such evidence).

(viii) Evidence about the future is particularly difficult to obtain and is less reliable than evidence about past events.

(b) (i) Those charged with governance are responsible for overseeing:

- the strategic direction of the entity
- obligations related to the accountability of the entity. This includes overseeing the financial reporting process.
- promotion of good corporate governance
- risk assessment processes
- the establishment and monitoring of internal controls
- compliance with applicable law and regulations
- implementation of controls to prevent and detect fraud and errors.

(ii) General audit matters that might be communicated to those charged with governance are addressed in ISA 260:

(1) *The auditor's responsibilities in relation to financial statement audit.*

This would include:

- A statement that the auditor is responsible for forming and expressing an opinion on the financial statements.

- That the auditor's work is carried out in accordance with ISAs and in accordance with local laws and regulations.

(2)   *Planned scope and timing of the audit.*

This would include

- The audit approach to assessing the risk of serious misstatement, whether arising from fraud or error.
- The audit approach to the internal control system and whether reliance will be placed on it.
- The timing of interim and final audits, including reporting deadlines.

(3)   *Significant findings from the audit.*

This heading could include:

- Significant difficulties encountered during the audit, including delays in obtaining information from management.
- Material deficiencies in internal control and recommendations for improvement.
- Audit adjustments, whether or not recorded by the entity, that have, or could have, a material effect on the entity's financial statements. For example, the bankruptcy of a material receivable shortly after the year-end that should result in an adjusting entry.

(4)   *A statement on independence issues affecting the audit.*

This would include:

- That the audit firm has ensured that all members of the audit team have complied with the ethical standards of ACCA.
- That appropriate safeguards are in place where a potential threat to independence has been identified.

Tutorial note

The lists of examples listed under the above headings are not exhaustive and in practice many more specific matters would be communicated to those charged with governance such as:

- *Modifications to the audit report.*
- *Any management representation points requested.*
- *Cases of suspected/actual fraud.)*

ACCA marking scheme			
			Marks
(a)		**Reliability of audit evidence**	
		Up to 1 mark for identification of factors, but maximum 4.	
		Independent source	
		Effective controls	
		Evidence obtained directly by auditor	
		Written evidence	
		Original documents	
		Normal course of business	
		Informed management	
		Evidence about the future	
		Maximum marks	4.0
(b)	(i)	**Responsibilities of those charged with governance**	
		½ mark for identification of responsibility and a further ½ if adequately described, but maximum 2.	
		Strategic direction	
		Accountability obligations	
		Financial reporting process	
		Promotion of good corporate governance	
		Risk assessment processes	
		Establishment and monitoring of internal controls	
		Compliance with law and regulations	
		Implementation of controls to prevent and detect fraud and errors	
		Maximum marks	2.0
	(ii)	**Matters to be communicated**	
		½ mark for identification of matter and a further ½ mark if explanation is adequate, but maximum 4.	
		Matters under the following headings	
		• Auditor's responsibilities	
		• Planned scope and timing	
		• Significant findings from audit	
		• Independence issues	
		• Modifications to the audit report	
		• Management representation points	
		• Cases of suspected/actual fraud	
		Maximum marks	4.0
Total			10.0

53   ISA 530/315/AUDIT REPORTS (A) *Walk in the footsteps of a top tutor*

Key answer tips

This is a straightforward knowledge based question. Note that four responses are required for parts (a) and (b) for four marks and that two marks are available for (c). Using the guidance in the 'Audit & Assurance Assistance' article you will get ½ for eah point listed with a further ½ mark for each linked explanation. For part (c) you need to introduce at least two points of explanation into your answer to get 1 mark each. You should fully explain your points to obtain the full mark though.

The highlighted words are key phases that markers are looking for.

(a)   **Sampling methods**

Methods of sampling in accordance with ISA 530 *Audit Sampling and Other Means of Testing:*

Random selection. Ensures each item in a population has an equal chance of selection, for example by using random number tables.

Systematic selection. In which a number of sampling units in the population is divided by the sample size to give a sampling interval.

Haphazard selection. The auditor selects the sample without following a structured technique – the auditor would avoid any conscious bias or predictability.

Sequence or block. Involves selecting a block(s) of contiguous items from within a population.

Tutorial note

Another method of sampling is:

Monetary Unit Sampling. *This selection method ensures that each individual $1 in the population has an equal chance of being selected.*

(b)   Assertions – classes of transactions

Occurrence. The transactions and events that have been recorded have actually occurred and pertain to the entity.

Completeness. All transactions and events that should have been recorded have been recorded.

Accuracy. The amounts and other data relating to recorded transactions and events have been recorded appropriately.

Cut-off. Transactions and events have been recorded in the correct accounting period.

Classification. Transactions and events have been recorded in the proper accounts.

(c) **Audit report term**

Modified. An auditor modifies an audit report in any situation where inappropriate to provide an unmodified report. For example, the auditor may provide additional information in an emphasis of matter (which does not affect the auditor's opinion) or modify the audit opinion because the financial statements as a whole are not free from material misstatement or the auditor is unable to obtain sufficient appropriate evidence to conclude.

54 ISA 620/AUDITOR RIGHTS/ASSERTIONS *Walk in the footsteps of a top tutor*

Key answer tips

This is a straightforward knowledge based question. Note that three responses are required for parts (a) and (b) for three marks and that four responses are required for (c) for four marks,

The highlighted words are key phases that markers are looking for.

(a) **Competence and objectivity of experts**

– The expert's professional qualification. The expert should be a member of a relevant professional body or have the necessary licence to perform the work.

– The experience and reputation of the expert in the area in which the auditor is seeking audit evidence.

– The objectivity of the expert from the client company. The expert should not normally be employed by the client.

(b) **Auditor rights**

– Right of access to the company's books and records at any reasonable time to collect the evidence necessary to support the audit opinion.

– Right to require from the company's officers the information and explanations the auditor considers necessary to perform their duties as auditors.

– Right to receive notices of and attend meetings of the company in the same way as any member of the company.

– Right to speak at general meetings on any matter affecting the auditor or previous auditor.

– Where the company uses written resolutions, a right to receive a copy of those resolutions.

(c) **Tangible non-current assets – assertions**

– Completeness – ensure that all non-current assets are recorded in the non-current asset register by agreeing a sample of assets physically verified back to the register.

– Existence – ensure non-current assets exist by taking a sample of assets from the register and physically seeing the asset.

ation and allocation – ensure assets are correctly valued by checking the onableness of depreciation calculations.

its and obligations – ensure the company owns the asset by seeing ropriate document of ownership for example, a purchase invoice.

sentation and disclosure assertions – ensure all necessary financial tements disclosures have been made by reviewing the financial statements.

ily four assertions were required.

55 INTERNAL AUDIT

(a) **Need for Internal Audit**

Having an internal audit department is generally considered to be 'best practice,' rather than being required by law. This allows flexibility in the way internal audit is established to suit the needs of a business.

In small, or owner managed businesses there is unlikely to be a need for internal audit because the owners are able to exercise more direct control over operations, and are accountable to fewer stakeholders.

The need for internal audit will therefore depend on:

- scale, diversity and complexity of activities;
- number of employees;
- cost/benefit considerations; and
- the desire of senior management to have assurance and advice on risk and control.

(b) **Contents of a Typical Internal Audit Review Report**

(i) **Cover**
The cover (or header for a shorter memorandum) would include the following items:
- Subject
- Distribution list
- Date of issue
- Any rating/evaluation.

(ii) **Detailed findings and agreed action**
The detailed findings will include agreed actions, timescale for action and responsibilities for resolution.

(iii) **Executive Summary**
The executive summary is a summary of the rest of the report.

(iv) **Key findings and recommendations**
Short, clear summaries of the key findings and recommendations from the review, including:
- Recommendations for solving the problem.
- Who is to carry out the necessary actions.
- Deadlines and timescales.
- The main problems found.
- Breaches in procedures.
- Ineffective procedures.

56   AUDITOR'S RESPONSIBILITIES

(a)   **Fraud**

In accordance with ISA 200 *Overall Objectives of the Independent Auditor* the external auditor is responsible for obtaining reasonable assurance that the financial statements, taken as a whole, are free from material misstatement, whether caused by fraud or error.

Therefore, the external auditor has some responsibility for considering the risk of material misstatement due to fraud.

In order to achieve this, auditors must maintain an attitude of professional scepticism. This means that the auditor must recognise the possibility that a material misstatement due to fraud could occur, regardless of the auditor's prior experience of the client's integrity and honesty.

ISA 315 *Identifying and Assessing the Risks of Material Misstatement Through Understanding the Entity and Its Environment* goes further than this general concept and requires that engagement teams discuss the susceptibility of their clients to fraud.

The engagement team should also obtain information for use in identifying the risk of fraud when performing risk assessment procedures.

To be able to make such an assessment auditors must identify, through enquiry, how management assesses and responds to the risk of fraud. The auditor must also enquire of management, internal auditors and those charged with governance if they are aware of any actual or suspected fraudulent activity.

If the auditor identifies a fraud they should communicate the matter on a timely basis to the appropriate level of management (i.e. those with the primary responsibility for prevention and detection of fraud). If the suspected fraud involves management the auditor shall communicate such matters to those charged with governance. If the auditor has doubts about the integrity of those charged with governance they should seek legal advice regarding an appropriate course of action.

In addition to these responsibilities the auditor must also consider whether they have a responsibility to report the occurrence of a suspicion to a party outside the entity. Whilst the auditor does have an ethical duty to maintain confidentiality, it is likely that any legal responsibility will take precedent.

In these circumstances it is advisable to seek legal advice.

(b)   **Laws and Regulations**

In accordance with ISA 200 *Overall Objectives of the Independent Auditor* the auditor is responsible for obtaining reasonable assurance that the financial statements taken as a whole, are free from material misstatement whether caused by fraud or error.

Noncompliance with laws and regulations can impact the financial statements because companies in breach of the law may need to make provisions for future legal costs and fines. In the worst case scenario this could affect the ability of the company to continue as a going concern.

In addition the auditor may need to report identified noncompliance with laws and regulations either to management or to a regulatory body, if the issue requires such action. An example of the latter would be when the client is in breach of money laundering regulations.

Therefore, in planning an audit of financial statements the auditor must take into account the applicable legal and regulatory framework.

More specifically the auditor must obtain sufficient, appropriate evidence regarding compliance with those laws and regulations generally recognised to have a direct effect on the determination of material amounts and disclosures in the financial statements.

The auditor must also perform specified audit procedures to help identify instances of noncompliance with those laws and regulations that may have a material impact on the financial statements. If noncompliance is identified (or suspected) the auditor must then respond appropriately.

ISA 250 *Consideration of Laws and Regulations in an Audit of Financial Statements* requires an auditor to perform the following procedures:

- obtaining a general understanding of the client's legal and regulatory environment;
- inspecting correspondence with relevant licensing and regulatory authorities;
- enquiring of management and those charged with governance as to whether the entity is compliant with laws and regulations;
- remaining alert to possible instances of noncompliance; and
- obtaining written representations that the directors have disclosed all instances of known and possible noncompliance to the auditor.

Section 3

PILOT PAPER EXAM QUESTIONS

1 WESTRA CO

Westra Co assembles mobile telephones in a large factory. Each telephone contains up to 100 different parts, with each part being obtained from one of 50 authorised suppliers.

Like many companies, Westra's accounting systems are partly manual and partly computerised. In overview the systems include:

(i)   Design software.

(ii)   A computerised database of suppliers (bespoke system written in-house at Westra).

(iii)   A manual system for recording goods inwards and transferring information to the accounts department.

(iv)   A computerised payables ledger maintained in the accounts department (purchased off-the-shelf and used with no program amendments).

(v)   Online payment to suppliers, also in the accounts department.

(vi)   A computerised general ledger which is updated by the payables ledger.

Mobile telephones are assembled in batches of 10,000 to 50,000 telephones. When a batch is scheduled for production, a list of parts is produced by the design software and sent, electronically, to the ordering department. Staff in the ordering department use this list to place orders with authorised suppliers. Orders can only be sent to suppliers on the suppliers' database. Orders are sent using electronic data interchange (EDI) and confirmed by each supplier using the same system. The list of parts and orders are retained on the computer in an 'orders placed' file, which is kept in date sequence.

Parts are delivered to the goods inwards department at Westra. All deliveries are checked against the orders placed file before being accepted. A hand-written pre-numbered goods received note (GRN) is raised in the goods inwards department showing details of the goods received with a cross-reference to the date of the order. The top copy of the GRN is sent to the accounts department and the second copy retained in the goods inwards department. The orders placed file is updated with the GRN number to show that the parts have been received.

Paper invoices are sent by all suppliers following dispatch of goods. Invoices are sent to the accounts department, where they are stamped with a unique ascending number. Invoice details are matched to the GRN, which is then attached to the invoice. Invoice details are then entered into the computerised payables ledger. The invoice is signed by the accounts clerk to confirm entry into the payables ledger. Invoices are then retained in a temporary file in number order while awaiting payment.

After 30 days, the payables ledger automatically generates a computerised list of payments to be made, which is sent electronically to the chief accountant. The chief accountant compares this list to the invoices, signs each invoice to indicate approval for payment, and then forwards the electronic payments list to the accounts assistant. The assistant uses online banking to pay the suppliers. The electronic payments list is filed in month order on the computer.

Required:

(a) List the substantive audit procedures you should perform to confirm the assertions of completeness, occurrence and cut-off for purchases in the financial statements of Westra Co. For each procedure, explain the purpose of that procedure.

(12 marks)

(b) List the audit procedures you should perform on the trade payables balance in Westra Co's financial statements. For each procedure, explain the purpose of that procedure. (8 marks)

(c) Describe the control procedures that should be in place over the standing data on the trade payables master file in Westra Co's computer system. (5 marks)

(d) Discuss the extent to which computer-assisted audit techniques might be used in your audit of purchases and payables at Westra Co. (5 marks)

(Total: 30 marks)

2 ENGAGEMENT LETTER (A)

(a) ISA 210 Agreeing the *Terms of Audit Engagements* explains the content and use of engagement letters.

Required:

State SIX items that could be included in an engagement letter. (3 marks)

 (b) ISA 500 *Audit Evidence* explains types of audit evidence that the auditor can obtain.

Required:

State, and briefly explain, four types of audit evidence that can be obtained by the auditor. (4 marks)

(c) ISA 700 *Forming an Opinion and Reporting on the Financial Statements* explains the form of audit reports.

Required:

State three ways in which an auditor's report may be modified and briefly explain the use of each modification. (3 marks)

(Total: 10 marks)

3   NORTHCEE CO

You are the audit manager in the audit firm of Dark & Co. One of your audit clients is NorthCee Co, a company specialising in the manufacture and supply of sporting equipment. NorthCee have been an audit client for five years and you have been audit manager for the past three years while the audit partner has remained unchanged.

You are now planning the audit for the year ending 31 December 2007. Following an initial meeting with the directors of NorthCee, you have obtained the following information.

(i)   NorthCee is attempting to obtain a listing on a recognised stock exchange. The directors have established an audit committee, as required by corporate governance regulations, although no further action has been taken in this respect. Information on the listing is not yet public knowledge.

(ii)   You have been asked to continue to prepare the company's financial statements as in previous years.

(iii)   As the company's auditors, NorthCee would like you and the audit partner to attend an evening reception in a hotel, where NorthCee will present their listing arrangements to banks and existing major shareholders.

(iv)   NorthCee has indicated that the fee for taxation services rendered in the year to 31 December 2005 will be paid as soon as the taxation authorities have agreed the company's taxation liability. You have been advising NorthCee regarding the legality of certain items as 'allowable' for taxation purposes and the taxation authority is disputing these items.

         Finally, you have just inherited about 5% of NorthCee's share capital as an inheritance on the death of a distant relative.

Required:

(a)   Identify, and explain the relevance of, any factors which may threaten the independence of Dark & Co's audit of NorthCee Co's financial statements for the year ending 31 December 2007. Briefly explain how each threat should be managed.   (10 marks)

(b)   Explain the actions that the board of directors of NorthCee Co must take in order to meet corporate governance requirements for the listing of NorthCee Co.   (6 marks)

(c)   Explain why your audit firm will need to communicate with NorthCee Co's audit committee for this and future audits.   (4 marks)

(Total: 20 marks)

4   SOUTHLEA CO

SouthLea Co is a construction company (building houses, offices and hotels) employing a large number of workers on various construction sites. The internal audit department of SouthLea Co is currently reviewing cash wages systems within the company.

The following information is available concerning the wages systems:

(i)   Hours worked are recorded using a clocking in/out system. On arriving for work and at the end of each day's work, each worker enters their unique employee number on a keypad.

(ii)   Workers on each site are controlled by a foreman. The foreman has a record of all employee numbers and can issue temporary numbers for new employees.

(iii) Any overtime is calculated by the computerised wages system and added to the standard pay.

(iv)   The two staff in the wages department make amendments to the computerised wages system in respect of employee holidays, illness, as well as setting up and maintaining all employee records.

(v)   The computerised wages system calculates deductions from gross pay, such as employee taxes, and net pay. Finally a list of net cash payments for each employee is produced.

(vi)   Cash is delivered to the wages office by secure courier.

(vii) The two staff place cash into wages packets for each employee along with a handwritten note of gross pay, deductions and net pay. The packets are given to the foreman for distribution to the individual employees.

Required:

(a)   (i)   **Identify and explain weaknesses in SouthLea Co's system of internal control over the wages system that could lead to mis-statements in the financial statements.**

      (ii)   **For each weakness, suggest an internal control to overcome that weakness.**

                                                                          (8 marks)

(b)   **Compare the responsibilities of the external and internal auditors to detect fraud.**

                                                                          (6 marks)

The computer system in the wages department needs to be replaced. The replacement will be carried out under the control of a specialist external consultant.

Required:

(c)   **Explain the factors that should be taken into consideration when appointing an external consultant.**   **(6 marks)**

                                                                    (Total: 20 marks)

5   EASTVALE CO (A)

EastVale Co manufactures a range of dairy products (for example, milk, yoghurt and cheese) in one factory. Products are stored in a nearby warehouse (which is rented by EastVale) before being sold to 350 supermarkets located within 200 kilometres of EastVale's factory. The products are perishable with an average shelf life of eight days. EastVale's financial statements year-end is 31 July.

It is four months since the year-end at your audit client of EastVale and the annual audit of EastVale is almost complete, but the auditor's report has not been signed.

The following events have just come to your attention. Both events occurred in late November.

(a)   A fire in the warehouse rented by the company has destroyed 60% of the inventory held for resale.

(b) A batch of cheese produced by EastVale was found to contain some chemical impurities. Over 300 consumers have complained about food poisoning after eating the cheese. 115 supermarkets have stopped purchasing EastVale's products and another 85 are considering whether to stop purchasing from EastVale. Lawyers acting on behalf of the consumers are now presenting a substantial claim for damages against EastVale.

Required:

In respect of EACH of the events at EastVale Co mentioned above:

(i) Describe the additional audit procedures you will carry out; **(8 marks)**

(ii) State, with reasons, whether or not the financial statements for the year-end require amendment; **(6 marks)**

(iii) Discuss whether or not the audit report should be modified. **(6 marks)**

Note: **The total marks will be split equally between each event.**

(Total: 20 marks)

Section 4

ANSWERS TO PILOT PAPER EXAM QUESTIONS

Tutorial note

Some answers are longer than could be expected from candidates sitting this examination. The answers may also include more points than would be necessary to obtain full marks in the examination. This is to provide examples of valid points that could be made.

1   WESTRA CO

(a)   **Audit procedures – purchases**

Audit procedure	Reason for procedure
Obtain a sample of list of parts documents from the computer. Trace individual parts to the goods received note (GRN).	Checks the *completeness* of recording of liabilities.
For entries in the list of parts where no GRN number has been entered, enquire with goods inwards staff why there is no GRN. Document reasons obtained.	Checks that goods have not been received but details not recorded. Possible *cut-off* error where goods have been received but GRN not raised.
Obtain a sample of GRNs. Agree details to the list of parts document on the computer.	Ensures that the parts received had been ordered by Westra, giving evidence for the *occurrence* assertion.
For a sample of GRNs from the goods inwards department, trace to the invoice held in the accounts department.	Ensures the *completeness* of recording of liabilities. GRNs with no matching invoice indicate a liability has been incurred. Unmatched GRNs should be included in the payables accrual. Note this test will be difficult because there is no cross reference maintained of the GRN to the invoice.
Review file of unmatched GRNs, investigate reasons for any old (more than one week) items.	Ensures the *completeness* of recording of liabilities. Unmatched items prior to the year end should be included in the payables accrual.

Audit procedure	Reason for procedure
Obtain a sample of paid invoices. Ensure that the GRN is attached.	Confirms that the invoice should be included in the payables ledger, meeting the completeness assertion.
For the sample of invoices, check details into the computerised payables ledger, ensuring the correct account has been updated and the invoice amount is accurate.	Confirms the *completeness* of recording of payables invoices in the ledger.
Obtain the unmatched invoices file. Investigate old items obtaining reason for GRN not being received/invoice not being processed.	Unmatched items at the year end could indicate unrecorded liabilities. Ensure included in the payables accrual if the goods had been received pre-year end.
For a sample of entries from the payables ledger, agree details back to the purchase invoice.	Ensures that the liability does belong to Westra, meeting the occurrence assertion.
For the sample of entries on the payables ledger, agree to the electronic payments list confirming that the supplier name and amount is correct.	Ensures that the liability has been properly discharged by Westra and that the payments list is therefore *complete*.
For a sample of entries on each electronic payments list, agree details to the purchase invoice.	Ensures that the payment has been made for a liability incurred by Westra, meeting the *occurrence* assertion.
For the sample of entries in the electronic payments list, agree details to the bank statement.	Shows that the payment was actually made to that supplier.
Obtain the bank statements. Trace a sample of payments to the electronic payments list.	Confirms that the payment made does relate to Westra, confirming the *occurrence* assertion.
For a sample of GRNs in the week pre- and post- year-end, trace to the supporting invoice and entry in the payables ledger, ensuring recorded in the correct accounting year.	Confirms the accuracy of *cut-off* in the financial statements.

(b)   **Audit procedures – payables**

Audit procedure	Reason for procedure
Obtain a list of payables balances from the computerised payables ledger as at Westra's year end. Cast the list.	To ensure that the list is accurate and that the total is represented by the individual balances (completeness assertion).
Agree the total of payables to the general ledger and financial statements.	To confirm that the total has been accurately recorded and that the balance in the financial statements is represented by valid payables (occurrence assertion).

Audit procedure	Reason for procedure
Perform analytical procedures on the list of payables. Determine reasons for any unusual changes in the total balance or individual payables in the list.	Provides initial indication of the accuracy and completeness of the list of payables.
For a sample of payables on the list, agree to supplier statements at the year-end.	Confirms that the payables balance is due from Westra meeting the occurrence assertion.
Reconcile supplier statement balances to the payables ledger.	Ensures that the liabilities exist and belong to Westra at the year-end.
For invoices on the statements not in the ledger, agree to invoices entered after the year-end. Check the date of goods receipt per the GRN attached to the invoice. Where goods received pre-year end agree invoice to the payables accrual.	Ensures that all liabilities were recorded at the year end, meeting the completeness and cut-off assertions.
For payments not included in the supplier statements, agree to the next month-end statement ensuring that the payment has been recorded.	Ensures that payments have been made to the correct supplier.
Review the payables ledger for old unpaid invoices. Enquire of the chief accountant the reason for non-payment.	Non-payment may be indicative of goods being returned for credit indicating that the payables figure may be overstated. Alternatively, taking additional credit from payables may be a going concern indicator.
Review credit notes received post-year end ensuring that where they relate to pre-year end purchases that the payables accrual has been reduced.	Ensures that payables are not over-stated at the year-end. Large credit notes may also be an indication of overstating payables deliberately to reduce profit.
Ensure that payables have been included in the financial statements under the heading of current liabilities.	Confirm the correct classification of payables in the financial statements.

(c) **Controls over standing data**

Controls include:

– Any amendment (addition, amendment or deletion) to the payables ledger should be authorised by a responsible official, for example, the chief accountant.

– Authorisation can be by a manual form being signed or by the chief accountant having restricted access password to amend the standing data.

– The computer should reject deletion of a supplier account where there is an outstanding balance (debit or credit).

–   A record of amendments made to the payables ledger should be maintained within the ledger and reviewed on a regular basis by the chief accountant to ensure that the changes are bona fide.

–   The chief accountant should review the list of suppliers on a regular basis (perhaps every four to six months) and delete those which are no longer used.

–   A comparison should be made regularly (perhaps every month) between the authorised list of suppliers on the computerised list of suppliers and the payables ledger. Any new supplier on the list of suppliers should be added to the payables ledger in preparation for payment.

–   A review of the computer control log regarding access to the payables standing data should be made on a regular basis and any unauthorised access identified and changes made under that access identified and if necessary reversed.

–   A list of suppliers should be printed out occasionally (about every three months) and kept in a secure location in the chief accountant's office. The chief accountant should then compare this list with the computerised list in three months time and account for any unauthorised additions.

(d)   **Use of CAATs**

Audit software may be used to identify old/obsolete balances in some of Westra's systems, e.g. outstanding deliveries and payments not being made to suppliers. However, the usefulness of the testing is limited and it is possible that the computer system already provides similar controls.

Test data input by the auditor would be useful in checking the online payments system, perhaps by setting up some 'dummy' accounts and ensuring that payments are sent to the correct suppliers. Other controls over payments such as access controls are more likely to be tested manually by the auditor.

Use of Computer-Assisted Audit Techniques (CAATs) may be limited in Westra due to the lack of integration of computer systems. For example, the suppliers' database is not connected to the payables ledger, limiting the use of test data to check transactions all the way through the purchases/payables system.

There is no indication provided in the scenario regarding the extent and effectiveness of computer controls. Controls would have to be identified and assessed for reliability prior to reliance being placed.

Given that some of Westra's systems are bespoke, then it may not be cost effective to use CAATs given the time required to write specific test data or program audit software to use Westra's data.

Use of CAATs in the suppliers' database may not be effective given that the database does not input directly into any financial accounting system. Testing GRNs to purchase invoice to ledgers, etc will provide greater assurance of the completeness and accuracy of purchases than testing the suppliers' database.

	Marking scheme	
(a)	Audit procedures – purchases 12 marks. 1 for procedure and 1 for the reason. Limit to 0.5 mark in each category where stated briefly without full detail.	*Marks*
	Audit procedure	**Reason for procedure**	
	Parts to GRN	Check completeness	
	Parts no GRN number	System error or cut-off error	
	GRN to computer	Parts received were ordered – occurrence	
	GRN agree to invoice	Completeness of recording	
	Review unmatched GRN file	Completeness of recording of liabilities	
	Paid invoice – GRN attached	Confirms invoice in PDB	
	Invoice details to payables ledger	Completeness and accuracy of recording	
	Review unmatched invoices file	Indicate understatement of liability (lack of completeness)	
	Payables ledger to purchase invoice	Liability belongs to Westra	
	Payables ledger to payments list	Liability properly discharged – payments complete	
	Payment list entries to invoice	Payment made for bona fide liability	
	Payments list to bank statement	Confirms payment to supplier	
	Bank statement entry to payments list	Confirms payment relates to Westra	
	GRN cut-off testing	Accuracy of cut-off	**12**
(b)	Audit procedures – payables 8 marks. 1 for procedure and 1 for the reason. Limit to 0.5 mark in each category where stated briefly without full detail.	
	Audit procedure	**Reason for procedure**	
	Obtain and cast list of payables	Ensure that the list is accurate	
	Total of payables to the general ledger and financial statements	Confirm that the total has been accurately recorded	
	Analytical procedures	Indicates problems with the accuracy and completeness of payables	
	Agree payables to supplier statements	Confirm balance due from Westra	
	Supplier statement reconciliation	Liabilities exist and belong to Westra	
	Reconcile invoices	Confirms completeness and cut-off assertions	
	Reconcile payments	Payment to correct supplier	
	Review ledger old unpaid invoices	Credits OS or going concern indicator	
	After date credit notes	Payables not overstated	
	FS categorisation creditors	Classification objective	**8**
(c)	Controls over standing data 5 marks. 1 mark for explaining each control. 0.5 for poor/limited explanation.	
	Amendments authorised	
	How authorised (form or access control)	
	Reject deletion where outstanding balance	
	Keep record of amendments	
	Review list of suppliers – unauthorised amendments	
	Update supplier list on computer regularly	
	Review computer control log	
	Review list of suppliers – unauthorised additions	
	Other relevant points (each)	**5**
(d)	Use of CAATs	
	Review computer control log	
	Identify old/obsolete – computer may already do this	
	Test data – online payments system	
	Use of CAATs – limited – lack of computer system integration	
	Need to assess computer controls prior to use of CAATs	
	Not cost effective – bespoke systems	
	Limited use of CAATs in supplier's ledger	
	Other relevant points (each)	**5**
	Total	**30**

2   ENGAGEMENT LETTER (A)

(a)   **Contents of an engagement letter**

-    Elaboration of the scope of the audit, including reference to applicable legislation and regulations;

-    The form of any report or other communication of the results of the engagement.

-    The risk that the auditor may not discover all material errors.

-    Provision of access to the auditor of all relevant books and records.

-    Arrangements for planning and performance of the audit.

-    Agreement of management to provide written representations.

-    Request that the client confirms in writing the terms of engagement.

-    Basis of fee calculation and billing arrangements.

(b)   **Types of audit evidence**

-    Inspection – examination of records or documents in whatever form,

     e.g. manual computerised, external or internal.

-    Observation – looking at the processes or procedures being carried out by others.

-    Enquiry – seeking information from knowledgeable persons, both financial or non-financial, either within or outside the entity being audited.

-    Confirmation – the process of obtaining a representation of an existing condition from a third party, e.g. a receivables letter.

-    Recalculation – checking the mathematical accuracy of documents or records.

-    Reperformance – this is the auditor's independent execution of procedures or controls that were originally performed as part of the entity's internal control system.

-    Analytical procedures – evaluation of financial information made by a study of plausible relationships among both financial and non-financial data.

(c)   **Modification of audit reports**

Emphasis of matter paragraph. Used where the auditor wishes to draw attention to an important item in the financial statements.

Modification because the auditor cannot obtain sufficient appropriate evidence regarding an item in the financial statements.

Modification because the auditor concludes that the accounts are not free from material misstatement.

	Marking scheme	
(a)	Contents of an engagement letter – 3 marks. 0.5 mark per point.	Marks
	Objective of the audit of the financial statements	
	Management's responsibility for the financial statements	
	The scope of the audit with reference to appropriate legislation	
	The form of any report or other communication of the results of the engagement	
	The auditor may not discover all material errors	
	Provision of access to the auditor of all relevant books and records	
	Arrangements for planning the audit	
	Agreement of management to provide a representation letter	
	Request that the client confirms in writing the terms of engagement	
	Description of any letters or reports to be issued to the client	
	Basis of fee calculation and billing arrangements	3

(b)	Types of audit evidence – 4 marks: 0.5 only for stating the type and 0.5 for explanation. Maximum 2 marks for simply providing a list of types of evidence. Inspection Observation Inquiry Confirmation Recalculation Reperformance Analytical procedures		**4**
(c)	Modification of audit reports. 3 marks. 0.5 for the type of report and 0.5 for explanation. Emphasis of matter paragraph Modification – lack of sufficient appropriate evidence Modification – material misstatement or omission		**3**
	Total		**10**

3   NORTHCEE CO

(a)   **Threats to independence**

Rotation of audit partner

NorthCee Co have had the same audit partner for the last five years. An audit partner's independence may be impaired where that position is retained for more than five years for a listed company. The reason being that the partner has become too close to the directors and staff in the firm and this may impair his judgement on the financial statements. However, NorthCee is currently not listed so this requirement does not apply.

As NorthCee is now being listed, Dark & Co should rotate the audit partner this year to avoid any familiarity threat. However, given that NorthCee was not a listed company up to this audit, may imply that the partner could continue this year, but would be recommended to be rotated before the 2008 audit.

Preparation of financial statements

Apparently Dark have been preparing NorthCee's financial statements as well as carrying out the audit in previous years. While this may not have been an independence issue in the past, it is likely to be now as in many jurisdictions auditors may not provide other services to their audit clients, especially listed clients. Preparing financial statements as well as auditing them would provide Dark with a self-review threat, that is they may not see any errors, or want to report errors in material that they have previously prepared.

Dark should therefore decline from preparation of NorthCee's financial statements.

Attendance at social event

Attending the social event with respect to the new listing may be inappropriate as Dark may be seen as supporting NorthCee in this venture. There is an advocacy threat to independence. Support for a client may imply that the audit firm are 'too close' to that client and may therefore lose their independent view regarding the audit. There is also a familiarity threat.

Dark should therefore politely decline the dinner invitation, clearly stating their reasons.

Unpaid taxation fee

The unpaid fee in respect of taxation services could be construed as a loan to the audit client. Audit firms should not make loans to or receive loans from audit clients. An outstanding loan will affect independence as closure of the loan may be seen as more important than providing an appropriate audit opinion.

Dark need to discuss the situation with NorthCee again, suggesting that a payment on account could be made to show that the whole fee will be paid. Alternatively, audit work on the 2007 financial statements can be delayed until the taxation fee is paid.

Inheritance

Under ACCA's Code of Ethics and Conduct, audit partners may not hold beneficial shares in a client company. This provision includes audit staff where they are involved in the audit. The independence issue is simply that the shareholder (the auditor in this case) may be more interested in the value of the shares than providing a 'correct' opinion on the financial statements.

The shares should be disposed of as soon as possible. However, given the inside knowledge of the listing, disposal now, or delaying disposal a few days to obtain a better price may be considered 'insider dealing'. It may be better that the audit manager resigns from the audit immediately to limit any real or potential independence problems. Professional advice may be needed on when to sell the shares.

(b) **Meeting corporate governance requirements**

Currently, the only action that the directors appear to have taken is to establish an audit committee. Given that NorthCee is going to be listed on a recognised stock exchange, then there are other corporate governance requirements to be met. These requirements include:

– Ensuring that the chairman and the company chief executive officer (CEO) are different people.

– Appointing non-executive directors (NEDs) to the board of NorthCee. The number of NEDs should be the same as the number of executive directors less the chairman.

– Ensuring that at least one NED has relevant financial experience.

– Appointing the NEDs to the audit committee, remuneration committee and possibly an appointments committee. The chairman will also have a seat on these committees.

– Establishing an internal audit department to review NorthCee's internal control systems and make reports to the audit committee.

– Ensure that NorthCee has an appropriate system of internal control and that the directors recognise their responsibilities for establishing and maintaining this system.

– Establishing procedures to maintain contact with institutional shareholders and any other major shareholders. The evening reception for shareholders could become a regular event in this respect.

– Checking that the annual financial report contains information on corporate governance required by the stock exchange (e.g. a report on how directors monitor the internal control systems).

(c)   **Communication with the audit committee**

Under most systems of corporate governance, the external auditor's primary point of contact with a company is the audit committee. There are various reasons for this:

- Initially, to ensure that there is independence between the board of directors and the audit firm. The audit committee consists of non-executive directors (NEDs), who by definition are independent of the company and can therefore take an objective view of the audit report.

- The audit committee will have more time to review the audit report and other communications to the company from the auditor (e.g. management letters) than the board. The auditor should therefore benefit from their reports being reviewed carefully.

- The audit committee can ensure that any recommendations from the auditor are implemented. The audit committee has independent NEDs who can pressurise the board to taking action on auditor recommendations.

- The audit committee also has more time to review the effectiveness and efficiency of the work of the external auditor than the board. The committee can therefore make recommendations on the re-appointment of the auditor, or recommend a different firm if this would be appropriate.

	Marking scheme	
(a)	0.5 for identifying risk area, 1 for explanation of risk and 1 for stating how to resolve. Maximum 2.5 for each area.	*Marks*
	Rotation of audit partner	
	Preparation of financial statements	
	Attendance at social event	
	Unpaid taxation fee	
	Inheritance	**10**
(b)	1 mark for each point	
	Chief executive officer (CEO)/chairman split	
	Appoint NED	
	NED with financial experience	
	NEDs to sub-committees of board	
	Internal audit	
	Internal control system	
	Contact institutional shareholders	
	Financial report information	**6**
(c)	1 for each point.	
	Independence from board	
	Time to review audit work	
	Check auditor recommendations implemented	
	Review work of internal auditor (efficiency, etc.)	**4**
	Total	**20**

4   SOUTHLEA CO

(a)   **Control weaknesses and recommendations**

Control weakness	Internal control recommendation
Employees can be paid for work not done. There appears to be no check to ensure that hours recorded in the computer system actually relate to hours worked.	A record of hours worked by each employee should be printed from the computerised wages system and signed by the site foreman to confirm that the hours are accurate.
There is no check to ensure that each employee inputs his/her employee number. One employee could input two numbers hiding the fact that one employee is absent.	The computerised wages system should print a list of employees present per the computer system during the day and the foreman should then sign this list to confirm it is accurate.
Fake or dummy employees can be put onto the payroll. The foreman can set up employee records for workers who do not exist. As payment is made automatically from the record of hours worked.	The wages office should check the list of employees against personnel records of authorised employees. Any new employees particularly should be verified in this way before payment is made.
The staff in the wages office could collude by setting up fake employee records in a similar way to the site foreman.	The list of employees on the payroll should be checked for accuracy by a person outside of the wages department, for example the personnel department or the chief accountant. The list of net payments should be signed by this person to show it is correct.
Gross pay inflated by wages department staff. The staff in the wages department could add extra hours to the records of some employees, and remove the net pay from the payment received from the courier prior to making up the pay packets.	The computerised payroll system should be programmed to produce a list of all amendments made to the payroll. This list should be reviewed by a responsible official outside of the wages department prior to wages being paid.
	Alternatively, the computerised payroll system should produce payslips for each employee showing the hours worked, gross and net pay etc. Employees should then check that the cash paid agrees to the net payment recorded on the payslip.

(b) **Fraud and External/Internal audit**

Guidance on the auditor's responsibility with respect to fraud can be found in ISA 240 *The Auditor's Responsibility Relating to Fraud in an Audit of Financial Statements*.

Main reason for audit work

The external auditor is primarily responsible for the audit opinion on the financial statements. The main focus of audit work is therefore to ensure that the financial statements show a true and fair view. The detection of fraud is therefore not the main focus of the external auditor's work.

The main focus of the work of the internal auditor is checking that the internal control systems in a company are working correctly. Part of that work may be to conduct detailed review of systems to ensure that fraud is not taking place.

Materiality

In reaching the audit opinion and performing audit work, the external auditor takes into account the concept of materiality. In other words, the external auditor is not responsible for checking all transactions. Audit procedures are planned to have a reasonable likelihood of identifying material fraud.

However, internal auditors may carry out a detailed review of transactions, effectively using a much lower materiality limit. It is more likely that internal auditors will detect fraud from their audit testing.

Identification of fraud

In situations where the external auditor does detect fraud, then the auditor will need to consider the implications for the entire audit. In other words, the external auditor has a responsibility to extend testing into other areas because the risk of providing an incorrect audit opinion will have increased.

Where internal auditors detect fraud, they may extend testing into other areas. However, audit work is more likely to focus on determining the extent of fraud and ensuring similar fraud has not occurred in other locations.

(c) **Use of expert**

Qualification

The consultant should have a relevant qualification to show ability to undertake the work. In this case being a member of a relevant computer society or the Institute of Internal Auditors would be appropriate.

Experience

The consultant should be able to show relevant experience from previous projects for example, upgrading or amending wages systems for other clients.

References

Hopefully the consultant will be able to provide references from previous employers showing capability to undertake the work.

Project management skills

The consultant should be able to display appropriate project management skills as managing a team will be an important element of the systems change work.

Access to information

The consultant will need access to important and sensitive information in SouthLea. The chief accountant must ensure that this information will be made available to third parties. The consultant will have to sign a confidentiality agreement.

Acceptance by other staff

Employing a consultant can be difficult as other internal audit staff may feel threatened or resentful that a consultant has been employed. The chief internal auditor must ensure that the reasons for employing the consultant are understood by members of the internal audit department.

	Marking scheme		Marks
(a)	Control weaknesses and recommendations 8 marks. 1 for explanation of weakness and 1 for internal control recommendation. Maximum 2 per weakness/recommendation.		*Marks*
	Control weakness	**Recommendation**	
	Employees can be paid for work not done.		
	No check hours actually worked	Authorise hours worked on computer	
	Fraudulent input employee number	Reconcile computer to actual employees	
	Fake or dummy employees can be put onto the payroll.		
	Foreman setup	Check employees against personnel records	
	Wages office staff setup	List of employees reviewed for accuracy	
	Gross pay inflated by wages department staff.		
	Add extra hours work done	List amendments to payroll produced	8
(b)	1 for internal audit work and 1 for external audit. Maximum 2 per point.		
	Main reason for audit work		
	Materiality		
	Identification of fraud		6
(c)	1 mark per valid point.		
	Qualification		
	Experience		
	References		
	Project management skills		
	Access to information		
	Acceptance by other staff		6
	Total		**20**

5   EASTVALE CO (A)

(a)   **Fire at warehouse**

   (i)   *Audit procedures*

   –   Discuss the matter with the directors checking whether the company has sufficient inventory to continue trading in the short term.

   –   Enquire that the directors are satisfied that the company can continue to trade in the longer term. Ask the directors to sign an additional letter of representation to this effect.

   –   Obtain a schedule showing the inventory destroyed and if possible check this is reasonable given past production records and inventory valuations.

          –   Enquire that the insurers have been informed. Review correspondence from the insurers confirming the amount of the insurance claim.

          –   Consider whether or not EastVale can continue as a going concern, given the loss of inventory and potential damage to the company's reputation if customer orders cannot be fulfilled.

  (ii)   *Amendment to financial statements*

          –   Enquire whether the directors have considered whether the event needs disclosure in the financial statements. Disclosure is unlikely given that the inventory was not in existence at the year-end and on the assumption that insurance is adequate to cover the loss.

          –   Amendment is not required as the fire did not affect any company property and the inventory would not have been in existence at the year end (inventory turn being very high).

  (iii) *Modification of audit report*

          –   Consider modifying the audit report with an emphasis of matter paragraph to draw attention to the disclosure of the note on the fire in the financial statements.

          –   If the going concern status of EastVale is in doubt, then consider modifying the audit report with an emphasis of matter paragraph to this effect.

          –   If disclosure made by the directors is considered to be inadequate, then modify the audit report with an 'except for' qualification.

(b) **Batch of cheese**

  (i)   *Audit procedures*

          –   Discuss the matter with the directors, determining specifically whether there was any fault in the production process.

          –   Obtain a copy of the damages claim and again discuss with the directors the effect on EastVale and the possibility of success of the claim.

          –   Obtain independent legal advice on the claim from EastVale's lawyers. Attempt to determine the extent of damages that may have to be paid.

          –   Review any press reports about the contaminated cheese. Consider the impact on the reputation of EastVale and whether the company can continue as a going concern.

          –   Discuss the going concern issue with the directors. Obtain an additional letter of representation on the directors' opinion of the going concern status of EastVale.

  (ii)   *Amendment to financial statements*

          –   The event should be disclosed in the financial statements in accordance with IAS 37 *Provisions, Contingent Liabilities and Contingent Assets* as it may have a significant impact on EastVale. Over two-thirds of EastVale's customers have either stopped purchasing products from the company or are considering taking this action.

          –   No adjustment is required for the event itself as it was not a condition at the balance sheet date.

— However, the event may become adjusting if the company's reputation has been damaged and the amount of the legal claim is significant. In this situation the directors may decide that EastVale is no longer a going concern so the financial statements may have to be re-drafted on a break-up basis. This action complies with International Accounting Standard 8; the break-up basis is used where the directors have no realistic alternative but to liquidate the company.

(iii) *Modification of audit report*

Modification of the audit report depends on the director's actions above.

— If the financial statements are prepared on a break-up basis, and the auditor agrees with that assessment, then a modified report can be issued with an emphasis of matter paragraph drawing attention to the accounting basis used.

— However, if the financial statements are prepared on a going concern basis then the auditor should consider modifying the audit report with an emphasis of matter paragraph to draw attention to the disclosure of the note on the fire in the financial statements. This is providing that the auditor agrees that the going concern basis is appropriate.

— If the going concern status of EastVale is in doubt, then consider modifying the audit report with an emphasis of matter paragraph to this effect, drawing attention to disclosure made by the directors.

— If EastVale is not a going concern, and the financial statements have been prepared using this assumption, modify the audit report with an adverse opinion stating that the company is not a going concern.

Marking scheme			
(a)	**Fire at warehouse**		*Marks*
	1 per well-explained point		
	(i)	Discuss the matter with the directors	
		Letter of representation point	
		Schedule of inventory destroyed – reasonable?	
		Insurance	
		Going concern status of company	4
	(ii)	Disclosure in FS – unlikely with reason	
		No amendment to B/S etc	3
	(iii)	Modification of report	
		Going concern status?	
		Inadequate disclosure by directors	3
(b)	**Batch of cheese**		
	1 per well-explained point.		
	(i)	Discuss with directors	
		Copy of damages claim	
		Legal advice	
		Press reports (or other third party) on cheese	
		Going concern?	4
	(ii)	Disclosure event – because significant impact	
		No adjustment	
		Going concern issue – reputation	
		May result in amendment to FS	3
	(iii)	Preparation of FS breakup basis	
		Prepared going concern basis – emphasis of matter	
		Prepared going concern – but in doubt – emphasis of matter	
		Prepared going concern and disagree – qualify report	3
	Total		**20**